Technology, Work and Globalization

Series Editors
Leslie P. Willcocks
Department of Management
London School of Economics and Political Science
London, UK

Mary C. Lacity
Sam M. Walton College of Business
University of Arkansas
Fayetteville, AR, USA

The Technology, Work and Globalization series was developed to provide policy makers, workers, managers, academics and students with a deeper understanding of the complex interlinks and influences between technological developments, including information and communication technologies, work organizations and patterns of globalization. The mission of the series is to disseminate rich knowledge based on deep research about relevant issues surrounding the globalization of work that is spawned by technology.

Albert Plugge • Shahrokh Nikou

Digitalisation of Global Business Services

Orchestrating the Enterprise Ecosystem

palgrave
macmillan

Albert Plugge
Nyenrode Business University
Breukelen, The Netherlands

Shahrokh Nikou
Department of Design, Organisation and Strategy
Delft University of Technology
Delft, The Netherlands

ISSN 2730-6623 ISSN 2730-6631 (electronic)
Technology, Work and Globalization
ISBN 978-3-031-51527-9 ISBN 978-3-031-51528-6 (eBook)
https://doi.org/10.1007/978-3-031-51528-6

This Palgrave Macmillan imprint is published by the registered company Springer Nature Switzerland AG.
The registered company address is: Gewerbestrasse 11, 6330 Cham, Switzerland

Paper in this product is recyclable.

Acknowledgements

Global Business Services (GBS) attracts the attention of enterprise leadership as their implementations are perceived to be challenging due to its multi-nature characteristics. As researchers, we were interested to study the following questions: Will digitalisation limit implementation challenges or create other effects on an enterprise level? How will orchestrating GBS in a plural sourcing context facilitate digital transformation? What are the antecedents of business services portfolio orchestration? These questions formed the starting point for our research journey.

First and foremost, we would like to express our gratitude to the anonymous reviewers who meticulously assessed our book proposal and offered invaluable suggestions and constructive comments. Their input has improved the overall concept of the book.

We would like to thank the representatives of multiple enterprises around the world, who include executives, managers and subject matter experts. They reserved their valuable time to participate in the survey and interviews and contributed to the realisation of our book. As a result, we learned a lot with regard to how to implement GBS, their challenges and contributions.

Furthermore, we extend our thanks to the representatives of the enterprises who actively participated in our case study interviews. Their valuable insights and perspectives on digitisation and GBS have played a crucial role in shaping our comprehensive cross-case analysis.

A special word of thanks goes out to Prof. mr. dr. ir. Sicco Santema (Delft University of Technology, The Netherlands) for the time that he spent on reviewing the book. Your valuable and pointed suggestions improved our book importantly. Highly appreciated!

We would also like to thank our good friend Piet Mul, who provided multiple suggestions to improve the book. Without any doubt, your help is much appreciated.

We would also like to take the opportunity to thank experts who were willing to write their endorsement based on reading the book and their experience in the field of GBS and sourcing. Many thanks, Prof. dr. Jochen Wirtz (National University of Singapore), Prof. dr. Julia Kotlarsky (University of Auckland Business School, New Zealand), and Alexander Raaijmakers, MSc (KPMG, The Netherlands).

In conclusion, this endeavour has been both challenging and rewarding, as we delved into the fascinating and significant phenomenon of GBS as an emerging field of research. We sincerely hope that scholars and practitioners will find enjoyment in reading this book and be inspired to embark on further research exploring new avenues within the realm of GBS.

Albert Plugge and Shahrokh Nikou

Praise for *Digitalisation of Global Business Services*

"Global Business Services (GBS) plays a crucial role as a driving force behind economic growth. However, many enterprises encounter challenges in effectively implementing GBS. In this context, enterprises adopt a plural sourcing strategy, bundling global business services into a diverse portfolio. In their groundbreaking book *Digitalisation of Global Business Services: Orchestrating the Enterprise Ecosystem*, Albert Plugge and Shahrokh Nikou delve into the factors influencing a successful GBS portfolio and explore the profound impact of digitalisation on GBS. Through meticulous research and analysis of an extensive international firm dataset, they have identified critical antecedents that demand constant attention to adapt to GBS changes effectively. Notably, the authors present four compelling case studies centred around financial business services, demonstrating that adopting an ecosystem approach empowers enterprises to skilfully orchestrate their GBS portfolio and align it with the essential antecedents. The multimethod approach employed in this book delivers cutting-edge insights into effectively managing a GBS portfolio. By reading this book enterprise management gains valuable insights to navigate the dynamic landscape of global business services successfully. This book offers practical and novel strategies to capitalise on GBS opportunities and drive organizational growth."

—Professor Jochen Wirtz, Ph.D., *Vice Dean, MBA Programmes, National University of Singapore*

"This book, written by outsourcing experts, provides unique insights into factors that are important for value (co-)creation in the context of an enterprise ecosystem for global business services. Based on extensive research that combines quantitative and qualitative methods the authors examine resource orchestration approaches to plural sourcing and offer detailed guidance to enterprises engaging with suppliers in the provision of global business services on how to organize their service portfolio within their enterprise ecosystem. Case studies that examine the implementation of global business services in major functions (Finance & Accounting, Supply Chain Management, Human Resources and Information Technology) discuss challenges and provide a range of practical examples that managers reading this book could easily relate to."

—Professor Julia Kotlarsky, Ph.D., *The University of Auckland Business School, New Zealand*

"The model of Global Business Services has been in place for well over a decade. Where it started with a small number of multi-nationals, it has evolved across multiple organisations, geographies and functions in scope. Initial focus predominantly on efficiency gains and breaking down the functional silos, nowadays the focus has moved to value add, innovation (like AI, ESG) and talent management. All leadership teams are somewhere on the journey, learning from each other and testing new concepts every day. Key in all of these developments is a business services portfolio with a clear supporting orchestration role. Without such an orchestration, impact will be limited and fragmented.

Within the field of global business services, academic studies are quite rare. A missed opportunity and therefore even more encouraging that Albert Plugge and Shahrokh Nikou have picked up the glove and created a great read. Both authors were able to bridge the day-to-day practice with in-depth research and academic perspectives. I encourage you as a reader to set aside some time and read the book; it will broaden your horizons."

—Alexander Raaijmakers, MSc, *Partner, KPMG*

Contents

List of Figures

List of Tables

1
Introduction

The degree in which enterprises have to compete today in a globalised market cannot be compared with primarily scale-based competition of the previous century (Teece & Linden, 2017). Acting in a turbulent and dynamic market, enterprises experience global competition, rapid technological developments, digitalisation, and sustainability requirements. As such business relationships and corresponding ties have become increasingly more complex. Traditional agreements with business partners, which have been based on bi-lateral relationships, have now been transformed into network structures. Consequently, enterprises are collaborating with business partners and suppliers to co-design and co-develop services to customers and business partners. Hence, enterprises, business partners and suppliers all become part of an ecosystem in which interdependencies and ties between them are paramount. As a result, enterprise management must develop new strategies and act more systemically on how to identify and address market demands and find relevant and valuable business partners to provide services to their customers. As such, enterprises have to transform, which is more difficult than before, to achieve a competitive advantage and market longevity and remain relevant in the market. Examples of enterprises that transformed successfully correspond to Lego, Nike and Disney. These enterprises

A. Plugge, S. Nikou, *Digitalisation of Global Business Services*, Technology, Work and Globalization, https://doi.org/10.1007/978-3-031-51528-6_1

collaborated with business partners and suppliers intensively and used digitalisation to create new products and services to their customers. Consequently, they transformed their enterprises and strengthened their market position.

To maintain their competitive position in the market, enterprises use their business services to respond to exogenous customer demands adequately. Originally, business services are often positioned as back-office services to support employees within an enterprise in fulfilling their tasks. As an increasing number of functions and corresponding processes of an enterprise become digitalised, business services rely on various sources of digital data. In addition, due to the rise of digitalisation, external customers raise demands that impact business services directly. An example can be found in the context of supply chain management (SCM) where customer demands and supplier requirements impact a manufacturer's information systems, which in turn also coordinates internal business units and teams to execute their supply chain tasks. To cater for tight schedules to complete customer orders, an enterprise needs to supply their partners with the necessary resources to prevent time wasting and delay in service delivery. In this situation, an enterprise information system automates the supply chain process and consolidates the actions and results into dashboards for internal use.

1.1 Global Business Services

To deal with customer demands directly, enterprises are transforming their business services into a hybrid mode, or in other words, modern business services support internal employees as well as external customers. Amongst the variety of business services as discussed in literature, the four commonly studied are deemed relevant for the current study. These four business services include: Finance and Accounting (Bangemann, 2005; Janssen & Joha, 2006; Wirtz et al., 2015), Human Resources (Maatman & Meijerink, 2017; Ulrich et al., 2008; McIvor et al., 2011), Supply Chain Management (Miles, 2005; Wang et al., 2015), and Information Technology (Fielt et al., 2014; Ulbrich & Schulz, 2014; Handley, 2017). Importantly, the business services in scope are interwoven, which increase the complexity to organise and manage them in practice. As an example, SCM activities are supported by financial services (i.e. F&A), which in turn are enabled by information systems and applications.

In particular, global operating enterprises which support customers, encounter various challenges due to their global operating model. For instance, enterprises operating with various types of delivery models (e.g. on-shore, off-shore) have to deal with geographically dispersed locations that requires intensive coordination and governance. To maintain the global operations, global enterprises started to shift their operating model to a Global Business Services (GBS) model during the last decade. GBS can be characterised by their "multi-nature" (Deloitte, 2018; KPMG, 2019), namely: multi-business, multi-function, multi-region, and multi-sourcing approach. The latter aspect is explained in more detail in Chap. 3. The goal of GBS is to create organisational responsiveness to support enterprises to cater for customer needs by creating a flexible way to organise and operate their business services. Consequently, GBS may enable an enterprise to enter new markets and adopt new processes more rapidly.

More importantly, due to digital transformation in the society and unpredictable incidents, enterprises face serious challenges that may affect the delivery of services internally and towards their customers. Although numerous challenges can be identified, we address three main challenges that impact enterprises GBSs, namely: technology (digital transformation), healthcare (COVID-19), and society (environmental, social, and governance (ESG)). Next, we elaborate on the effects that these challenges will have on enterprise level.

1.2 Global Business Services Challenges

1.2.1 Technology Challenge (Digital Transformation)

In the last decade, the emergence of digital transformation has impacted both academia (Bharadwaj et al., 2013) and practitioners (Majchrzak et al., 2016). Digital transformation can be characterised as a process where digital technologies transform the development and provisioning of existing products and services, and as such enabling to innovate the existing value creation and capturing practices. Vial (2021) conducted an extensive literature review on digital transformation, and indicated that the use of digital technologies, such as social, analytics, platforms, and ecosystems, creates changes in value creation paths. The effect of changes in value creation paths, however, is twofold. On the one hand, operational efficiency may increase due to automating business processes. In a similar vein, organisational performance may be improved as the coordination effort between organisational departments and teams can be limited in aligning production activities. On the other hand, digital transformation creates organisational barriers that may affect existing organisational structures. Therefore, it is vital that organisations implement strategies that tackle digitalisation challenges successfully (Kane et al., 2015; Matt et al., 2015).

The last decade has witnessed a significant interest in the automation of business services, such as Robotic Process Automation (RPA), Machine Learning (ML), process mining and complex algorithms. Willcocks (2020) argues that these digital technology solutions, which are often referred to as variants of Artificial Intelligence (AI), are expected to impact enterprises. For example, RPA refers to the automation of manual business process management tasks that can be characterised by repetitive and rule-based functions, typically executed by back-office employees (Leyh et al., 2017). ML relies on different algorithms to solve data problems, while the type of algorithm that is used is dependent on the kind of problem that need to be solved and as such may vary. Some commonly used ML algorithms refer to supervised and unsupervised learning, neural networks, and instance-based learning (Mahesh, 2020). To further strengthen existing business processes, process mining technologies aim to discover, monitor, and improve these processes (Van der Aalst et al., 2011).

Process mining tools experienced a spectacular growth as data and techniques have matured. In practice, enterprise management focuses to improve business processes and compliance by applying process mining technologies. Another relevant example of digital technologies is the rise of digital platforms that support various internal and external activities (e.g. internal use, supply chain platforms, digital industry platforms) (Gawer, 2014). Digital platforms are based on the assumption that seamless integration of information and data is provided to support business services. Enterprises may use digital platforms to support the exchange of external demand-supply processes with their customers, and in parallel support internal business services in the context of back-office functions. Digital platforms are closely related to ecosystems (Iansiti & Levien, 2004), as they facilitate enterprise functions that are often organised in a fragmented structure. Importantly, digital technologies refer to both business processes and data that in case of data inconsistencies or lack of quality may result in incorrect decision making. Consequently, GBSs, which rely on business processes and corresponding data, may be affected negatively.

1.2.2 Healthcare Challenge (e.g. COVID-19)

The COVID-19 pandemic demonstrated a major disruption that affected enterprises globally in ordering and delivering products and services to their customers, which forced them to change their operations (Nagar, 2020). Based on a review of Maital and Barzani (2020), the authors discussed three important effects of COVID-19 on enterprises, namely, a direct effect on production (supply), supply chain disruption (supply), and financial impact on enterprises (demand). Recent research shows that many enterprises focused on surviving the pandemic by transforming their supply by means of distributed leadership, workforce, and adaptive culture to sustain their business operations (Obrenovic et al., 2020). The authors found that more informed and decentralised decision making contributed to become a more resilient enterprise. This finding aligns with that of Janssen and Van der Voort (2020) who argue that adaptive governance calls for both centralised and decentralised decision making in the context of innovation and bureaucracy. The disruption of supply chains, for instance, forced policymakers to change their global supply chain and transform to establish local value chains (Seric et al., 2020). Research illustrates that global operating enterprises proved to be more resilient to the COVID-19 crisis than domestic enterprises. As an explanation, Borino et al. (2021) found that global operating enterprises "were less likely than their domestic counterparts to lay off workers or file for bankruptcy and more likely to adopt countermeasures to continue production, such as telework" (p. 44). During the pandemic enterprises faced a decrease of demand regarding regular products and services, which caused financial impacts, and next affected their financial business services. An exception is formed by enterprises that operate in a health manufacturing industry to produce sanitisers, gloves, and other hygiene products, which experienced significant, and sudden increase of demand.

In hindsight, various enterprise GBSs (e.g. SCM, F&A, IT) were seriously affected. Besides the effects on SCM, financial accounting was also impacted. Managerial accounting faced difficulties as some enterprises had to close down locations for months, because of lockdowns that impacted their accounting (Atienza & Tabuena, 2021). COVID-19 accelerated the use of information technology (IT) specifically as enterprises transformed various physical activities into virtual activities that range from increased remote working performed through, e.g., Zoom and Teams, and remote learning to keep supply chains functioning. A survey conducted by McKinsey (2022) has confirmed a rapid shift of enterprises towards interacting with their customers through digital channels. As a next step, enterprises invested in creating digital or digitally enhanced product offerings. Overall, the COVID-19 pandemic increased enterprises' awareness on their information systems and speeding up of their digital transformation.

1.2.3 Environmental, Social and Governance (ESG) Challenge

A relevant topic that will affect enterprises is the phenomenon referred to Environmental, Social, and Governance (ESG). ESG can be seen as a method and approach to invest or assess an enterprise's ESG performance while also addressing financial return. This is closely related to the 17 sustainable development goals (SDG) initiated by the United Nations 2030 agenda for sustainable development. Since the introduction in the United Nations report in 2006, ESG have captivated the attention of enterprises, governments, and academics (Atkins, 2021). ESG issues impact enterprises seriously and are considered to be a global concern.

The principles for responsible investments are defined as "a strategy and practice to incorporate environmental, social and governance (ESG) factors in investment decisions and active ownership" (Principles for Responsible Investment (PRI), 2022). Various events such as frequent financial and energy crises, the COVID-19 pandemic, Black Lives Matter protests, and enterprises being delisted due to fraud have increased global attention to handle ESG issues. Hence, enterprises address ESG issues by increasing their maturity by means of establishing ESG evaluation systems and apply ESG disclosure standards. Although ESG factors have been studied separately, today we notice a shift towards an integrated approach driven by regulation. Enterprises that solely focus on financial performance are lacking assets based on the assumption of socially and environmentally responsible business. The release of industry-based standards by the Sustainability Accounting Standards Board (SASB) accelerated acceptance that to deal with ESG issues, enterprises must pay attention on material factors. As enterprises initiated ESG strategies during the last decade, they are measuring, managing, and reporting ESG issues regularly (Ioannou et al., 2016).

Importantly, reporting on ESG goals and issues assumes that these topics are monitored by nature which corresponds to GBSs. For instance, monitoring and reporting financial-related ESG topics involves the presence of finance and accounting (F&A) systems to track and trace ESG progress. The same goes for ESG human resources (HR) factors in which topics such as enterprises' degree of inclusiveness and education of employees are registered and reported, which in turn requires an HR strategy, policies, and systems.

An example in the context of SCM shows that most of the Fortune 250 enterprises in the United States defined different ESG goals, ranging from travel emissions to responsible procurement (Dai & Tang, 2022). This addresses the need to avoid waste of physical products in supply chains. The examples demonstrate that ESG affects the GBSs in scope, as F&A, HR and SCM functions all use IT systems and applications to support the monitoring, measurement, analysis, and reporting of ESG issues. This shows how GBS is interconnected, with various services being dependent on each other. From another view, enterprises GBS facilitates both internal use (e.g. monitoring, analysis) and external use (reporting), indicating the dual position and importance of GBSs.

1.3 Enterprise as an Ecosystem

To facilitate the provisioning of GBSs, enterprises predominantly use two different theoretical organisational models, namely: the coalitional model and rational model. The coalitional model uses the perspective of an organisation that corresponds to a market-like partnership where departments are bounded together in a loosely coupled system of other subunits (Astley & Zajac, 1991). The related tasks and activities in this system are not directly interdependent, but more isolated and often comprise of specific expertise. The loosely coupled system model builds on the resource dependency logic where enterprise departments or units are seen as rather autonomous (Andersson et al., 2002). Each department or unit has its own distinct network and strives either for autonomy or to affect other departments or units to shift in a direction that supports the development of their own business.

In contrast, the rational model organises tasks in dedicated subunits (e.g. highly specialised) in which each subunit is tightly coupled to other units, often labelled as a machine-like system. Value creation is viewed as "one system" that can be optimised further. The rational model divides tasks into modules and activities and can be perceived as a sequential dependent model (Astley & Zajac, 1991; Mackenzie, 1986). This value-chain-driven view fits with Porter's focus to achieve efficiencies in similar business processes. The value chain interlinks activities to decrease the cost level and maximise the value as perceived by customers. These value chains are often increasingly fragmented and specialised. Importantly, as business services activities have become more globalised, internal transfers between intra-units have increased, which in turn result in less strategic activities for each department or unit.

In this way, enterprises organise their departments or business units by means of smaller subunits that focus on specialisation. Bento and Garotti (2019) argue that the emergent and evolving structure of webs of interactions often result in organisational clusters. These clusters are often termed as "silos" (Centola, 2018), a term that in many organisational discourses implies a negative perception of value. The term "silo" goes back to agriculture silos in the 1800s in Europe, which were trenches dug to store grains during the winter (Bento et al., 2020), while in North

America, silos are seen as storage towers separating different grains from each other. More importantly, "organisational silos" are a metaphor to illustrate the presence of barriers that may hinder the exchange of knowledge and information. Organisational silos encompass a multi-perspective approach, or in other words, organisational decision making and economics that refer to the role of financial incentives. Addressing the relevance of GBSs, we noticed that these services are interwoven in practice. However, when enterprises organise their GBS services in fragmented organisational units (silos), the exchange of knowledge and information may be hindered due to potential conflicting decision making or financial interests between these organisational units.

Addressing various organisational units within an enterprise and their internal transfers, we argue that an enterprise can be portrayed as an ecosystem that represents an environment of distributed heterogeneous organisms (or units) in dispersed geographical locations. The concept of ecosystems, amongst other typologies, is well described in literature and is generally described as a network in which all entities have their own individual interests and goals but are bounded together as a collective whole. These entities, or units in the context of an enterprise, share ties among communities, processes and technologies. As such an enterprise ecosystem serve as a foundation to support business strategies and intra-organisational collaboration between organisational units. This corresponds to research of Lyytinen et al. (2016) in which the authors argue that applying an ecosystem lens redefines the way of working of an enterprise regarding competition and innovation.

Defining the term ecosystems is not that easy as various interpretations exists, which are often context specific. Starting with the metaphor of a biological ecosystem the Merriam-Webster Third New International Dictionary of the English Language (1986) defines a biological ecosystem as "a community of living organisms with air, water and other resources". Based on this metaphor, various interpretations have been made in which we show the most common ones below.

> Ecosystems are groups of firms that must deal with either unique or super modular complementarities that are nongeneric, requiring the creation of a specific structure of relationships and alignment to create value. (Jacobides et al., 2018, p. 2263)

> An ecosystem is defined by the alignment structure of the multilateral set of partners that need to interact in order for a focal value proposition to materialize. (Adner, 2017, p. 42)

> In a business ecosystem, companies coevolve capabilities around a new innovation: they work cooperatively and competitively to support new products, satisfy customer needs, and eventually incorporate the next round of innovations. (Moore, 1993, p. 76)

> A service ecosystem can be defined as a "relatively self-contained, self-adjusting system of resource integrating actors connected by shared institutional arrangements and mutual value creation through service exchange. (Lusch & Vargo, 2014, p. 161)

In the context of digitalisation, more recently, scholars highlighted the roles of platform-owners, complementors and intermediaries (Benlian et al., 2015; Foerderer et al., 2018) in which digital platforms support an enterprise in achieving their business strategic goals. These studies show distinctive properties that characterise a digital business ecosystem and the interactions between enterprise units to commercialise their business services (Jacobides et al., 2018). Literature shows various examples of digital business ecosystem definitions. For example:

> Digital Business Ecosystem (DBE) is a specific type of business ecosystem defined as an IT-enabled business network of entities with differing interests bound together in a collective whole. (Iansiti & Levien, 2004)

> A DBE is a socio-technical environment of individuals, organisations and digital technologies with collaborative and competitive relationships to co-create value through shared digital platforms. (Senyo et al., 2016, p. 53)

As we focus on an enterprise as an ecosystem in the context of GBSs, we build the following definition:

> *An enterprise ecosystem is a socio-technical environment in which individuals within organisational units, which are supported by digital interactions, collaborate in co-creating, implementing and orchestrating GBSs in order to create business value.*

With regard to the provisioning of GBSs, an enterprise ecosystem comprises of multiple specialists that are organised in a fragmented way across an enterprise and contribute to establish these services. An example can be found in the context of financial and accounting services that besides financial processes, knowledge and skills rely on information systems and applications that are often organised in various departments. As enterprises need to act more dynamically to handle servitisation developments, digitalisation challenges, and to achieve sustainability goals, and thus applying an enterprise ecosystem perspective may benefit to achieve these goals. Consequently, enterprises that organise their GBSs by means of an ecosystem view may achieve new synergies, internal partnerships, and collaboration formats to cater for competitiveness and ultimately profitable business models (Kohtamäki et al., 2020). An enterprise ecosystem amplifies the available capacities without additional investments. Hence, enterprises are more able to cater for changing circumstances such as volatile markets and changing production locations as generative knowledge and cognitive organised competence centres are accessible from anywhere.

Rasoulian et al. (2023) argue that to achieve competitive advantage in globalised markets, enterprises that view their organisation as an ecosystem need to coordinate the integration of complementary resources. As the GBSs are both provided in-house and outsourced, enterprises have to orchestrate the integration of resources adequately. A lack of resource integration will result in failures that may negatively impact an enterprise's business services portfolio and ultimately their service performance (Kotzab et al., 2015). We argue that the orchestration of continuous resource integration creates strongly tied resource-integrating patterns that become institutionalised in a GBS context. The interaction process between business services units enables resource integration patterns that simultaneously constrain change (e.g. adoption of new digital technologies). Resource orchestration theory (ROT), which is an extension of the resource-based view theory (RBV) and dynamic capabilities theory (DC), addresses the integration of asset orchestration and resource management (Sirmon et al., 2007, 2011). The authors posit that managers need to orchestrate their resources to effectively structure, bundle, mobilise, and deploy resources to create value. As such ROT is useful for creating insights in how enterprises' business services portfolios need to be orchestrated as the provisioning of business services may change over time (e.g. in-house or outsourced).

As an effect, an enterprise ecosystem is influenced in various ways. First, customer demands influence business services directly and in turn supporting business processes. McLoughlin et al. (2021) propose that enterprises engaging in business networks are embracing a modularised approach to their business processes, seeking to adapt efficiently to evolving circumstances. As a result, GBS functionality must be developed and implemented with the aim to support a hybrid model (e.g. in-house or outsourced) in which business processes as mediator fulfils an essential role to achieve firm performance (Aydiner et al., 2019). Second, an enterprise ecosystem affects the delivery model of business services in scope as some functions can be provided in-house or outsourced. This corresponds to existing capabilities needed to design, develop, and provide business services. Third, managing a complex enterprise ecosystem requires a governance model that takes a complex delivery model into account. As such, business services as part of an enterprise ecosystem can be considered as a monolithic system, and that governance mechanisms are often used to manage interdependencies between internal and external suppliers. Although an enterprise ecosystem aims to create business value, the conditions of internal and external stakeholders might be different. This may result in tensions between internal and external suppliers' objectives that may be conflicting. Therefore, orchestrating an enterprise ecosystem is necessary to ensure a sound functioning.

1.4 Demarcation

In this book, we focus on digitalised GBSs in the context of an enterprise ecosystem. The GBSs as described are perceived as mature services in the market that makes it possible to compare the different business services with each other. With respect to GBS delivery models, we can identify two main enterprise delivery strategies, namely: in-house and outsourced services. To obtain a comprehensive overview on orchestration, it is worthwhile to address both delivery models within an enterprise. To define the boundaries of this book, it is important to note that other forms or types of GBSs, such as Software Development, Research and Development, and Customer Contact Centres will not be discussed in this study. The logic behind such demarcation is that other business services are more focused on providing external customer related services rather than supporting both external customers and internal employees. As such, these business services are based on a different concept that includes another context. Hence, the results will be to diffuse to extract any conclusions.

1.5 Problem Definition

Due to their nature, GBS is considered to be a complex model, and various aspects (e.g. business processes, internal and external suppliers, business services portfolio) need to be coordinated continuously to ensure the proposed benefits. Reflecting the degree of GBS complexity, enterprises' struggle to implement business services effectively (see Sect. 2.3). Digitalisation may provide, however, new opportunities due to additional automation of business services. As a result, limited manual interactions between global departments may decrease GBS implementation challenges.

From an academic perspective the review of Holmlund et al. (2016) of business and management literature related to service-orientation underpins the call for more research on business services implementation and usage contexts. The authors argue that management, leadership, and decision making in organisations that rely on business services and which are engaged in the transition towards service-based approaches, face many challenges for managers that researchers could tap into (p. 2460). In a similar vein, Richter and Brühl (2017) call for more research examining the mediating effects between the antecedents of the business services and the outcomes. The authors argue that previous studies on business services failed to identify which antecedents directly influence or operate as mediators to business services outcomes (e.g. a business services portfolio).

To address this research gap, the current study adopts ROT and aims to examine the direct and indirect relationships between the antecedents of business services to enterprise business services portfolio. In addition, this research is interested in assessing the role of modularised business processes as mediator between antecedents of business services and orchestration of business services portfolio.

1.6 Main Objectives of the Book

The main objective of this book is to offer enterprise management a fresh perspective to use an ecosystem view when organising GBSs in the context of both in-house and outsourced delivery models. Applying an ecosystem view as an alternative for managing a classical organisational structure that is based on silos, may result in improved value creation, and enhanced organisational performance. However, applying an ecosystem view in the context of an increased complex delivery context is not enough. Importantly, enterprise management also have to integrate internal and external resources to provide GBSs, and as such cater for dynamic changes. By further digitalising business services, enterprise management will obtain new insights to overcome organisational barriers between business units and ultimately strengthen its competitive advantage. The main objectives of the book are to:

1. Identify which antecedents form a part of an enterprise orchestration capability that aims at integrating internal and external resources.
2. Theoretically develop and empirically validate a business services portfolio model and its corresponding antecedents.
3. Show how business processes act as a mediator towards a business services portfolio.
4. Demonstrate how digitalisation may overcome business services implementation barriers.

1.7 Research Approach

Since empirical research on the implementation of global business services (GBS) and the influencing role of digital technologies is scarce, we conducted a mixed-method research study. A more detailed and in-depth explanation is found in Appendix A. First, based on an extensive literature review we identified essential antecedents that potentially affect a GBSs services portfolio in which services are partially provided in-house and outsourced. The hybrid governance mode of bundling in-house and outsourced business services fits with the concept of plural sourcing in which firms make, buy or ally similar goods and services (Gulati & Puranam, 2006). Based on quantitative research we developed a research model and tested the relationships between the antecedents of GBSs by confirming or rejecting hypotheses, which assumed to predict the dependent variable (Bacharach, 1989). Second, we conducted four case studies in the context of GBS financial services to create a better understanding in how digitalisation affects GBSs in a practical setting. We opted to study digitalisation in the context of financial services as this GBS function is considered to be one of the first functions that was based on in-house as well as outsourced services (Borman, 2006; Currie et al., 2008) and we may assume that enterprises are experienced in this field to some degree.

1.8 Contribution

The contribution to the literature is threefold. First, as we demonstrated how internal and external resources can be integrated, we contribute to the business services, Operation Management (OM), and sourcing literature by validating a proposed research model. Based on a unique dataset, by studying global business services and influencing antecedents within the context of a plural sourcing strategy, the present research investigated the direct and indirect effects of several antecedents on an enterprise's orchestration of business services portfolio. We contributed to orchestration literature to study effects across countries or geographical regions

(Hitt et al., 2016, p 83). Our study partially fills that gap as we used an enterprise degree of outsourcing, size, geographical location (e.g. region and country) and maturity as control variables to examine whether the proposed relationships in the research model are affected by these variables. We identified how these control variables act as moderators and found moderating effects between various path relationships specifically in situations where enterprises apply a low degree of outsourcing.

Second, building on the theoretical perspectives of Resource Orchestration Theory (ROT), and employing two different methodological approaches, we examine the dependencies between antecedents and the orchestration of a GBSs portfolio. The findings explain why specific antecedents require continuous management attention, as they affect the complexity of orchestrating a GBS portfolio directly or indirectly. We contribute to OM literature by operationalising Sirmon et al.'s (2011) resource orchestration framework and followed resource management and asset management elements. Our results suggest that adapting a business services portfolio requires both sensing and seizing capabilities to cater for changes effectively. As a result, enterprise management needs to use a holistic view to coordinate changes that affect the antecedents under study to ensure coherence. Our case studies demonstrate that enterprises need to be mature to orchestrate internal and external resources adequately. Hence, we argue that enterprise management have to invest in building a dynamic orchestration capability.

A third contribution emphasises the dynamics to orchestrate a business services portfolio. We find that digital technologies accelerated the need to apply an enterprise ecosystem approach, which in turn strengthened the ties between various departments, management, and experts as each of them is aware of mutual dependencies. From a management and organisation perspective, we find that a coalitional model creates a better fit to handle enterprise dynamics. Our findings provide novel and powerful insights that enterprises' who apply an ecosystem approach to orchestrate their business services portfolio, taking a plural sourcing strategy and corresponding antecedents into account, are better capable to deal with orchestration complexity. By conducting this study, we extend the research of Holmlund et al. (2016) to examine management and leadership challenges in business services companies during the transition to service orientation (p. 2460). By applying ecosystem characteristics enterprises are able to transform their organisation and adapt to the dynamics to orchestrate a business services portfolio. As far as we know, this is the first study that explored that enterprises can be considered as an ecosystem, taking global business services in a plural sourcing context into account.

1.9 Structure of the Book

First, in Chap. 2 we address the positioning of global business services by studying three perspectives, namely: (1) the rise of business services and corresponding delivery modes, (2) the growth and position of GBSs, and their multi-nature, and (3) the importance of digitalisation as a means to overcome GBSs implementation challenges. Chapter 3 describes the theoretical background of our research model that draws on the Resource Orchestration Theory (ROT), plural sourcing and GBSs portfolio, addresses the development of hypotheses, and the introduction of a research model. Chapter 4 shows the findings of our quantitative research through the research method, data analysis and results. Chapter 5 illustrates various business services configurations by making use of a relatively new methodological approach; namely, fuzzy-set Qualitative Comparative Analysis (fsQCA), while the Chaps. 6, 7, 8, and 9 provide insights in the digitalisation of GBS by means of four case studies, a European logistic service provider, a global employment agency, a global building and construction enterprise, and a global financial service provider respectively. Chapter 10 provide insights in a cross-case analysis and in Chapter 11 we discuss our conclusions and managerial implications.

References

Adner, R. (2017). Ecosystem as structure: An actionable construct for strategy. *Journal of Management, 43*(1), 39–58.

Andersson, U., Forsgren, M., & Holm, U. (2002). The strategic impact of external networks: Subsidiary performance and competence development in the multinational corporation. *Strategic Management Journal, 23*(11), 979–996.

Astley, W. G., & Zajac, E. J. (1991). Intraorganizational power and organizational design: Reconciling rational and coalitional models of organization. *Organizational Science, 2*(4), 399–411.

Atienza, M. A., & Tabuena, A. C. (2021). The impact of COVID-19 pandemic on managerial accounting and its adjustments in financial markets. *International Journal of Business, Technology and Organizational Behavior, 1*(4), 287–296.

Atkins, B. (2021). *ESG history & status.* Retrieved August 10, 2021, from https://insights.diligent.com/wp-content/uploads/2020/06/ESGHistory-Status.pdf

Aydiner, A. S., Tatoglu, E., Bayraktar, E., Zaim, S., & Delen, D. (2019). Business analytics and firm performance: The mediating role of business process performance. *Journal of Business Research, 96*, 228–237.

Bacharach, S. B. (1989). Organizational theories: Some criteria for evaluation. *Academy of Management Review, 14*, 496–515.

Bangemann, T. O. (2005). *Shared Services in Finance and Accounting* (1st ed.). Routledge.

Benlian, A., Hilkert, D., & Hess, T. (2015). How open is this platform? The meaning and measurement of platform openness from the Complementers' perspective. *Journal of Information Technology, 30*(3), 209–228.

Bento, F., & Garotti, L. (2019). Resilience beyond formal structures: A network perspective towards the challenges of an aging workforce in the oil and gas industry. *Journal of Open Innovation, Technology, Market, and Complexity, 5*(1), 1–10.

Bento, F., Tagliabue, M., & Lorenzo, F. (2020). Organizational silos: A scoping review informed by a behavioural perspective on systems and networks. *Societies, 10*(56), 1–27.

Bharadwaj, A., El Sawy, O., Pavlou, P., & Venkatraman, N. (2013). Digital business strategy: Toward a next generation of insights. *MIS Quarterly, 37*(2), 471–482.

Borino, F., Carlson, E., Rollo, V., & Solleder, O. (2021). International firms and COVID-19: Evidence from a global survey. *COVID Economics, 75*, 30–59. Brighton: Harvard Business Press.

Borman, M. (2006). Applying multiple perspectives to the BPO decision: A case study of call centres in Australia. *Journal of Information Technology, 21*(2), 99–115.

Centola, D. (2018). *How behaviour spreads: The science of complex contagions.* Princeton University Press.

Currie, W., Michell, V., & Abanishe, A. (2008). Knowledge process outsourcing in financial services: The vendor perspective. *European Management Journal, 26*(2), 94–104.

Dai, T., & Tang, C. (2022). Frontiers in service science: Integrating ESG measures and supply chain management: Research opportunities in the post-pandemic era. *Service Science, 14*(1), 1–12.

Deloitte GBS. (2018). *Future of global business services: catalyst for enterprise digital transformation.* https://www2.deloitte.com/us/en/pages/operations/articles/globalbusiness-services-digital-transformation.html

Fielt, E., Bandara, W., Miskon, S., & Gable, G. (2014). Exploring shared services from an IS perspective: A literature review and research agenda. *Communications of the Association for Information Systems, 34*(1), 1001–1040.

Foerderer, J., Kude, T., Mithas, S., & Heinzl, A. (2018). Does platform Owner's entry crowd out innovation? Evidence from Google photos. *Information Systems Research, 29*(2), 444–460.

Gawer, A. (2014). Bridging differing perspectives on technological platforms: Toward an integrative framework. *Research Policy, 43*(7), 1239–1249.

Gulati, R., & Puranam, P. (2006). *Complementarity and constraints: Why firms both make and buy the same thing.* Working paper, Social Sciences Research Network, Copenhagen Business School. http://www.cbs.dk/content/download/

Handley, S. (2017). How governance misalignment and outsourcing capability impact performance. *Production and Operations Management, 26*(1), 134–155.

Hitt, M. A., Xu, K., & Matz Carnes, C. (2016). Resource based theory in operations management research. *Journal of Operations Management, 41*, 77–94.

Holmlund, M., Kowalkowski, C., & Biggemann, S. (2016). Organisational behavior in innovation, marketing, and purchasing in business service contexts: An agenda for academic inquiry. *Journal of Business Research, 69*(7), 2457–2462.

Iansiti, M., & Levien, R. (2004). *The keystone advantage: What the new dynamics of business ecosystems mean for strategy, innovation, and sustainability.*

Ioannou, I., Li, S. X., & Serafeim, G. (2016). The effect of target difficulty on target completion: The case of reducing carbon emissions. *The Accounting Review, 91*(5), 1467–1492.

Jacobides, M. G., Cennamo, C., & Gawer, A. (2018). Towards a theory of ecosystems. *Strategic Management Journal, 39*(8), 2255–2276.

Janssen, M., & Joha, A. (2006). Motives for establishing shared service centers in public administrations. *International Journal of Information Management, 26*(2), 102–115.

Janssen, M., & van der Voort, H. (2020). Agile and adaptive governance in crisis response: Lessons from the COVID-19 pandemic. *International Journal of Information Management, 55*, 102180.

Kane, G. C., Palmer, D., Phillips, A. N., Kiron, D., & Buckley, N. (2015). *Strategy, not technology, drives digital transformation* (Vol. 14(1–25)). MIT Sloan Management Review and Deloitte University Press.

Kohtamäki, M., Parida, V., Patel, P. C., & Gebauer, H. (2020). The relationship between digitalization and servitization: The role of servitization in capturing the financial potential of digitalization. *Technological Forecasting and Social Change, 151*, 119804.

Kotzab, H., Teller, C., Grant, D. B., & Friis, A. (2015). Supply chain management resources, capabilities and execution. *Production Planning & Control, 26*(7), 525–542.

KPMG Insights. (2019). Global business services at a crossroads: Results From the KPMG/HFS research state of operations survey. https://advisory.kpmg.us/articles/2019/gbs-crossroads.html

Leyh, C., Bley, K., & Seek, S. (2017). Elicitation of processes in business process management in the era of digitization—The same techniques as decades ago? In F. Piazolo, V. Geist, L. Brehm, & R. Schmidt (Eds.), *Innovations in Enterprise information systems management and engineering* (pp. 42–56). Springer International Publishing.

Lusch, R., & Vargo, S. (2014). *Service-dominant logic: Premises, perspectives, possibilities*. Cambridge University Press.

Lyytinen, K., Yoo, Y., & Boland, R. J., Jr. (2016). Digital product innovation within four classes of innovation networks. *Information Systems Journal, 26*(1), 47–75.

Maatman, M., & Meijerink, J. (2017). Why sharing is synergy: The role of decentralized control mechanisms and centralized HR capabilities in creating HR shared service value. *Personnel Review, 46*(7), 1297–1317.

Mackenzie, K. D. (1986). *Organizational design: The organizational audit and analysis technology*. Ablex Pub. Corp.

Mahesh, B. (2020). Machine learning algorithms—A review. *International Journal of Science and Research, 9*(1), 381–386.

Maital, S., & Barzani, E. (2020, March 2–11). The global economic impact of COVID-19: A summary of research. *Samuel Neaman Institute for National Policy*.

Majchrzak, A., Markus, M. L., & Wareham, J. (2016). Designing for digital transformation: Lessons for information systems research from the study of ICT and societal challenges. *MIS Quarterly, 40*(2), 267–277.

Matt, C., Hess, T., & Benlian, A. (2015). Digital transformation strategies. *Business & Information Systems Engineering, 57*(5), 339–343.

McIvor, R., McCracken, M., & McHugh, M. (2011). Creating outsourced shared services arrangements: Lessons from the public sector. *European Management Journal, 29*(6), 448–461.

McKinsey. (2022). Retrieved January 2, 2023, from https://www.mckinsey.com/capabilities/strategy-and-corporate-finance/our-insights/how-covid-19-has-pushed-companies-over-the-technology-tipping-point-and-transformed-business-forever

McLoughlin, K., Lewis, K., Lascelles, D., & Nudurupati, S. (2021). Sustainability in supply chains: Reappraising business process management. *Production Planning & Control, 34*(1), 19–52.

Miles, I. (2005). Knowledge intensive business services: Prospects and policies. *Foresight, 7*(6), 39–63.

Moore, J. F. (1993). Predators and prey: A new ecology of competition. *Harvard Business Review, 71*(3), 75–86.

Nagar, T. (2020). *How will the coronavirus impact the software industry?* Retrieved June 22, 2020, from https://customerthink.com/how-will-the-coronavirus-impact-the-software-industry/

Obrenovic, B., Du, J., Godinic, D., Tsoy, D., Khan, M. A. S., & Jakhongirov, I. (2020). Sustaining enterprise operations and productivity during the COVID-19 pandemic: "Enterprise effectiveness and sustainability model". *Sustainability, 12*(15), 5981.

Principles for Responsible Investment (PRI). (2022). *What is responsible investment?* Retrieved December 24, 2022, from https://www.unpri.org/an-introduction-to-responsible-investment/what-is-responsible-investment/4780.article

Rasoulian, S., Grégoire, Y., Legoux, R., & Sénécal, S. (2023). The effects of service crises and recovery resources on market reactions: An event study analysis on data breach announcements. *Journal of Service Research, 26*(1). https://doi.org/10.1177/10946705211036944

Richter, P. C., & Brühl, R. (2017). Shared service Centre research: A review of the past, present, and future. *European Management Journal, 35*(3), 26–38.

Senyo, P. K., Liu, K., Sun, L., & Effah, J. (2016). Evolution of norms in the emergence of digital business ecosystems. In M. Baranauskas, K. Liu, L. Sun, V. Neris, R. Bonacin, & K. Nakata (Eds.), *Socially aware organisations and technologies. Impact and challenges* (pp. 79–84). Springer.

Seric, A., Görg, H., Mösle, S., & Windisch, M. (2020). *Managing COVID-19: How the pandemic disrupts global value chains.* https://iap.unido.org/articles/managing-covid-19-how-pandemic-disruptsglobal-value-chains

Sirmon, D. G., Hitt, M. A., & Ireland, R. D. (2007). Managing firm resources in dynamic environments to create value: Looking inside the black box. *Academy of Management Review, 32*(1), 273–292.

Sirmon, D. G., Hitt, M. A., Ireland, R. D., & Gilbert, B. A. (2011). Resource orchestration to create competitive advantage breath, depth, and life cycle effects. *Journal of Management, 37*(5), 1390–1412.

Teece, D. J., & Linden, G. (2017). Business models, value capture, and the digital enterprise. *Journal of Organizational Design, 6*(8). https://doi.org/10.1186/s41469-017-0018-x

Ulbrich, F., & Schulz, V. (2014). Seven challenges management must overcome when implementing IT-shared services. *Strategic Outsourcing: An International Journal, 7*(2), 94–106.

Ulrich, D., Younger, J., & Brockbank, W. (2008). The twenty-first-century HR organization. *Human Resource Management, 47*(4), 829–850.

Van der Aalst, W., Schonenberg, M., & Song, M. (2011). Time prediction based on process mining. *Information Systems, 36*(2), 450–475.

Vial, G. (2021). Understanding digital transformation: A review and a research agenda. In *Managing digital transformation*. Routledge.

Wang, Y., Wallace, S. W., Shen, B., & Choi, T. M. (2015). Service supply chain management: A review of operational models. *European Journal of Operational Research, 247*(3), 685–698.

Willcocks, L. P. (2020). Robo-apocalypse cancelled? Reframing the automation and future of work debate. *Journal of Information Technology, 35*(4), 286–302.

Wirtz, J., Tuzovic, S., & Ehret, M. (2015). Global business services: Increasing specialization and integration of the world economy as drivers of economic growth. *Journal of Service Management, 26*(4), 565–587.

2

Positioning Business Services

2.1 Increasing Demand of Business Services

2.1.1 Business Services

Originally, business services were established within an enterprise with the focus on sustaining their internal organisation rather than on business services to end users (consumers or other businesses). We build on the definition of Wirtz et al. (2015) and define business services as "services that are provided both in-house and to other businesses and can be characterised by their knowledge-intensive nature". Business services consist of a variety of services such as, Finance and Accounting (Janssen & Joha, 2006), Administration (Ono, 2003), Human Resources (Maatman & Meijerink, 2017), Supply Chain Management (Wang et al., 2015), Procurement (Van der Valk & Rozemeijer, 2009), Legal (Lacity et al., 2014; Massini & Miozzo, 2012), and Information Technology (Handley, 2017; Lacity et al., 2010). To focus on their core business competences, business services are perceived as a federation of capabilities that collaborate with other business services in an ecosystem (Cherbakov et al., 2005). Since early 2000, academics studied business services from various perspectives including business strategy (Albertoni et al., 2017;

A. Plugge, S. Nikou, *Digitalisation of Global Business Services*, Technology, Work and Globalization, https://doi.org/10.1007/978-3-031-51528-6_2

Lacity et al., 2016; Murray et al., 2009), international business (Love & Mansury, 2009; Miles, 2005; Sako, 2006), information systems (Legner et al., 2017; Tan & Gallupe, 2006; Willcocks et al., 2017), and economics (Barber & Strack, 2015; Wirtz et al., 2015). However, between 2005 and 2011, researchers paid ample attention to service orientation to improve internal business services by building these out of readily available building blocks (e.g. Aier et al., 2011; Cherbakov et al., 2005; Janssen, 2008). Due to the convergence of rapid business developments and digitisation challenges, enterprises nowadays again seek various approaches, putting business services back in the limelight to achieve organisational responsiveness (Deloitte, 2018; KPMG, 2019).

As such, organisations decompose their enterprise and corresponding business services into smaller autonomous business components that may interact with other business components in order to improve effectiveness. The decomposition of enterprises makes complexity manageable and, as such, business services can be integrated and/or disintegrated across an organisation. In this way, business processes, which enable business services delivery are managed across an enterprise that requires breaking down siloed business processes into modular independent services (Demirkan et al., 2007), which result in dynamic business processes. Considering dynamic processes, each subsequent process step may be based on the full or partial results of previous steps. Consequently, dynamic processes increase an enterprise organisational responsiveness to cater for market changes. On the one hand, literature shows that to support business services, information systems must be loosely coupled to create dynamic business processes (Janssen, 2008), and therefore, form a prerequisite to enable strategic decision making. On the other hand, tightly coupled business services and IS may hinder the degree of business services effectiveness. Due to the evolution of IS (e.g. web services, architectures, application, practices) and of corresponding business processes, Alreemy et al. (2016) state that appropriate governance is essential to achieve organisational success.

Importantly, business services can be provided by an enterprise internal organisation or by the market. As there are many business services, it can result in sourcing strategies in which multiple modes of sourcing decisions are managed simultaneously. Today, sourcing remains an essential topic that needs further attention as the market continues to grow both from a content and size perspective. As we address the effects of business services in the context of plural sourcing specifically, we illustrate the rise of business services sourcing options from this perspective. Next, we address four perspectives of business services sourcing modes that emerged over time in the context of global business services.

2.1.2 Shared Services Centres

Since the rise of shared service centres (SSCs) in the late 1980s, the concept has gained its popularity in public and private organisations to deliver shared services to internal departments (Niehaves & Krause, 2010; Ulbrich, 2006; Wirtz et al., 2015). Examples relate to General Electrics, Baxter Healthcare and AT Kearney (Quinn et al., 2000). In that period, shared services were predominantly used within the Finance and Accounting function (Hammer, 2001). However, by the year 2000 approximately 80% of the top 20 Fortune 500 used shared services and many other top Fortune 500 implemented some form of shared services. Sourcing arrangements related to shared services often focus on providing services in the most efficient way, creating economies of scale. The basic premise regarding shared services is that one entity is responsible for providing services to internal departments with relatively little effort (Bergeron, 2003; Ulbrich & Borman, 2012).

Based on the literature, we define shared services as "a collaborative strategy in which a subset of existing business functions are concentrated into a new semi-autonomous business unit that has a management structure designed to promote efficiency, value generation, costs savings, and improved service for the internal customers of the parent corporation (Bergeron, 2003, p. 3). Because of the mix of rapid business advancements and challenges created by digitisation, organisations demand services provided by SSCs to ensure organisational responsiveness (e.g. KPMG, 2019). As such, organisations' SSC strategies are becoming crucial, as decision making has far reached implications for offering shared services. Examples of common SSC are Finance and Accounting (F&A) (Janssen & Joha, 2006), Human Resources (HR) (Maatman & Meijerink, 2017) and Information Technology (IT) (Ulbrich & Schulz, 2014).

Service delivery modes (centralised, decentralised) related to shared services can be seen as strategic instruments, which are dependent on an enterprise's business objectives. The main rationale to establish centralised shared services is often determined by cost reduction that may be achieved when individually provided services are consolidated. When multiple internal departments within an enterprise provide similar types of services, synergies may be realised by means of standardisation and consolidation. A mechanism to decrease the cost of providing services is to achieve high economies of scale striving to provide internal services as most efficient as possible (Ulbrich & Borman, 2012). The same goes for bundling in-depth expertise in an SSC in which specific skills and experience can be shared to support end users. Consequently, this service delivery mode can be seen as an operational excellence strategy to deliver services at the lowest cost in the most effective way. The trade-off of this approach is that the internal end users' perspective is less important. Internal business demands to customise services are often neglected as this may disturb process standardisation and increase the cost level. Previous research revealed that if internal business departments feel less served, this might affect their perception of the provided performance of the services (Ulbrich & Borman, 2012).

The decentralised service delivery mode can be perceived as the opposite strategy of the centralised shared services. Organisational motives to establish decentralised shared services arise from business needs per department. When an enterprise can be characterised as a heterogeneous organisation, business service needs per department may vary. To meet specific business needs of internal departments and have a significant degree of flexibility, enterprises choose this form of delivery mode. However, decentralised shared services focus on process standardisation in order to benefit from cost reductions, but it might be on a lower level when compared with centralised shared services. In turn, capabilities as utilised by decentralised shared services may develop and provide services that are fully aligned with internal departments' needs that be geographically dispersed (Lacity & Fox, 2008).

Today, SSCs are driven by IT technology (data, cloud) and as such, can be considered as a platform that provides services by means of technical modules to internal business units. An SSC often connects users of services and providers of services as some services are provided in-house, whereas for others, the SSCs source the services on the market. From this view, SSCs can be viewed as a modular platform providing services. Literature shows that SSCs have extensively been investigated (see e.g. Janssen & Joha, 2006; Fielt et al., 2014). However, numerous terms for the same notion have been offered; for example, challenges (Knol et al., 2014), determinants (Richter & Brühl, 2017), and critical success factors (Borman & Janssen, 2013). More importantly, different factors may affect the implementation of an SSC, such as the type of service and the importance of business processes (Joha & Janssen, 2014). As such, there is a scarcity of knowledge about the factors that lead to a successful SSC implementation (Miskon et al., 2012), despite a handful of descriptive case studies that thoroughly investigated how businesses adopt SSCs.

2.1.3 Captives

Captive centre is a strategy that is investigated by enterprises when thinking about how to offshore work. Oshri (2011, p. 9) defines a captive centre as "wholly owned facilities with the purpose of processing activities that were previously done in a company's back office in the domestic country. The concept of captive centres is directly related to SSCs as an enterprise may establish captive centres in other countries compared to their home destination. As such, captives can be considered as a particularisation of SSC's. Captives emerged at the end of the twentieth century as enterprises established captives to reduce cost and create access to expertise and skills (e.g. General Electric, Philips).

Recent research of Oshri et al. (2023) on captive centres shows that there are over 75,000 SSCs on a global level in 2022, in which the Compound Annual Growth Rate (CAGR) has grown by 30% in the period 2015 up to 2022. Regarding the maturity of captive centres some advanced SSCs have turned into official operating business units of their respective enterprises. Besides captive customers, they serve third-party customers as well and operate as profit centres. While external customers are being served with comprehensive and advanced pricing models, internal captive customers are handled differently by applying internal agreements and related pricing (internal accounting). Taking the growth and success of captive centres into account, literature illustrates that captive centre faces difficulties in offering benefits within the enterprise such as limited financial profitability, challenges from a product or service development view, and increased employee wages (Oshri, 2011). Although the type of captive may vary, such as basic captives (all tasks are performed within the captive), hybrid captives (partially outsourced tasks), and shared captives (business services provided to both the own enterprise and external clients), the implementation of captive centre is challenging. In this regard, aspects like organisational redesigns (demarcation of business services tasks), aligning business processes, governing renewed roles and responsibilities, redesign of supporting information systems (e.g. infrastructure, applications), and increased employee attrition rate within captive centres, may all hinder the implementation phase. Consequently, operational performance of business services may be affected negatively.

2.1.4 Outsourcing

Research on information technology outsourcing (ITO) and business process outsourcing (BPO) market literature shows that enterprises are more inclined to outsource their business services (Oshri et al., 2023). As the outsourcing market matured over time, multiple suppliers offer various type of business services in which some suppliers focus on a limited number of business services and/or industries. A survey conducted by Loughborough University in 2014 shows that multiple business services have been outsourced to the market, ranging from IT infrastructure, software testing, data warehousing to legal services and research and development. Recent research on outsourcing shows that robotic process automation and artificial intelligence (AI) solutions are outsourced too (Beulen et al., 2022; Willcocks et al., 2019). Oshri et al. (2023) define outsourcing of business services as "contracting to a third-party supplier for the management and completion of a certain amount of work, for a specified length of time, cost, and service level". A vast landscape of ITO and BPO suppliers has evolved over the past decade, providers are also essential to further improve business services as they offer their services based on various delivery models (e.g. offshoring, captives). Interestingly, the chain of parties involved include enterprise business units, their captives, retained organisation, outsourcing suppliers and next third parties.

As enterprises have to manage uncertainties in the provisioning of external business services (Krancher et al., 2022), governance is a prerequisite to encourage desirable behaviour in the use of resources. Literature reveals two main research streams that include formal and relational governance. Formal governance addresses the need to coordinate tasks between outsourcing service providers to prevent opportunistic behaviour (Chang et al., 2017). Other scholars, such as Rai et al. (2012) considered relationships that attempts to address some of the deficiencies in contract governance; namely, the failure to account for social structures within which the inter-organisation exchanges are embedded (Xiao et al., 2012). For example, literature on information systems governance shows more complex and dynamic interrelationships between formal and relational governance than the previously assumed dichotomy of complementarity and substitution (Lacity et al., 2016). These studies emphasise the role of relation-specific boundary conditions and find that formal and relational governance mechanisms can act as substitutes (Rai et al., 2012), simultaneously work as substitutes and complements (Lioliou et al., 2014), or have an impact that oscillates over time. This finding illustrates the complexity of applying an outsourcing strategy in governing internal and external suppliers.

However, outsourcing arrangements have evolved from dyadic client–provider relationship toward an environment that includes multiple suppliers (Palvia et al., 2010). The shift from single sourcing toward multi-sourcing arrangements provides enterprises with benefits, like quality improvements, by being able to select the best suppliers, having access to external capabilities and skills and mitigating the risks of supplier lock in (Hawk et al., 2012; Gonzalez et al., 2013). Literature shows that enterprises that engage in global collaborative networks invest in time, commitment, and trust-building to create and capture common value (Romero & Molina, 2011), or by interacting with multiple sourcing participants.

In the 2010s, scholars and practitioners alike defined IT multi-sourcing as the use of two or more external suppliers as part of an outsourcing arrangement (Su & Levina, 2011). These authors refer to Wiener and Saunders (2014), who define IT multi-sourcing as "the situation where a client firm delegates IT projects and services to multiple external vendors who must, at least partly, work cooperatively to achieve the client's business objectives" (p. 211). Information Systems (IS) research shows that enterprises should govern an IT multi-sourcing arrangement beyond the traditional contractual agreements and build trust relationships between individual suppliers and the client to support the exchange of information (Rai et al., 2012). Importantly, to build trust, clients and suppliers have to work together intensively to exchange information. However, literature shows that collaboration within a multi-sourcing context is often problematic because it is difficult to establish and monitor control and coordination mechanisms (Rao et al., 2007), including and specifically in international settings. Furthermore, Wiener and Saunders (2014) argue that, in a competing IT multi-sourcing arrangement, collaboration between actors is essential to aligning their interests, avoiding tensions, and creating common value. A study by Huber et al. (2017) showed that a lack of collaboration prevents actors from creating value together due to a lack of governance cost. The authors argue that this issue is addressed more successfully if the IT multi-sourcing environment is conceptualised as an ecosystem (Moore, 1996), where actors exchange information and knowledge to create and capture value together.

2.1.5 Offshoring

Offshoring of business services have become a significant trend in which enterprises may benefit from various objectives such as cost reduction, access to external capabilities, improved lead times, process streamlining and strategic repositioning (Beulen & Ribbers, 2021; Oshri, 2011). The concept of offshoring is closely related to outsourcing as suppliers may establish offshore locations to execute ITO and BPO tasks more efficiently. In a similar vein to the concepts of SSC's and captive, offshoring can be considered as a particularisation of outsourcing. The offshore provisioning of IT outsourcing services has shown a rapid increase in the past 20 years while it is expected to continue its growth. Oshri et al. (2015) defined offshoring as "the relocation of organisational activities (i.e. information technology, finance and accounting, back office, and human resources) to a wholly owned subsidiary or an independent service provider in another country", (p. 8). When being confronted with fierce competition from over-seas firms, enterprises increased to offshore their operations to achieve cost reductions (Farrel, 2004). This trend started in the manufacturing industry and gradually permeating the service industry in particular with establishing call centres.

Carmel and Tjia (2005), who studied the offshoring market intensively, identified the important role that India plays by dominating the global ITO market. As an example, we can refer to worldwide anticipation of IT problems at the turn of the millennium and dubbed Y2K problems, where enterprises outsourced the solution of the Y2K problems to suppliers who offered available resource capacity in offshore locations. Although literature on offshoring critique addressed the importance of service quality and potential language barriers (Oshri, 2011), business services offshoring continued to grow. Today suppliers offer various sourcing delivery models that include outsourcing and offshoring options and span multiple countries such as: Argentina, Brazil, China, Egypt, India, Hungary, Lithuania, Philippines, Poland, Portugal, Romania, Ukraine, and South Africa amongst others. As such, the demarcation between offshoring locations (originally Asia) and nearshoring have become blurred.

From a historical perspective of sourcing models, the concept of make and buy which are applied to support the provisioning of business services has evolved over time. The variety of sourcing models are summarised in Fig. 2.1.

All in all, we conducted an extensive literature study in the context of global business services and corresponding sourcing modes; shared service centres and captives, outsourcing and offshoring. Next, we discussed and elaborated on these essential research insights. As shown in Table 2.1 below, we bundled relevant and impactful research insights as studied. Interestingly, the four perspectives of business services sourcing modes emerged over time and followed various paths to end up in the concept

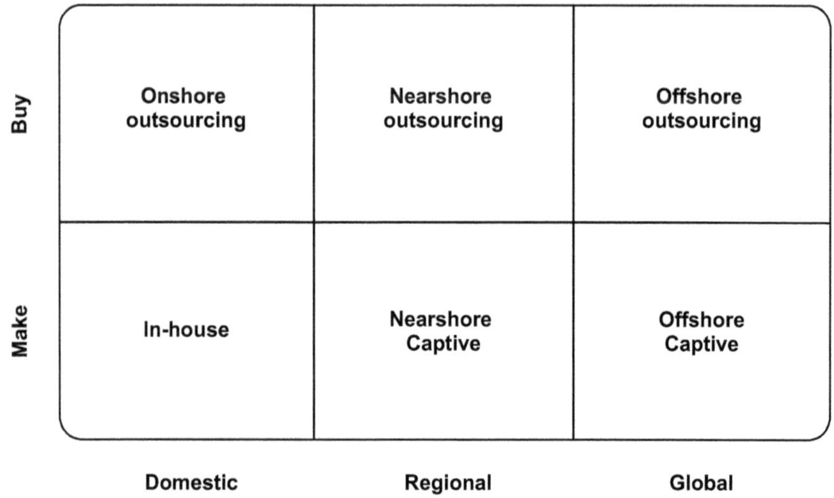

Fig. 2.1 Sourcing models. (Adapted from Oshri, 2011)

of global business services (GBS). Next, we elaborate on GBS and explain the richness as well as the complexity of implementing GBSs.

2.2 Global Business Services

The emergence of GBSs can be linked to the impacts of the financial crisis of 2007–2008 on businesses. This severe worldwide economic crisis, also mentioned as the Global Financial Crisis (GFC) forced enterprises to focus on cost reduction, lower their quality of services, and as a consequence changed their operating model. More specifically, an enterprise operating model is based on a coherent structure of an enterprise strategy, sourcing delivery models, business processes and employees' skills and expertise. The first concepts of GBS were described by various market research firms such as Deloitte, Gartner, Horses for Sources (HfS), KPMG, and PWC. These market research firms find that enterprises sourced their business services from both an SSC perspective and an outsourcing perspective. For example, research of HfS (2011, p. 1) illustrates that the objective of a global business services strategy is not

Table 2.1 Literature review

	Source	Journal (research discipline)	Type of research	Key attributes
(Global) Business Services	Esteves and Pastor (2001)	Communications of the Association for Information Systems	Literature review	Information Systems, Lifecycle, Business processes
	Fremantle et al. (2002)	Communications of the ACM	Literature review	Web Services, Information systems, Integration
	Sako (2006)	Oxford Review of Economic Policy	Literature review	Business Services, Outsourcing, Offshoring
	Demirkan et al. (2007)	Electronic Commerce Research and Applications	Literature review	Customer Perspective, Economics, Information Technology Strategy
	Van der Aalst (2012)	IEEE Transactions on Services Computing	Literature review	Business Processes, Process Aware Information Systems
	Ciarli et al. (2012)	Journal of Economic Surveys	Qualitative research	Business Services, Knowledge Dynamics, Geography
	Wynstra et al. (2015)	Journal of Operations Management	Literature review	Governance, Capabilities, Contracting, Management
	Alreemy et al. (2016)	International Journal of Information Management	Literature review	Information Systems, Governance, Success factors
	Holmlund et al. (2016)	Journal of Business Research	Literature review	Financial Issues, Management, Decision-making
	Wirtz et al. (2015)	Journal of Service Management	Literature review, Desk research	Economic Growth, Service Economy, Outsourcing, Offshoring
	Lacity et al. (2017)	The Journal of Strategic Information Systems	Qualitative research	Business Services Outsourcing, Inter-Organisational Conflicts
	Lu et al. (2020)	Journal of Service Theory and Practice	Literature review	Service Robots, Artificial Intelligence, Service Employees
	Peng (2022)	Book—Cengage Learning	Qualitative research	Strategy, Structure, Global Business Services, F&A, HR, SCM

(continued)

Table 2.1 (continued)

	Source	Journal (research discipline)	Type of research	Key attributes
Shared Service Centres and Captives	Ulbrich (2006)	Business Process Management Journal	Literature review	Shared Services, Business Process Reengineering, Organisational Processes
	Janssen and Joha (2006)	International Journal of Information Management	Literature review, Qualitative research	Services, Outsourcing, Information Networks
	Niehaves and Krause (2010)	Transforming Government: People, Process and Policy	Qualitative research	Shared Services, Resource Sharing, Networking
	Oshri (2011)	Book—The MIT Press	Qualitative research	Shared Services, Captives, Outsourcing, Offshoring
	Dreher (2013)	Finance Bundling and Finance Transformation	Literature review	Captive Shared Service Centre, Scoring Model, Business Unit, SLA
	Knol et al. (2014)	European Management Journa	Literature review	Shared Services, Challenges, Resource Dependence Perspective
	Lacity et al. (2017)	Journal of Information Technology	Literature review	Business Services, IT Outsourcing, Business Process Outsourcing
	Maatman and Meijerink (2017)	Personnel Review	Quantitative research	Shared Services, Dynamic Capabilities, Value, Control Mechanisms
	Richter and Brühl (2017)	European Management Journal	Literature review	Shared Service, Business Services, Outsourcing, Configurations
	Richter and Brühl (2020)	European Management Journal	Quantitative research	Shared Service, Dynamic Capabilities, Operational Capabilities
	Plugge et al. (2022)	Industrial Management & Data Systems	Qualitative research	Shared Service Centre, Configurations, Service Portfolio, Standardisation
	Oshri et al. (2023)	MIS Quarterly	Qualitative research	Shared Service Centre, Captive, Outsourcing

Outsourcing and offshoring	Carmel and Tjia (2005)	Book—Cambridge University Press	Qualitative research	Outsourcing, Offshoring, Geography, Governance, Relationships
	Cohen and Young (2006)	Book—Harvard Business Press	Qualitative research	Outsourcing, Multisourcing, Governance, Service Providers
	Bapna et al. (2010)	Information Systems Research	Literature review	Multisourcing; Offshore outsourcing, Governance, Cooperation, Coordination
	Palvia et al. (2010)	Decision Sciences	Quantitative research	Offshoring, Capability, Quality, Performance, Vendors
	Su and Levina (2011)	IEEE Transactions on Engineering Management	Qualitative research	IT Outsourcing, Multisourcing, Financial Business Services, Configurations
	Rai et al. (2012)	MIS Quarterly	Quantitative research	Business Process Outsourcing, Formal Contract, Hybrid Governance
	Lioliou et al. (2014)	Information Systems Journal	Qualitative research	Outsourcing, Formal and Relational Governance, Psychological Contract
	Wiener and Saunders (2014)	The Journal of Strategic Information Systems	Qualitative research	IT Multisourcing, Outsourcing, Forced Coopetition, Competition, Cooperation
	Willcocks et al. (2018)	Book—Palgrave Macmillan	Qualitative research	Outsourcing, Innovation, Governance, Automation
	Oshri et al. (2019)	Journal of Management Information Systems	Quantitative research	Multisourcing, Joint Performance, Governance, Architectural Knowledge
	Kotlarsky et al. (2023)	MIS Quarterly	Qualitative research	Information Technology Outsourcing, Business Partner, Reputation Formation
	Beulen and Ribbers (2021)	Book—Routledge 3rd edition	Qualitative research	IT Outsourcing, Digitalisation, Robotic Process Automation, Governance
	Krancher et al. (2022)	Journal of the Association for Information Systems	Quantitative research	Multisourcing, Bilateral and Collective Governance, Performance

only "to source globally, but also to leverage shared services, outsourcing and third-party investments to advance the objectives of the enterprise". A recent market study conducted by BCG (2022) shows that the concept of GBS matured over time and currently there are more than 10.000 GBS centres around the world. BCG projected the growth of the GBS market from USD 1.8 trillion in 2022 to USD 2.5 trillion USD by 2025. This finding shows that GBS is expected to contribute to the value equation for global enterprises. In addition, due to COVID-19 and Brexit, the importance of GBS has increasingly been valued as enterprises had to cater for changing circumstances and searched for organisational responsiveness. Today, GBS is being applied to a variety of models attempting to coordinate service delivery across multiple functions (Deloitte, 2018). According to Huber and Danino (2012) GBS can be characterised as an integrated compilation of service offerings for any (multiple) support functions within a company [...] global in nature and with respect to both delivery centres and customers. As a result, GBS models are different from the traditional approach of shared services and the past wave of outsourcing/offshoring, as it seeks to leverage the capabilities of suppliers (McIvor et al., 2011).

Market research conducted in 2021 by Deloitte shows that various business services are organised by means of SSCs and outsourcing. The four most common global business services are: (1) Finance and Accounting (F&A), (2) Human Resources (HR), (3) Information Technology (IT), and (4) Supply Chain Management (SCM). Based on market insights of Deloitte, HfS, KPMG, and PWC, GBS is described as an operating model for business services that encompass SSCs, captives, outsourcing, and centres of excellence to support enterprises' business units.

2.2.1 Multi-nature Aspects

Market research shows that GBS models can be characterised by their "multi-nature" (Deloitte, 2018; KPMG, 2019), namely: multi-business, multi-function, multi-region, and multi-sourcing approach. Applying a multi-sourcing strategy fit with the concept of plural sourcing. Many enterprises have seen their shared services and outsourcing initiatives evolve out of a single business unit, often the largest one. In some cases, internal politics may hinder GBS adoption by other business units, forcing them to go it alone. Enterprises that apply GBS typically serve multiple business units, applying the best, and most sophisticated practices to the entire organisation. Often enterprises that have started their journey with a single function or business process, extended their business functions over time. As market research shows, GBS organisations are multifunctional by nature. Historically, shared services and outsourcing programmes stated to support one geographical region. Today, however, GBS may support multiple regions within an organisation at the same time, often divided into various regions that include the Americas, Europe, and Asia-Pacific. GBS often starts with multiple centres in each region for each function. GBS organisations focus on providing an increased performance by consolidating the footprint to fewer locations. Some enterprises continue to rely on a regional delivery model, while others choose a hub-and-spoke approach, with the bulk of work typically performed in an Asian hub to achieve cost reductions. To implement a plural sourcing strategy, both firms and suppliers need to focus on mutual collaboration as they have to work together intensively to exchange business service information. However, literature shows that collaboration within a plural sourcing context is often problematic because it is difficult to establish and monitor control and coordination mechanisms (Rao et al., 2007). Due to the characteristics of GBS, the degree of complexity to govern business services increases. Consequently, an enterprise must delegate resources, processes, and managerial control to independent external suppliers. Wirtz et al. (2015) argue that firms have to apply a centralised approach when governing their business services in order to integrate into corporate strategies. Importantly, due to plural sourcing, the supply chains of technology-intensive business services become more fragmented. This creates a new source of complexity because GBS is introduced in the context of plural sourcing that may require new service governance approaches.

Enterprises that apply GBS are increasingly agnostic when it comes to sourcing delivery models. Some enterprises continue to rely exclusively on shared services or outsourcing, while other enterprises are combining the two driven by business needs. In practice, transactional activities are often being outsourced, with higher value advisory activities delivered through captive centres. The most mature enterprises focus on what type of business services are supported in-house or outsourced, while associated delivery units focus on how business services are provided supporting the multi-nature of GBS. The evolution of business services and corresponding delivery models over time is depicted in Fig. 2.2.

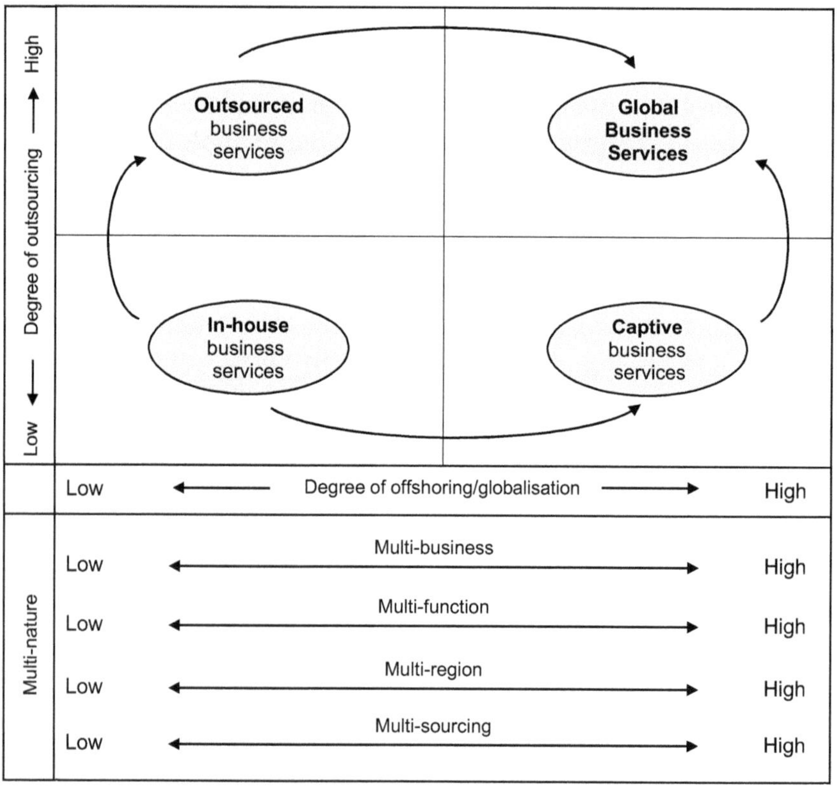

Fig. 2.2 Evolution of business services. (Adapted from Wirtz et al., 2015)

2.2.2 GBS Drivers

We conducted a survey to identify the rationales of the enterprises in scope why they started the implementation of the GBS concept. Participants were asked to enter the digit 1 to 5 that corresponds with the rationales to implement GBSs (see Appendix A). The rationales and corresponding outcomes are illustrated in Table 2.2. We included seven rationales (perspectives) that can be considered to achieve enterprises' strategic objectives when implementing the GBS concept.

First, we focused on a merger and acquisitions view as global operating enterprises may focus on growth and achieve synergies. This is supported by the second rationale to achieve growth by accessing new markets. Third, an enterprise operating model is complex by nature, and includes various aspects that need to be managed in a coherent and consistent manner (e.g. business processes, organisational structure, technology, and employees' skills). Therefore, we address the rationale to align an operating model, and consequently reducing the degree of business risks. The next rationale focuses on how to optimise global operations in order to scale up when relevant. The fifth rationale discusses the added value of applying data and analytics to support strategic decision making. Next, we address the importance of process excellence in order to support the added value of GBSs. Finally, the last rationale focuses on to what degree an internal repository of talent can be built to support a GBS implementation.

Applying a rationale view across industries, we find that the enterprises address the importance of aligning their operating model to support the provisioning of business services on a global level. As a result, business risks such a lack of governance or unclear or even lacking quality policies are mitigated, which in turn contribute to achieve compliance. In this regard, the findings of the fourth rationale is coherent with the findings of the third rationale as optimisation of global operations create opportunities to scale up business services on a global level. Importantly, the outcomes of the sixth rationale "process excellence and collaboration" is recognised by the majority of the enterprises in scope. This finding supports extant literature that argues that the coordination of business

Table 2.2 Overview of enterprises' rationales[a] to apply GBS

Rationale	Consumer products	Diversified conglomerate	Education	Energy & utilities	Financial & professional services	Food & beverages	Manufacturing & logistics	Pharma	Public sector	Technology & telecom	Other
Drive growth & realise synergies from acquisitions	3.83	2.87	4.33	2.17	2.75	3.00	3.25	3.46	1.54	3.16	2.94
Drive growth in emerging markets	2.66	2.25	2.66	1.88	2.37	2.33	1.75	2.21	2.09	3.16	2.35
Align the operating model to mitigate business risk and ensure compliance	4.33	3.75	4.33	2.77	3.77	3.55	3.62	4.20	4.66	4.50	4.55
Optimise the global operations footprint and ability to scale	4.00	2.87	1.66	3.64	3.66	4.11	3.62	4.06	2.66	3.83	3.22
Unlock the power of data & analytics to drive greater insight	3.83	3.25	3.66	3.88	3.44	2.77	3.25	3.60	3.00	3.33	3.70
Drive process excellence and collaboration	4.75	4.20	2.66	4.41	4.16	4.14	3.85	4.25	1.54	4.50	4.12
Build internal repository of high-quality talent	3.50	3.00	2.66	3.90	3.16	3.28	3.00	3.00	3.45	2.66	3.50
Total number of enterprises	N = 6	N = 8	N = 10	N = 18	N = 9	N = 9	N = 8	N = 15	N = 11	N = 6	N = 21

[a]Rationales were evaluated based on the importance of the following statements on a 5-point rating scale, ranged from 1 being "totally disagree" to 5 being "totally agree"?

processes is related to the integration of internal and external business services (Narayanan et al., 2011; Van der Aalst, 2012). In case business services are outsourced to the market, the degree in which business process coordination need to take place will increase. Taking both internal and external business services into account business processes also need to be flexible to support business services that can be managed in various configurations.

From an industry perspective, we find that enterprises operating on Consumer Products and Pharma focus on aligning their operating model, optimise their global operations and drive process excellence. This finding shows the coherence between business services supported by business processes on a global level. Various industries have also noticed the need to align their operating model or global operations supported by excellent business processes (e.g. Food and Beverages, Public Sector, Technology and Telecom, others). These findings illustrate the significant importance of both global operations, and operating model related to business processes.

2.2.3 Benefits

Several market research firms such as BCG (2022), Deloitte (2017, 2018), HfS (2011), and KPMG (2019), shows six key benefits for enterprises' when applying GBS. First, as GBS spans multiple functions, geographies, and delivery channels, it creates opportunities that may foster new value propositions. Consequently, enterprises may benefit from one integrated organisation with end-to-end processes, and clear accountability. In addition, GBS may enable an enterprise to enter new markets and adopt new processes more rapidly. Hence, applying GBS offers enterprises the opportunity to better serve the end users and customers. Second, GBS provides flexibility, as an integrated set of management and back- and middle-office delivery capabilities enable enterprises to focus on their front-office activities and as such, striving for the growth of their business. The degree of flexibility contributes to create an agile enterprise with scalability to respond to changing business needs such as mergers, acquisitions, and divestitures. Third, GBS offers a standard approach to globally manage back- and middle-office services. As such, it offers the scale to drive cost and operational efficiencies on a global level across business services and internal business units. This makes it easier for end users and customers to do business. Fourth, centres of excellence are identified and integrated into the business services portfolio. As a result, an enterprise can maximise its talent and resources to focus on innovation and opportunities. Fifth, GBS may support enterprises to effectively manage risks; for example, decrease business disruptions and apply global control frameworks across business services and geographies. Finally, GBS becomes an incubator for digital ways of working and a catalyst for enterprise-wide digital transformation programs. This may be strengthened by improved data analytics and insights from access to cross-functional, enterprise-wide data.

2.3 GBS Implementation Challenges

Due to their multi-nature, GBS is considered to be a complex model, and various aspects (e.g. business processes, internal and external suppliers, business services portfolio) need to be aligned and coordinated continuously to ensure the proposed benefits. Prior studies have explored the antecedents contributing the success of business services implementation. However, implementation success stories are relatively scarce and predominantly based on stand-alone case studies. Studying the literature that includes SSC, outsourcing, offshoring, captives, and GBS, we may bundle implementation challenges to four groups: (1) strategy and organisation, (2) operating and delivery model, (3) business processes, and (4) geography.

Regarding *strategy and organisation*, we found examples of power struggles due to the loss of FTE and financial agreements of specific business units within an enterprise. The way in which business services are governed has been found to be a challenge as sometimes it is unclear who is responsible for managing business services and make decisions to adjust them if necessary. Tensions were found on how to implement a GBS strategy such as a big-bang scenario or a more gradual implementation strategy (step-by-step approach) of business services. In addition, unclarity about organisational boundaries may hinder the provisioning of business services, which are provided by internal and or external suppliers. The same goes for challenges that may occur with regard to the geographic dispersion of various business services (e.g. global, regional, local). Finally, a lack of executive and management attention may rise problems and complaints to formulate clear objectives which in turn cannot be measured to identify the degree of implementation success.

In addition, an enterprise decision to outsource business services to the market has serious impact on an *operating and delivery model* as the relationships towards external suppliers are formalised compared to in-house delivery of business services. As a result, enterprise management must invest in additional governance and coordination towards external suppliers to continue service provisioning, mitigating business and operational risks and ensure compliance. Massini and Miozzo (2012) studied outsourcing and offshoring challenges on a global level by analysing case studies that include various type of business services (e.g. administrative services, call centres, information technology services, procurement, and product development). The authors argue that challenges arise with regard to outsourcing decision making (e.g. accountability, responsibility), impact of globalisation on value-adding tasks, and the organisation of technical centres of excellence that comprise of specific skills and expertise to support business services specifically. The latter is in line with the findings of Wirtz et al. (2015) in which the authors state that from a strategic perspective, business services outsourcing will be a key challenge in maintaining a viable resource base. In other words, does the enterprise have viable and skilled resources to manage and govern the provisioning of external business service. Lacity et al. (2011) studied business services in an outsourcing and offshoring context and found that enterprises expect that suppliers innovate business services over time. Importantly, practice shows that when enterprises focus on lower costs and improving service quality innovation, suppliers exclude innovation that in turn often relate to investments. As a result, innovations will be “out of scope”.

To support business services effectively, implementing *business processes* are essential to enable an enterprise to continue their businesses. The challenge of business processes, however, arises from the fact that there is no one-size-fits-all solution (Blasini et al., 2017). Business processes are context dependent, which means that they have to be adapted taking various aspects into account, such as: an enterprise's industry, their role in its industry (e.g. service integrator, service provider, or intermediate), and more particular an enterprise's underlying processes and services. From a historical view, business processes have been tightly coupled and optimised for specific needs and contexts of businesses and industries and supported by information systems. Although tightly coupled business processes and information systems can perform well, enterprises may encounter face challenges in scalability, flexibility, agility, and innovation needs of firms. To deal with these limitations, enterprises increasingly rely on modular business process and information systems. Due to the complexity of business services functionality, implementing modular business processes is risky and may hinder business continuity. In case business services are outsourced or offshored, implementation risks will increase as the chain of parties is extended (enterprise departments, multiple supplier delivery units). These business process challenges correspond with our research findings on enterprises' rationale to achieve process excellence and collaboration that in turn contributes to business continuity.

Literature shows that country attractiveness and *geography* play an essential role when implementing business services (Lacity et al., 2011; Oshri et al., 2023). The cultural difference, which refers to the extent to which the members of two distinct groups (such as an enterprise and supplier personnel) are different, was found to be important factor as they may differ on one or more cultural dimensions. Prior studies demonstrate that cultural distance negatively affects business services outcomes. A second factor that relate to geography is financial attractiveness. This relate to the degree to which a country is attractive to business services enterprises due to favourable financial factors. Examples are labour costs, taxes, regulatory, and other costs (e.g. Doh et al., 2009; Malos, 2010). Creating access to skills and expertise is often an important motivation to organise business services tasks abroad. This relate to human attractiveness that may be limited in practice due to a limited size of a labour pool and quality of education. The multi-nature of GBS demonstrates its complexity when the concept is implemented in practice.

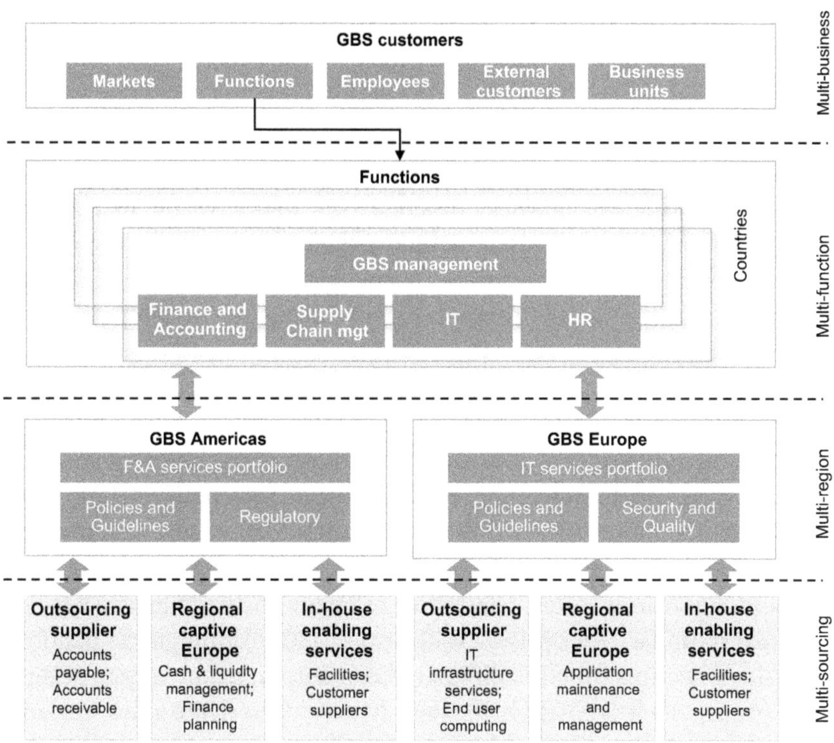

Fig. 2.3 Example of a GBS structure

Figure 2.3 shows an example of the GBS multi-function characteristics and corresponding delivery models (multi-sourcing) in a geographic dispersed view (multi-region) that may support various businesses (multi-business).

To summarise, the challenges as described above potentially hinder an effective implementation of business services in practice. Considering the multi-nature of GBSs and the associated degree of complexity, it can be argued that enterprises have to develop strategies to overcome implementation barriers effectively. Due to the convergence of rapid business developments and challenges imposed by digitisation of work processes, enterprises may explore how digital solutions may decrease implementation challenges.

2.4 Importance of Digitalisation

Today, enterprises cannot neglect the impact of the digitalisation on their business services. When enterprises have outsourced their business services, suppliers have to cater for digitalisation too as business services are intertwined with the business processes. As digitalisation increasingly encompasses entire enterprises, including their employees in which many of them corresponds to generation Z, emerging digital technologies may increasingly serve as a key operant resource during the implementation of global business services. As such, digitalisation may be seen as a valuable solution to overcome implementation challenges.

Market research (BCG, 2022) on GBS demonstrates that enterprises invest in digitalisation, such as cloud-based solutions, building analytics and reporting capabilities, apply robotic process automation (RPA) solutions that will support hybrid delivery models (e.g. virtual and physical location strategies). Emerging technologies, such as RPA, process mining, and algorithms, often referred to as Artificial Intelligence (AI), are expected to impact enterprises (Willcocks, 2020). Although the majority of business services functionality have been automated by means of digital platforms such as SAP, Oracle, and Microsoft to name a few, remaining tasks are still performed by humans. By automating repetitive and rule-based functions typically handled by back office, enterprises are able to digitalise the last mile. An example is RPA that digitally support process tasks (e.g. cost accounting, payables and receivables) which were previously performed by humans (Frank et al., 2017). A second example corresponds to process mining that combine various data sets from internal and external sources (suppliers) (Barbosa et al., 2019). Process mining is often used to optimise business process tasks and preventive identification of problems, forecasting and recommendations, like F&A and supply chain related tasks. Next, chatbots refers to software applications, which are used with the intent of backing up employees of customers in service sectors; for example, customer service to imitate written or verbal human words/speaking (Ulas, 2019).

The impact of digitalisation on enterprises is significant, as the basic assumption is that digital technologies may help to overcome GBS implementation challenges as described earlier. For instance, enterprises that use RPA and process mining solutions may overcome duplicated or ignored tasks conducted by humans. These solutions automate the "*last mile*" as an extension of existing digital platforms that support business services like F&A, HR and SCM. By digitalising routine-based decisions made by humans, existing enterprises' operating, and delivery model challenges may be limited as manual coordination is reduced or even absent.

To illustrate the effects of digitalisation, we provide two examples. First, the trend to apply digitalisation in enterprises actually merges with the transformation from functional silos (e.g. F&A, HR, SCM, IT) into end-to-end process management. Based on end-to-end business processes, enterprise managers are no longer responsible for a specific function, like purchase-to-pay or order-to-cash but become responsible for an enterprise end-to-end business process. Such an end-to-end business process comprises functionalities that are supported by various business services. As a result, an enterprise organisational structure will change by breaking down silos and focus on employees and customers need first. IT services will play an essential role to support the transformation into digital end-to-end oriented processes that may even go beyond their own organisation in case outsourced business service are provided by suppliers.

Second, market research conducted by Deloitte (2017) illustrates that intelligent automation will have severe impact on new ways of working, challenging enterprises' ability to cope with changing circumstances that comprise augmenting human work with smart machines. As (chat)bots and humans collaboratively conduct tasks, failing to augment them will have negative consequences for both human and bot performance. As another effect of digitalisation, enterprises have the opportunity to design and implement their global business services from the perspective of employees and customers. As such, customer centricity becomes the focal point in a digital enterprise's thinking and acting. Consequently, data-driven decision making affects managers in designing value-added business services functionality to support employees and customers. In turn, these new functionalities need to be supported by an operating and delivery model, which include both in-house and outsourced solutions. The latter are supported by digital solutions like self-service solutions based on chatbots and algorithms. In doing so, digitalised GBSs become customer-centric and create the opportunity to cater for changing circumstances more easily.

2.5 Conclusion

Enterprises nowadays seek various approaches in delivering global business services to achieve organisational responsiveness and efficiency. The gradual transformation of business services delivery models into a GBS concept contributes to organisational flexibility as a service management option for globally operating enterprises. The multi-nature characteristics of GBS, however, may result in various implementation challenges, but digitalisation and the use of emerging digital technologies may help to overcome GBS implementation challenges. As such, more far-reaching digitalisation solutions, which exclude manual interactions in business services functionality, may be a fruitful strategy to overcome GBS implementation challenges.

References

Aier, S., Bucher, T., & Winter, R. (2011). Critical success factors of service orientation in information systems engineering. *Business and Information Systems Engineering, 3*(2), 77–88.

Albertoni, F., Elia, S., Massini, S., & Piscitello, L. (2017). The reshoring of business services: Reaction to failure or persistent strategy? *Journal of World Business, 52*(3), 417–430.

Alreemy, Z., Chang, V., Walters, R., & Wills, G. (2016). Critical success factors (CSFs) for information technology governance (ITG). *International Journal of Information Management, 36*(6), 907–916.

Bapna, R., Barua, A., Mani, D., & Mehra, A. (2010). Cooperation, coordination, and governance in multisourcing: An agenda for analytical and empirical research. *Information Systems Research, 21*(4), 785–795.

Barber, F., & Strack, R. (2015). The surprising economics of a 'People Business'. *Harvard Business Review, 83*(6), 80–90.

Barbosa, A. C., Moraes, T. M., Tesima, D. T., Pontes, R. C., Lima, A. D. S. M., & Azevedo, B. Z. (2019). Smart planning: Tools, concepts, and approaches for a sustainable digital transformation. In *Smart and digital cities* (pp. 221–236). Springer.

BCG. (2022). GBS-Yielding the butterfly effect: The changing role of Global Business Services. https://bcg.com

Bergeron, B. (2003). *Essentials of shared services*. John Wiley & Sons.

Beulen, E., & Ribbers, P. M. (2021). *Managing information technology outsourcing* (3rd ed.). Routledge.

Beulen, E., Plugge, A. G., & Van Hillegersberg, J. (2022). Formal and relational governance of artificial intelligence outsourcing. *Information Systems and e-Business Management, 20*(4), 719–748.

Blasini, J., Leist, S., & Merkl, W. (2017). Developing and implementing a process-performance management system—Experiences from S-Y systems technologies Europe GmbH—A global automotive supplier. In J. vom Brocke & J. Mendling (Eds.), *Business process management cases: Digital innovation and business transformation in practice*. Springer.

Borman, M., & Janssen, M. (2013). Reconciling two approaches to critical success factors: The case of shared services in the public sector. *International Journal of Information Management, 33*(2), 390–400.

Carmel, E., & Tjia, P. (2005). *Offshore outsourcing of information technology work*. Cambridge University Press.

Chang, Y. B., Gurbaxani, V., & Ravindran, K. (2017). Information technology outsourcing: Asset transfer and the role of contract. *MIS Quarterly, 41*(3), 959–973.

Cherbakov, L., Galambos, G., Harishankar, R., Kalyana, S., & Rackham, G. (2005). Impact of service-orientation at the business level. *IBM Systems Journal, 44*(4), 653–668.

Ciarli, T., Meliciani, V. & Savona, M. (2012). Knowledge dynamics, structural change and the geography of business services. *Journal of Economic Surveys, 26*(3), 445–467.

Cohen, L., & Young, A. (2006). *Multisourcing: Moving beyond outsourcing to achieve growth and agility*. Harvard Business Press.

Deloitte. (2017). The robots are ready. Are you? Untapped advantage in your digital workforce. https://www2.deloitte.com/content/dam/Deloitte/nl/Documents/strategy/deloitte-nl-consulting-robots-are-ready.pdf

Deloitte. (2018). Future of global business services: Catalyst for enterprise digital transformation. https://www2.deloitte.com/us/en/pages/operations/articles/globalbusiness-services-digital-transformation.html

Deloitte. (2021). Global shared services and outsourcing survey report. 2021 Deloitte Development LLC. All rights reserved.
Demirkan, H., Goul, M., & Brown, G. W. (2007). Minitrack: Towards 'the service-oriented enterprise'. *Proceedings of the 40th Annual Hawaii International Conference on System Sciences (HICSS 07)*, IEEE, Hawaii, 62–62.
Doh, J., Bunyaratavej, K., & Hahn, E. (2009). Separable but not equal: The location determinants of discrete services offshoring activities. *Journal of International Business Studies, 40*(6), 926–943.
Dreher, N. (2013). Developing and Selling New Portfolio Elements in a Captive Shared Services Environment. In *Finance Bundling and Finance Transformation: Shared Services Next Level* (pp. 315–337). Wiesbaden: Springer Fachmedien Wiesbaden.
Esteves, J., & Pastor, J. (2001). Enterprise Resource Planning Systems Research: An Annotated Bibliography. *Communications of the Association for Information Systems, 7*, 386–446.
Farrel, D. (2004). Beyond offshoring: Assess your company's global potential. *Harvard Business Review, 82*(12), 1–10.
Fielt, E., Bandara, W., Miskon, S., & Gable, G. (2014). Exploring shared services from an is perspective: A literature review and research agenda. *Communication of the Association for Information Systems, 34*(1), 1001–1040.
Frank, M., Roehrig, P., & Pring, B. (2017). *What to do when machines do everything: How to get ahead in a world of AI, algorithms, bots, and big data.* John Wiley & Sons.
Fremantle, P., Weerawarana, S. & Khalaf, R. (2002). Enterprise services: Examining the emerging files of web services and how it is integrated into existing enterprise infrastructures. *Communications of the ACM, 45*(10), 77–82.
Gonzalez, R., Llopis, J., & Gasco, J. (2013). Information systems offshore outsourcing: Managerial conclusions from academic research. *International Entrepreneurship and Management Journal, 9*(2), 229–259.
Hammer, M. (2001). *Agenda: What every business must do to dominate the decade.* Crown Publishing Group, Inc.
Handley, S. (2017). How governance misalignment and outsourcing capability impact performance. *Production and Operations Management, 26*(1), 134–155.
Hawk, S., Kaiser, K. M., Goles, T., Bullen, C. V., Simon, J. C., Beath, C. M., et al. (2012). The information technology workforce: A comparison of critical skills of clients and service providers. *Information Systems Management, 29*(1), 2–12.

Holmlund, M., Kowalkowski, C. & Biggemann, S. (2016). Organisational behavior in innovation, marketing, and purchasing in business service contexts: An agenda for academic inquiry. *Journal of Business Research, 69*(7), 2457–2462.

Horses for Sources (HfS). (2011). *The evolution of global business services: Enhancing the benefits of shared services and outsourcing*. HfS Research, Ltd | www.hfsresearch.co, July 2011.

Huber, B., & Danino, S. (2012). *Global business services: Taking business support functions to the next level.* Information Services Group.

Huber, T. L., Kude, T., & Dibbern, J. (2017). Governance practices in platform ecosystems: Navigating tensions between cocreated value and governance costs. *Information Systems Research, 28*(3), 563–584.

Janssen, M. (2008). Exploring the service-oriented enterprise: Drawing lessons from a case study. *Proceedings of the 41st Annual Hawaii International Conference on System Sciences*, HICSS, IEEE, Hawaii, p. 101.

Janssen, M., & Joha, A. (2006). Motives for establishing shared service centers in public administrations. *International Journal of Information Management, 26*(2), 102–115.

Joha, A., & Janssen, M. (2014). Factors influencing the shaping of shared services business models: Balancing customization and standardization. *Strategic Outsourcing: An International Journal, 7*(1), 47–65.

Knol, A., Janssen, M., & Sol, H. (2014). A taxonomy of management challenges for developing shared services arrangements. *European Management Journal, 32*(1), 91–103.

Kotlarsky, J., Rivard, S., & Oshri, I. (2023). Building a Reputation as a Business Partner in Information Technology Outsourcing. The University of Auckland Business School Research Paper Series, Forthcoming, MIS Quarterly (Open Access). https://doi.org/10.25300/MISQ/2022/15554

KPMG Insights. (2019). Global business services at a crossroads: Results from the KPMG/HFS research state of operations survey, Boston. https://advisory.kpmg.us/articles/2019/gbs-crossroads.html

Krancher, O., Oshri, I., Kotlarsky, J., & Dibbern, J. (2022). Bilateral, collective, or both? Formal governance and performance in multisourcing. *Journal of the Association for Information Systems, 23*(5), 1210–1234.

Lacity, M. C., & Fox, J. (2008). Creating global shared services: Lessons from Reuters. *MISQ Executive, 7*(1), 17–32.

Lacity, M. C., Khan, S., Yan, A., & Willcocks, L. P. (2010). A review of the IT outsourcing empirical literature and future research directions. *Journal of Information Technology, 25*(4), 395–433.

Lacity, M. C., Salomon, S., Yan, A., & Willcocks, L. P. (2011). Business process outsourcing studies: A critical review and research directions. *Journal of Information Technology, 26*(4), 215–258.

Lacity, M. C., Willcocks, L. P., & Burgess, A. (2014). *The rise of legal services outsourcing: Risk and opportunity*. A&C Black Business Information and Development.

Lacity, M. C., Khan, S. A., & Yan, A. (2016). Review of the empirical business services sourcing literature: An update and future directions. *Journal of Information Technology, 31*(3), 269–328.

Lacity, M. C., Khan, S. A. & Yan, A. (2017). Review of the empirical business services sourcing literature: An update and future directions. In *Outsourcing and Offshoring Business Services* (499–651). Palgrave Macmillan, Cham.

Legner, C., Eymann, T., Hess, T., et al. (2017). Digitalization: Opportunity and challenge for the business and information systems engineering community. *Business Information Systems Engineering, 59*(4), 301–308.

Lioliou, E., Zimmermann, A., Willcocks, L. P., & Gao, L. (2014). Formal and relational governance in IT outsourcing: Substitution, complementarity and the role of the psychological contract. *Information Systems Journal, 24*(6), 503–535.

Love, J. H., & Mansury, M. A. (2009). Exporting and productivity in business services: Evidence from the United States. *International Business Review, 18*(6), 630–642.

Lu, V. N., Wirtz, J., Kunz, W. H., Paluch, S., Gruber, T., Martins, A. & Patterson, P. G. (2020). Service robots, customers and service employees: What can we learn from the academic literature and where are the gaps? *Journal of Service Theory and Practice, 30*(3), 361–391.

Maatman, M., & Meijerink, J. (2017). Why sharing is synergy: The role of decentralized control mechanisms and centralized HR capabilities in creating HR shared service value. *Personnel Review, 46*(7), 1297–1317.

Malos, S. (2010). Regulatory Effects and Strategic Global Staffing Profiles: Beyond cost concerns in evaluating offshore location attractiveness. *Employee Responsibilities and Rights Journal, 22*, 113–131.

Massini, S., & Miozzo, M. (2012). Outsourcing and offshoring of business services: Challenges to theory, management and geography of innovation. *Regional Studies, 46*(9), 1219–1242.

McIvor, R., McCracken, R., & McHugh, M. (2011). Creating outsourced shared services arrangements: Lessons from the public sector. *European Management Journal, 29*(6), 448–461.

Miles, I. (2005). Knowledge intensive business services: Prospects and policies. *Foresight, 7*(6), 39–63.
Miskon, S., Bandara, W., Gable, G., & Fielt, E. (2012). Success factors for ICT shared services in the higher education sector. *Journal of Information Technology Research, 5*(3), 1–24.
Moore, J. F. (1996). *The death of competition: Leadership and strategy in the age of business eco-systems*. Harper Business.
Murray, J. Y., Kotabe, M., & Westjohn, S. A. (2009). Global sourcing strategy and performance of knowledge-intensive business services: A two-stage strategic fit model. *Journal of International Marketing, 17*(4), 90–105.
Narayanan, S., Jayaraman, V., Luo, Y., & Swaminathan, J. M. (2011). The antecedents of process integration in business process outsourcing and its effect on firm performance. *Journal of Operations Management, 29*(1–2), 3–16.
Niehaves, B., & Krause, A. (2010). Shared service strategies in local government: A multiple case study exploration. *Transforming Government. People, Process and Policy, 4*(3), 266–279.
Ono, Y. (2003). Outsourcing business services and the role of central administrative offices. *Journal of Urban Economics, 53*(3), 377–395.
Oshri, I. (2011). *Offshoring strategies: Evolving captive center models*. MIT Press.
Oshri, I., Kotlarsky, J., & Willcocks, L. P. (2015). *The handbook of global outsourcing and offshoring* (3rd ed.). Palgrave Macmillan.
Oshri, I., Lioliou, E., Gerbasi, A., & Zimmermann, A. (2019). Organizational Controls, Social Ties and Performance in Plural Sourcing. In Digital Services and Platforms. Considerations for Sourcing: 12th Global Sourcing Workshop 2018, La Thuile, Italy, February 21–24, 2018, Revised Selected Papers 12 (164–185). Springer International Publishing.
Oshri, I., Kotlarsky, J., & Willcocks, L. P. (2023). *The handbook of global outsourcing and offshoring* (4th ed.). Palgrave Macmillan.
Palvia, P. C., King, R. C., Xia, W., & Palvia, S. C. J. (2010). Capability, quality, and performance of offshore IS vendors: A theoretical framework and empirical investigation. *Decision Science, 41*(2), 231–270.
Peng, M. W. (2022). *Global business*. Cengage learning.
Plugge, A. G., Nikou, S, & Janssen, M. F.W.A.H. (2022). A Fuzzy-set Qualitative Comparative Analysis of Factors Influencing Successful Shared Service Centre Implementation. *Industrial Management and Data Systems, 122*(4), 920–941.
Quinn, B., Cooke, R., & Kris, A. (2000). *Shared services: Mining for gold*. Pearson Education.

Rai, A., Keil, M., Hornyak, R., & Wüllenweber, K. (2012). Hybrid relational-contractual governance for business process outsourcing. *Journal of Management Information Systems, 29*(2), 213–256.
Rao, M. T., Earls, T. W., & Sanchez, G. (2007). International collaboration in trans-organizational systems development: The challenges of global insourcing. *Journal of Global Information Technology Management, 10*(3), 52–69.
Richter, P. C., & Brühl, R. (2017). Shared service centre research: A review of the past, present, and future. *European Management Journal, 35*(3), 26–38.
Richter, P. C., & Brühl, R. (2020). Ahead of the game: Antecedents for the success of shared service centers. *European Management Journal, 38*(3) 477–488.
Romero, D., & Molina, A. (2011). Collaborative networked organisations and customer communities: Value co-creation and co-innovation in the networking era. *Production Planning & Control, 22*(5–6), 447–472.
Sako, M. (2006). Outsourcing and offshoring: Implications for productivity of business services. *Oxford Review of Economic Policy, 22*(4), 499–512.
Su, N., & Levina, N. (2011). Global multisourcing strategy: Integrating learning from manufacturing into IT service outsourcing. *IEEE Transactions on Engineering Management, 58*(4), 717–729.
Tan, F. B., & Gallupe, R. B. (2006). Aligning business and information systems thinking: A cognitive approach. *IEEE Transactions on Engineering Management, 53*(2), 223–237.
Ulas, D. (2019). Digital transformation process and SMEs. *Procedia Computer Science, 158*, 662–671.
Ulbrich, F. (2006). Improving shared service implementation: Adopting lessons from the BPR Movement. *Business Process Management Journal, 12*(2), 191–205.
Ulbrich, F., & Borman, M. (2012). Preventing the gradual decline of shared service centers. *Proc of the Eighteenth Americas Conference on Information Systems*, Seattle, Washington, August 9–12.
Ulbrich, F., & Schulz, V. (2014). Seven challenges management must overcome when implementing IT-shared services. *Strategic Outsourcing: An International Journal, 7*(2), 94–106.
Van der Aalst, W. M. P. (2012). A decade of business process management conferences: Personal reflections on a developing discipline. In A. Barros, A. Gal, & E. Kindler (Eds.), *Business Process Management* (LNCS 7481). Springer-Verlag Berlin Heidelberg.
Van der Valk, W., & Rozemeijer, F. (2009). Buying business services: Towards a structured service purchasing process. *Journal of Services Marketing, 23*(1), 3–10.

Wang, Y., Wallace, S. W., Shen, B., & Choi, T. M. (2015). Service supply chain management: A review of operational models. *European Journal of Operational Research, 247*(3), 685–698.

Wiener, M., & Saunders, C. (2014). Force coopetition in IT multi-sourcing. *Journal of Strategic Information Systems, 23*, 210–225.

Willcocks, L. P. (2020). Robo-apocalypse cancelled? Reframing the automation and future of work debate. *Journal of Information Technology, 35*(4), 286–302.

Willcocks, L. P., Lacity, M. C., & Craig, A. (2017). Robotic process automation: Strategic transformation lever for global business services? *Journal of Information Technology Teaching Cases, 7*(1), 17–28.

Willcocks, L. P., Oshri, I., & Kotlarsky, J. (2018). Why Innovation and Why Now? In Willcocks, L., Oshri, I., Kotlarsky, J. (Eds.), *Dynamic Innovation in Outsourcing*. Technology, Work and Globalization. Palgrave Macmillan, Cham.

Willcocks, L. P., Hindle, J., & Lacity, M. C. (2019). *Becoming strategic with robotic process automation*. SB Publishing.

Wirtz, J., Tuzovic, S., & Ehret, M. (2015). Global business services: Increasing specialization and integration of the world economy as drivers of economic growth. *Journal of Service Management, 26*(4), 565–587.

Wynstra, F., Spring, M. & Schoenherr, T. (2015). Service triads: A research agenda for buyer–supplier–customer triads in business services. *Journal of Operations Management, 35*, 1–20.

Xiao, J., Xie, K., & Hu, Q. (2012). Inter-firm IT governance in power-imbalanced buyer–supplier dyads: Exploring how it works and why it lasts. *European Journal of Information Systems, 22*(5), 512–528.

3

Literature Review

3.1 Resource Orchestration Theory

Resource Orchestration Theory (ROT), which is an extension of the resource-based view theory (RBV) and dynamic capabilities theory (DC), addresses the integration of resource management and asset orchestration management (Sirmon et al., 2007, 2011), and posits that "managers need to orchestrate their resources to realise any potential advantage" (Chirico et al., 2011, p. 310). An essential element of ROT is the role of managers in structuring, bundling, and leveraging firm resources (Sirmon et al., 2011). Literature shows that the role of managers is underdeveloped in terms of initiating resource-related processes and actions to initiate oversight (Kraaijenbrink et al., 2010). For example, a study of Crook et al. (2008) identified unspecified contingences related to managers' "strategic choices" while Sirmon et al.'s (2007) resource management framework focuses on process-oriented managerial actions that are important in achieving creating value. Sirmon et al. (2011) argued that empirical testing is required to identify and understand managers' actions to coordinate resources. The authors developed a resource orchestration framework that includes resource management and asset orchestration elements. Sirmon et al. (2007) defined the management of resources as "dynamic,

A. Plugge, S. Nikou, *Digitalisation of Global Business Services*, Technology, Work and Globalization, https://doi.org/10.1007/978-3-031-51528-6_3

with change resulting from adapting to environmental contingencies and from exploiting opportunities created by those contingencies" (p. 275). Asset orchestration has been described as "the ability to combine selected technologies, individuals, and other resources in new products and processes regardless of location and across organisational boundaries" (Lessard et al., 2016, p. 214). The assets that need to be orchestrated can be found inside or outside of the firm (Teece, 2014, p. 23), and can be intangible as well as physical. Due to the two views, the resource orchestration framework is helpful to explicate the role and actions of managers within an enterprise when orchestrating internal and external resources. Managers should aim to create value for customers and end users and ultimately improve enterprise competitive advantage.

ROT highlights the role of resource orchestration in creating value for organisations and their stakeholders as well as states that resources must be structured, bundled, and then leveraged in order to gain competitive advantage (Ahuja & Chan, 2017; Sirmon et al., 2007). Chadwick et al. (2015) state that after resources have been acquired, management must cooperate to effectively structure, bundle, mobilise, and deploy resources to create value (Sirmon et al., 2011). In other words, firms depend on managers' skills in generating synergetic effects by deploying resources (Sirmon et al., 2007). Hitt et al. (2016) acknowledges the importance of management and indicate that to orchestrate resources effectively, business managers must focus on the coordination and synchronisation of their assets and capabilities. Although business managers may imitate practices, it is much more difficult to imitate the way in which these resources are synchronised (Burin et al., 2020). ROT is useful for creating insights in how enterprises' business services portfolios need to be orchestrated as the provisioning of business services may change over time (e.g. in-house or outsourced). From this perspective, the ROT arguments could be further developed by theorising that a business services portfolio is dependent on an enterprise's plural sourcing strategy and affected by various business services antecedents, which, in turn, need to be orchestrated carefully (Sako et al., 2016).

3.2 Plural Sourcing Strategy

The hybrid governance mode of bundling in-house and outsourced business services fits with the concept of plural sourcing in which enterprises make, buy or ally similar goods and services (Gulati & Puranam, 2006). However, literature lacks a clear definition of plural sourcing. For instance, Gulati and Puranam (2006, p. 3) argued that "[F]irms often make and buy the same thing" while *same* has a seemingly clear meaning as "identical". Parmigiani (2007) state that similar input similarity is measured as a control variable while results show that more similar inputs are rather concurrently sourced than bought. Krzeminska et al. (2013) reconceptualised the problematic term of "same" into degrees of similarity, that can be "conceptualised as a spectrum anchored at one end by identical inputs and extending towards infinite dissimilarity" (p. 1616). In the present research, plural sourcing is defined as "the degree of simultaneous insourcing and outsourcing (make-and-buy) of the same business service activities by a firm but differ from each other in their capabilities and limitations" (adaptation based on Tiwana & Kim, 2016, p. 103). During the past decade plural sourcing has attracted interest of scholars to study this phenomenon, specifically from a governance perspective (e.g. Parmigiani, 2007; Puranam et al., 2013).

Applying a plural sourcing strategy provides a variety of benefits, such as enhanced supplier competition, a lower risk of supply chain interruption, and increased flexibility in responding to changing market conditions (Puranam et al., 2013). However, it also has its own set of challenges, like coordinating delivery, managing multiple suppliers, governance mode (e.g. combine governance modes), and assuring constant quality (Krzeminska et al., 2013). From an enterprise procurement perspective, an unbalanced power-dependency relationship may result in supplier failures caused by a dominant power position of an enterprise. This relates to Kraljic purchasing portfolio matrix that provides guidance in power and interdependence in buyer-supplier relationships. Literature reveals an important relational challenge as external suppliers may not be willing to cooperate or behave opportunistically (Das & Teng, 1996). A strategy to overcome such a challenge is to establish a joint partnership with suppliers to decrease performance ambiguity. Research of Oshri et al. (2019) shows that organisational controls may mitigate performance risks when governing a plural sourcing arrangement. The authors found that outcome controls can be used to govern internal suppliers, while behavioural controls are more effective in case of external suppliers. In addition, to a certain degree social ties affect the relationships between organisational control and performance.

An essential aspect of plural sourcing corresponds to complementarities, for example, certain procured services or exchanged knowledge and experience by providers (Puranam et al., 2013). Parmigiani and Mitchell (2009) argue that complementarities between two or more product or service components will influence firms' knowledge and production boundaries, as firms will produce sets of complementary components both internally and outsourced. However, this leads to the challenge of coordinating interdependencies between in-house and outsourced business services as the interdependencies may have an impact on their criticality, for example, on firm performance and overall business success. Mishra et al. (2021) underpin the criticality of resource interdependencies as they find that the efficiency of IT projects execution is lower when their sourcing structures cross a country boundary relative to when their sourcing structures do not cross a country boundary. The authors' findings correspond to orchestration challenges as various in-house and outsourced business services need to be bundled and effectively orchestrated to avoid cross-service spillovers. Complex sourcing arrangements, such as plural sourcing, need to be strategically evaluated by enterprises to remain competitive in the market. Contractual agreements and relationship management principles are essential to evaluate that may result in an adjusted business services portfolio. Addressing the importance of both contractual agreements and relationship principles is reflected in the Best Value method (Van de Rijt & Santema, 2012) in which enterprises focus on improved procurement by selecting suppliers who provide an excellent performance. In a similar way, if enterprises and suppliers increase their collaboration and both contribute to shared value creation they focus on a "what's in it for all of us" mindset as argued by Vitasek and Manrodt (2012).

3.3 Business Services Portfolio

Developing a portfolio of business services helps an enterprise efficiently manage its operations in information-intensive and resource-intensive services (Arora et al., 2021). Kohlborn et al. (2009) define a business services portfolio as "a dynamic decision-making process that is dedicated to the continuous and strategically aligned revision of service portfolios" (p. 1). In nutshell, a business services portfolio is a strategic tool that allows enterprises to offer a range of services that can be tailored to specific customer segments and can be used to achieve a variety of strategic goals. The co-production relationship between in-house and outsourced suppliers implies that design choices must be made to configure a business services portfolio by using design archetypes (Roels, 2014). Design choices such as degree of suppliers' collaboration, service delivery model (service factories), and level of in-house services strategically affect an enterprise's business services portfolio due to their interdependent antecedents. For example, on the one hand, Joha and Janssen (2014) identified the importance of customer orientation to identify changing internal customer needs that may result in an adaptation of a business services portfolio. On the other hand, Ulbrich and Borman (2012) stressed the importance of business processes to support business services. Literature shows that factors shaping a business services portfolio have been studied individually rather than in combination with one another (Richter & Brühl, 2017). Therefore, an integrative approach is needed to understand factors that lead to business services, their interdependencies, and how they have a direct or indirect impact on a business services portfolio. In doing so, the positioning of a business services portfolio contributes to service differentiation (Guajardo & Cohen, 2018). The concepts and corresponding references and antecedents are illustrated in Table 3.1.

Table 3.1 Literature overview

Concepts	References	Journal (research discipline)	Type of research	Key antecedents
Business services portfolio	Sako (2006)	Oxford Review of Economic Policy	Literature review	Business services, Specialisation, Standardisation, Business process
	Lacity et al. (2008)	Strategic Outsourcing: An Internal Journal	Empirical research (qualitative)	International business, Outsourcing
	Abramovsky and Griffith (2006)	Journal of the European Economic Association	Empirical research (quantitative)	Business services, Outsourcing, Offshoring, ICT
	Wirtz and Ehret (2009)	European Business Review	Literature review	Service industries, Property rights, Entrepreneurialism
	Ciarli et al. (2012)	Journal of Economic Surveys	Empirical research (qualitative)	Business services; Knowledge; Regional specialisation; Structural change
	Wirtz et al. (2015)	Journal of Service Management	Empirical research (qualitative)	Global business services, Outsourcing, Offshoring, Resource-based view, Property-rights theory
	Lacity et al. (2016)	Journal of Information Technology	Literature review	Business services sourcing literature, IT outsourcing, business process outsourcing
	Willcocks et al. (2017)	Palgrave Macmillan	Empirical research (qualitative)	Business services, Governance, Offshoring, Supplier relationships
	Lacity and Willcocks (2017)	The Journal of Strategic Information Systems	Empirical research (qualitative)	BSO conflicts, Conflict types, Conflict styles, Conflict outcomes

Plural sourcing strategy	Levina and Su (2008)	Decision Sciences	Empirical research (qualitative)	Plural sourcing, Offshoring, Outsourcing, Sourcing selection, Strategic decision making
	Bapna et al. (2010)	Information Systems Research	Literature review	Cooperation, Coordination, Output verifiability, Observability, Relational governance
	Su and Levina (2011)	IEEE Transactions on Engineering Management	Empirical research (qualitative)	Information technology (IT) outsourcing, Plural sourcing, Strategy, Service supply chain
	Wiener and Saunders (2014)	The Journal of Strategic Information Systems	Empirical research (qualitative)	Plural sourcing, Forced coopetition, Plural sourcing models, Vendor competition, Vendor collaboration
	Oshri et al. (2019)	Journal of Management Information Systems	Empirical research (quantitative)	Plural sourcing, Joint performance, Guardian, Governance, Architectural knowledge
	Lioliou et al. (2019)	Journal of Business Research	Empirical research (qualitative)	Plural sourcing, Opportunism, Transaction costs, Uncertainty, Coopetition
	Hurni et al. (2021)	European Journal of Information Systems	Empirical research (quantitative)	Platform ecosystems, Complementor dedication, Platform governance, Governance practices
	Krancher et al. (2018)	Journal of the Association for Information Systems	Empirical research (quantitative)	Bilateral and Collective outcome control, Conflict management procedures, Plural sourcing outcomes

(continued)

Table 3.1 (continued)

Concepts	References	Journal (research discipline)	Type of research	Key antecedents
Orchestration of business services portfolio	Hasselbring (2000)	Communications of the ACM	Literature review	Enterprise Application Integration, Business processes, Complex systems, Heterogeneity
	Sadiq and Racca (2004)	Cambridge University Press	Empirical research (qualitative)	Business process management, Business services, Information Systems, Tooling, Interfaces
	Rai and Sambamurthy (2006)	Information Systems Research	Literature review	Service management, End-to-end business processes, Information technology services
	Janssen et al. (2006)	Information Systems Management	Empirical research (qualitative)	Cross-agency processes, Service orchestration architecture, Information systems
	Janssen and Joha (2006)	International Journal of Information Management	Empirical research (qualitative)	Shared service centres, Outsourcing, Orchestration, Information systems, Motives
	Bharadwaj et al. (2013)	MIS Quarterly	Empirical research (qualitative)	Digital business strategy, Orchestration of digital resources, Value creation and capture
	Liu et al. (2016)	Journal of Operations Management	Empirical research (quantitative)	Resource orchestration theory, supply chain integration, IT competency, Fit
	Parida et al. (2019)	Journal of Business Research	Empirical research (qualitative)	Orchestration, Inter-organisational relationships, Business model, Servitisation
	Tian et al. (2021)	Industrial Marketing Management	Empirical research (qualitative)	Orchestration capability, platform, co-evolution, value co-creation

3.4 Development of Hypotheses

The literature review is used to identify the antecedents that have an impact on orchestration of business services portfolio, and from that, hypotheses will be formulated. The chapter will end with developing a conceptual research model that illustrates the identified factors and path relationships between them.

3.4.1 Method for Factors Influencing Business Services

A systematic literature review using three databases—namely: Scopus, Web of Science and Google Scholar—was performed to identify antecedents that affect an enterprise's orchestration of business services portfolio, and publications from 2000 to 2021 were collected. Search terms used, either separately or in combination, included "global business services", "business services", "strategy", "organisation", "management", "plural sourcing", "implementation", "determinants", "antecedents", and "factors". The selection was based on two criteria.

First, publications have been selected that include at least one search term in the title, abstract or keywords. Second, to ensure the reliability of the data collection, only peer-reviewed journals, book chapters and conference proceedings with more than 50 citations were selected. As the aims were on assessing business services antecedents from an organisational perspective, computing and modelling views were excluded. Based on the analysis of selected key publications, the following five overarching antecedents (see Table 3.2), in the context of business services, were identified: modularisation, standardisation, decision rights, business services portfolio, and customer orientation. Following that, these antecedents are examined in greater depth to demonstrate how they affect the implementation of a business services portfolio in the context of a plural sourcing strategy.

Table 3.2 Overview of relevant antecedents

Antecedents	References	Journal (research discipline)	Type of Research	Key attributes
Modularised business processes	Demirkan et al. (2008)	Electronic Commerce Research and Applications	Literature review	Business Processes, Modularisation, Management, SOA Technology
	Rai et al. (2012)	Journal of Management Information Systems	Empirical research (quantitative)	Contractual and Relational Governance, Satisfaction
	Van der Aalst (2012)	LNCS Springer	Literature review	Business Processes, Modularisation, Process Aware Information Systems
	Vom Brocke et al. (2014)	Business Process Management Journal	Empirical research (qualitative)	Context Awareness, Involvement, Enablement, Simplicity
	Eissens-Van der Laan et al. (2016)	International Journal of Operations & Production Management	Literature review	Modularisation, Decomposition logic, Service routineness

Orchestration of business services portfolio	Jeffery and Leliveld (2004)	MIT Sloan Management Review	Empirical research (qualitative)	IT Portfolio Management, Maturity, Strategy
	Beulen et al. (2005)	European Management Journal	Empirical research (qualitative)	Outsourcing, IT Infrastructure, Service Portfolio
	Janssen and Joha (2006)	Strategic Outsourcing: An International Journal	Empirical research (qualitative)	Application Portfolio, Management Challenges
	Roseman and vom Brocke (2014)	Handbook on Business Process Management	Literature review	Strategic Alignment, Governance, Information Technology, People
IS standardisation	Lee et al. (2008)	Information Systems Research	Empirical research (quantitative)	IT Outsourcing, Integration, Control, Performance
	Izza (2009)	Enterprise Information Systems	Empirical research (quantitative)	Integration approach
	Goh et al. (2007)	Industrial Management & Data Systems	Empirical research (qualitative)	SSC model, IT capabilities, Governance
	Aksin and Masini (2008)	Journal of Operations Management	Empirical research (quantitative)	Shared Services, Outsourcing, Capabilities, Information Systems

(*continued*)

Table 3.2 (continued)

Antecedents	References	Journal (research discipline)	Type of Research	Key attributes
Customer orientation	Osterwalder et al. (2005)	Com. of the Association for Information Systems	Literature review	Customer Value, Business Model
	Grant et al. (2007)	Government Information Quarterly	Empirical research (qualitative)	Governance, Oversight, Accountability, Culture, Management of resources
	Al-Debei and Avison (2010)	European Journal of Information Systems	Literature review	Customer Value, Business Model, Information Systems
	Holmlund et al. (2016)	Journal of Business Research	Literature review	Customer Orientation, Innovation, Business Services
Managing decision rights	Aier et al. (2011)	Business & Information Systems Engineering	Empirical research (quantitative)	Service Oriented Design, Decision making, Information Systems
	Alreemy et al. (2016)	International Journal of Information Management	Literature review	IT Governance, Critical Success Factors
	Lacity et al. (2016)	Journal of Information Technology	Empirical research (qualitative & quantitative)	Business Services, Governance, Insourcing, Outsourcing, Decision making
	Johnson et al. (2021)	International Journal of Operations & Production Management	Conceptual	Governance, Decision making

Plural Sourcing and Orchestration of Business Services Portfolio

Based on ROT, the integration of internal and external resources must be deployed and coordinated in a collaborative manner to create value. Different levels of plural sourcing have various foci and business services' needs, thus impacting the degree in which antecedents directly or indirectly influence an enterprise's business services portfolio (Sako et al., 2016; Tiwana & Kim, 2016). For instance, a low degree of outsourcing may require limited attention on business processes and governance as they are already implemented internally. In contrast, a high degree of outsourcing demands more effort to orchestrate an extended business process chain and supporting information systems to provide external business services. Enterprises strategically need to centralise and standardise their critical functions (Daub et al., 2020) into a unified entity known as GBS division. For example, the integration of F&A services within GBS ensures transparent and standardised financial reporting, enabling timely insights into the organisation's financial health (Aman & Fernandez, 2022). Similarly, the HR function within GBS fosters a unified talent management approach, promoting a consistent organisational culture and employee engagement practices worldwide (Küppers, 2016). Within GBS, SCM plays a pivotal role in optimising procurement, logistics, and inventory management, fostering synergies across the supply chain and enhancing supplier collaboration to meet dynamic market demands efficiently (Arlbjørn & Lüthje, 2012). Finally, IT under GBS leads digital transformation initiatives, orchestrating innovative technology solutions and enhancing cybersecurity measures across the enterprise (Rainer et al., 2007). It can be concluded that by embracing GBSs as a strategic framework, an enterprise can leverage the collective strengths of these critical functions, which are bundled in a business services portfolio.

Brahm et al. (2021) argue that an enterprise's business management ability is to administer, orchestrate, and coordinate the entire enterprise's activities that relates to management capabilities. These capabilities include resource orchestration and the ability of strategic decision making to expand, allocate, and redeploy resources both within the enterprise and across businesses (Helfat & Martin, 2015; Sirmon et al., 2011). Sako et al. (2016) reveals that an enterprise's choice to apply a plural sourcing strategy is closely associated with the design of a business service portfolio. In information-intensive enterprises, suppliers may control vital services and technology that can be internalised to build a portfolio of services that is based on cutting-edge technology. ROT stresses the need to transcend enterprise's boundaries to obtain and manage resources, which in turn requires managers' skills to structure and manage a enterprise's portfolio of resources. As such, a business services portfolio can be seen as an instrument that requires intensive management attention to orchestrate the allocation and deployment of internal and external resources in a flexible way. Thus, management's proficiency to orchestrate a business services portfolio increases an enterprise's overall performance by effectively monitoring the delivery of products or services (Heide et al., 2014), and by managing the boundaries of the enterprise and of its suppliers (Galbraith, 1995). This suggests that a plural sourcing strategy affects an enterprise's business services portfolio in which the orchestration of in-house and outsourced resources can be considered as a prerequisite. This reasoning leads to the first hypothesis:

H1: *A plural sourcing strategy is positively related to the orchestration of a business services portfolio.*

Customer Orientation

Enterprises must improve their business services on a regular basis and strengthen their resources to deliver higher value to customers and remain relevant to them (Roels, 2014). This requirement refers to customer orientation, which is defined as a "means of demonstrating the business rationale of producing value for customers that meets the needs of their target groups" (Osterwalder et al., 2005). This definition is in line with the findings of McIvor et al. (2011) who suggest "to pay close attention to interacting and communicating with employees who are impacted by changes in order to address challenges related to development (p. 458)". Customer orientation implies that business services fit with internal customers' needs. To actualise an enterprise's business services portfolio regularly, it is vital to verify if the required quality of business services (e.g. service levels) still fits with the provided business services functionality (Buell et al., 2016). Consequently, and according to ROT, enterprises' managers must evaluate internal customers' needs and ultimately adapt the deployment of in-house and outsourced resources. Thus, managers may orchestrate the demand and supply of business services via internal distribution channels as a means of value exchange (Sjödin et al., 2022). This includes attention to identify relationship expectations and actor interaction issues that may affect the provisioning of business services (Witell et al., 2020). It can be concluded that managers may safeguard the quality of business services by applying a customer orientation view. This reasoning leads to the second hypotheses:

H2a: *Customer orientation is positively related to the orchestration of a business services portfolio.*

Modularisation Business Processes

To support a business services portfolio that orchestrates both in-house and outsourced business services, enterprises are modularising business processes and unbundling their value chains into independent services (McLoughlin et al., 2021). Sanchez and Mahoney (1996) define modularity as "a special form of design that intentionally creates a high degree of independence or 'loose coupling' between component designs by standardising component interface specifications (p. 65)". Reijers (2021) argues that applying a modular approach to design business processes results in sub-processes that contributes to service flexibility. Hence, modularisation requires the dynamic coordination of business processes as opposed to procedures developed from a specified static sequence, in which the preceding process must be completed before beginning the next. From an ROT view, an enterprise's management aims to synchronise their business services portfolio via dynamic orchestration of their business processes, and as such contributes to enterprise performance (i.e. service portfolio) (Cui et al., 2022). By verifying customers' needs regularly, enterprises can align their portfolio with their business strategy, and in doing so maximise the value of their business services portfolio. Thus, it can be concluded that not only customer orientation is positively related to modularised business processes, but also modularising business processes and adapting them on a regular basis contribute to a synchronised business service portfolio. The next hypotheses follow from this reasoning:

H2b: *Customer orientation is positively related to modularised business processes.*

H3: *Modularisation of business processes is positively related to the orchestration of a business services portfolio.*

Information Systems Standardisation

In practice, Information Systems (IS) are interconnected as applications that support business services increasingly need to work together (Yoshikuni et al., 2023). Van der Aalst et al. (2007) defines an IS as a system that "support[s] the operations of an organisation and its processes involved" (p. 6). Enterprises often use generic IS such as Workflow Management (WFM) systems and Business Process Management (BPM) systems. Research of Gronwald (2017) demonstrates that enterprise IS have become integrated and as such, are based on standardised components to cater for business changes adequately. Burin et al.'s (2020) research on the influence of ambidexterity on supply chain flexibility shows that standardised IS may cause moderation effects on that relationship. Hence, IS standardisation is perceived to be a valuable approach to deal with complex service systems (Dos Santos & Da Silva, 2021). To handle changing customers' needs adequately, IS standardisation is applied to create agility and to overcome customisation. According to ROT, managers must coordinate such interconnected in-house and outsourced IS to remain standardised to support a business services portfolio effectively. Therefore, standardisation seems not only relates to related to modularised business processes, but also plays an important role in orchestrating the business services portfolio. This reasoning leads to the following hypotheses:

H4a: *IS standardisation is positively related to the orchestration of a business services portfolio.*

H4b: *IS standardisation is positively related to modularised business processes.*

Managing Decision Rights

Literature shows that governance is associated with an enterprise's responsibilities to manage business services (Lacity et al., 2017). We define governance, and more in particular termed as managing decision rights, as "an enterprise's overarching capacity and responsibility for directing and monitoring organisational responsibilities to manage business services activities as well as its operations" (Westphal & Sohal, 2013). Handley (2017) emphasises the importance of governance, as misalignment of an enterprise's outsourcing capability may result in inferior business process performance. Zhao et al. (2021) analysed the effects of different resource allocations and their impacts on the development of strategic alliances (e.g. plural sourcing). The authors find that managing decision rights need to be perceived as a dynamic process rather as unchanging decision results that effect the applicability of various resource allocations. This is consistent with previous research of Mukhopadhyay and Bouwman (2019) who argue that decision rights can be seen as a mechanism for value co-creation in the context of multi-industry ecosystems. Taking a plural sourcing context into account, managing decision rights form a condition to orchestrate an enterprise's business services portfolio that is based on in-house and outsourced resources. Consequently, and based on ROT, managers need to manage the decision rights of in-house and outsourced suppliers regularly, as services that require a significant amount of information have become more spread out, and this can impact the business services portfolio. This reasoning leads to the following hypotheses:

H5a: *Managing decision rights is positively related to the orchestration of a business services portfolio.*

H5b: *Managing decision rights is positively related to modularised business processes.*

In addition, literature shows that the coordination of business processes is related to the integration with an enterprise's outsourced business services (Narayanan et al., 2011). From an outsourcing perspective, both internal and external business processes need to be integrated to support make-and-buy provisioned business services. In doing so, modularisation of business processes forms a prerequisite for integration effectiveness. Kock et al. (2020) find evidence that portfolio related business processes act as a mediator in the relationship between portfolio applications and portfolio success. Although literature demonstrates various examples in which business processes act as mediator (Peng et al., 2016; Shi & Liao, 2013) it lacks the context of business services portfolio. As such, we conceptualise that the factors (1) customer orientation, (2) IS standardisation, and (3) managing decision rights all form necessary preconditions to implement modularised business processes, see Fig. 3.1. Hence, our assumption is that modularised business processes act as a mediator between these three antecedents and business services portfolio. Hence, we posit the next more detailed hypotheses:

H2c: *Modularised business processes mediate the relationship between customer orientation and orchestration of a business services portfolio.*

H2d: *Modularised business processes mediate the relationship between IS standardisation and orchestration of a business services portfolio.*

H2e: *Modularised business processes mediate the relationship between managing decision rights and orchestration of a business services portfolio.*

Figure 3.1 depicts the proposed conceptual model of the study and shows the expected path relationships.

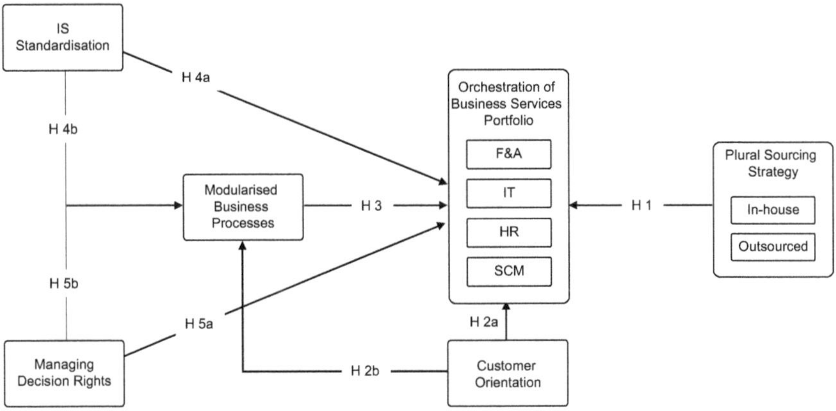

Fig. 3.1 Conceptual research model

3.5 Conclusions

This chapter addresses the main objective 1: *Identify which antecedents form a part of an enterprise orchestration capability that aims at integrating internal and external resources.*

Based on an extensive literature study we explored essential constructs that corresponds to our first objective. We explored and analysed GBS in a plural sourcing context by applying a resource orchestration lens. In particular, five antecedents were found, namely: business services portfolio, modularised business processes, IS standardisation, managing decision rights, and customer orientation.

References

Abramovsky, L., & Griffith, R. (2006). Outsourcing and offshoring of business services: How important is ICT? *Journal of the European Economic Association, 4*(2–3), 594–601.

Ahuja, S., & Chan, Y. E. (2017). Resource orchestration for IT-enabled innovation. *Kindai Management Review, 5*(1), 78–96.

Aier, S., Bucher, T., & Winter, R. (2011). Critical success factors of service orientation in information systems engineering. *Business and Information Systems Engineering, 3*(2), 77–88.

Aksin, O. Z., & Masini, A. (2008). Effective strategies for internal outsourcing and offshoring of business services: An empirical investigation. *Journal of Operations Management, 26*(2), 239–256.

Al-Debei, M. M., & Avison, D. (2010). Developing a unified framework of the business model concept. *European Journal of Information Systems, 19*(3), 359–376.

Alreemy, Z., Chang, V., Walters, R., & Wills, G. (2016). Critical success factors (CSFs) for information technology governance (ITG). *International Journal of Information Management, 36*(6), 907–916.

Aman, A., & Fernandez, D. (2022). Finance and accounting shared services and outsourcing firms in Malaysia: Growth and challenges. *Journal of Strategic Digital Transformation in Society, 2*(1), 1–29.

Arlbjørn, J. S., & Lüthje, T. (2012). Global operations and their interaction with supply chain performance. *Industrial Management & Data Systems, 112*(7), 1044–1064.

Arora, A., Belenzon, S., & Patacconi, A. (2021). Knowledge sharing in alliances and alliance portfolios. *Management Science, 67*(3), 1569–1585.

Bapna, R., Barua, A., Mani, D., & Mehra, A. (2010). Research commentary—Cooperation, coordination, and governance in multisourcing: An agenda for analytical and empirical research. *Information Systems Research, 21*(4), 785–795.

Beulen, E., Van Fenema, P., & Currie, W. (2005). From application outsourcing to infrastructure management: Extending the offshore outsourcing service portfolio. *European Management Journal, 23*(2), 133–144.

Bharadwaj, A., El Sawy, O. A., Pavlou, P. A., & Venkatraman, N. (2013). Digital Business Strategy: Toward a next generation of insights. *MIS Quarterly, 37*(2), 471–482.

Brahm, F., Parmigiani, A., & Tarziján, J. (2021). Can firms be both broad and deep? Exploring interdependencies between horizontal and vertical firm scope. *Journal of Management, 47*(5), 1219–1254.

Buell, R. W., Campbell, D., & Frei, F. X. (2016). How do customers respond to increased service quality competition? *Manufacturing & Service Operations Management, 18*(4), 585–607.

Burin, A. R. G., Perez-Arostegui, M. N., & Llorens-Montes, J. (2020). Ambidexterity and IT competence can improve supply chain flexibility? A resource orchestration approach. *Journal of Purchasing and Supplier Management, 26*(2), 100610.

Chadwick, C., Super, J. F., & Kwon, K. (2015). Resource orchestration in practice: CEO emphasis on SHRM, commitment-based HR systems, and enterprise performance. *Strategic Management Journal, 36*(3), 360–376.

Chirico, F., Sirmon, D. G., Sciascia, S., & Mazzola, P. (2011). Resource orchestration in family firms: Investigating how entrepreneurial orientation, generational involvement, and participative strategy affect performance. *Strategic Entrepreneurship Journal, 594*, 307–326.

Ciarli, T., Meliciani, V., & Savona, M. (2012). Knowledge dynamics, structural change and the geography of business services. *Journal of Economic Surveys, 26*(3), 445–467.

Crook, T. R., Ketchen, D. J., Jr., Combs, J. G., & Todd, S. Y. (2008). Strategic resources and performance: A meta-analysis. *Strategic Management Journal, 29*(11), 1141–1154.

Cui, T., Ye, J. H., & Tan, C. H. (2022). Information technology in open innovation: A resource orchestration perspective. *Information & Management, 59*(8), 103699.

Das, T. K., & Teng, S. T. (1996). Risk types and inter-firm alliance structures. *Journal of Management Studies, 33*(6), 827–843.

Daub, M., Ess, A., Silver, J., & Singh, S. (2020). Does the global business services model still matter. *McKinsey Digital*. Retrieved July 18, 2023, from https://www.bcg.com/publications/2015/centralize-or-not-to-centralize.aspx

Demirkan, H., Kauffman, R. J., Vayghan, J. A., Fill, H. G., Karagiannis, D., & Maglio, P. P. (2008). Service-oriented technology and management: Perspectives on research and practice for the coming decade. *Electronic Commerce Research and Applications, 7*(4), 356–376.

Dos Santos, J. C., & Da Silva, M. M. (2021). Optimising IT outsourcing services by managing the balance between standardisation and customisation: A providers' perspective. *International Journal of Business Information Systems, 37*(1), 78–105.

Eissens-Van der Laan, M., Broekhuis, M., van Offenbeek, M., & Ahaus, K. (2016). Service decomposition: A conceptual analysis of modularizing services. *International Journal of Operations & Production Management, 36*(3), 308–331.

Galbraith, J. R. (1995). *Designing organizations: An executive briefing on strategy, structure, and process*. Jossey-Bass.

Goh, M., Prakash, S., & Yeo, R. (2007). Resource-based approach to IT shared services in a manufacturing firm. *Industrial Management & Data Systems, 107*(2), 251–270.

Grant, G., McKnight, S., Uruthirapathy, A., & Brown, A. (2007). Designing governance for shared services organizations in the public service. *Government Information Quarterly, 24*(3), 522–538.

Gronwald, K. D. (2017). *Integrated business information systems: A holistic view of the linked business process chain ERP-SCM-CRM-BI-Big Data*. Springer.

Guajardo, J. A., & Cohen, M. A. (2018). Differentiation and operating segments: A framework and an application to after-sales services. *Manufacturing & Service Operations Management, 20*(3), 440–454.

Gulati, R., & Puranam, P. (2006). *Complementarity and constraints: Why firms both make and buy the same thing*. Working paper, Social Sciences Research Network, Copenhagen Business School, Copenhagen, Denmark. http://www.cbs.dk/content/download/

Handley, S. (2017). How governance misalignment and outsourcing capability impact performance. *Production and Operations Management, 26*(1), 134–155.

Hasselbring, W. (2000). Information system integration. *Communications of the ACM, 43*(6), 32–38.

Heide, J. B., Kumar, A., & Wathne, K. H. (2014). Concurrent sourcing, governance mechanisms, and performance outcomes in industrial value chains. *Strategic Management Journal, 35*(8), 1164–1185.

Helfat, C. E., & Martin, J. A. (2015). Dynamic managerial capabilities: Review and assessment of managerial impact on strategic change. *Journal of Management, 41*(5), 1281–1312.

Hitt, M. A., Xu, K., & Matz Carnes, C. (2016). Resource based theory in operations management research. *Journal of Operations Management, 41*, 77–94.

Holmlund, M., Kowalkowski, C. & Biggemann, S. (2016). Organisational behavior in innovation, marketing, and purchasing in business service contexts: An agenda for academic inquiry. *Journal of Business Research, 69*(7), 2457–2462.

Hurni, T., Huber, T. L., Dibbern, J., & Krancher, O. (2021). Complementor dedication in platform ecosystems: Rule adequacy and the moderating role of flexible and benevolent practices. *European Journal of Information Systems, 30*(3), 237–260.

Izza, S. (2009). Integration of industrial information systems: From syntactic to semantic integration approaches. *Enterprise Information Systems, 3*(1), 1–57.

Janssen, M., & Joha, A. (2006). Motives for establishing shared service centers in public administrations. *International Journal of Information Management, 26*(2), 102–115.

Janssen, M., Gortmaker, J., & Wagenaar, R. W. (2006). Web service orchestration in public administration: Challenges, roles, and growth stages. *Information Systems Management, 23*(2), 44.

Jeffery, M., & Leliveld, I. (2004). Best practices in IT portfolio management. *MIT Sloan Management Review*.

Joha, A., & Janssen, M. (2014). Factors influencing the shaping of shared services business models. *Strategic Outsourcing: An International Journal, 7*(1), 47–65.

Johnson, M., Roehrich, J. K., Chakkol, M., & Davies, A. (2021). Reconciling and reconceptualising servitization research: Drawing on modularity, platforms, ecosystems, risk and governance to develop mid-range theory. *International Journal of Operations & Production Management, 41*(5), 465–493.
Kock, A., Schulz, B., Kopmann, J., & Gemünden, H. G. (2020). Project portfolio management information systems' positive influence on performance: The importance of process maturity. *International Journal of Project Management, 38*(4), 229–241.
Kohlborn, T., Fielt, E., Korthaus, A., & Roseman, M. (2009). Towards a service portfolio management framework. In M. Davern & H. Scheepers (Eds.), *Proceedings of the twentieth Australasian conference on information systems understanding shared services: An exploration of the IS literature.* Monash University, CD Rom, pp. 1–10.
Kraaijenbrink, J., Spender, J.-C., & Groen, A. J. (2010). The resource-based view: A review and assessment of its critiques. *Journal of Management, 36*, 349–372.
Krancher, O., Dibbern, J., & Meyer, P. (2018). How social media-enabled communication awareness enhances project team performance. *Journal of the Association for Information Systems, 19*(9), 3. https://doi.org/10.17705/1jais.00510
Krzeminska, A., Hoetker, G., & Mellewigt, T. (2013). Reconceptualizing plural sourcing. *Strategic Management Journal, 34*(13), 1614–1627.
Küppers, T. (2016). *Role of organisational culture when shaping a shared service organisation into a lean system.* Doctoral dissertation, University of Gloucestershire. https://eprints.glos.ac.uk/4431/
Lacity, M., & Willcocks, L. (2017). Conflict resolution in business services outsourcing relationships. *The Journal of Strategic Information Systems, 26*(2), 80–100.
Lacity, M. C., Khan S. A., & Yan, A. (2016). Review of the empirical business services sourcing literature: an update and future directions. *Journal of Information Technology, 31*(3), 269–328.
Lacity, M. C., Khan, S. A., & Yan, A. (2017). Review of the empirical business services sourcing literature: An update and future directions. In *Outsourcing and Offshoring Business Services* (pp. 499–651). Palgrave Macmillan.
Lacity, M. C., Willcocks, L. P., & Rottman, J. W. (2008). Global outsourcing of back office services: Lessons, trends, and enduring challenges. *Strategic Outsourcing: An International Journal, 1*(1), 13–34.
Lee, J. N., Huynh, M. Q., & Hirschheim, R. (2008). An integrative model of trust on IT outsourcing: Examining a bilateral perspective. *Information Systems Frontiers, 10*, 145–163.

Lessard, D., Teece, D. J., & Leih, S. (2016). The dynamic capabilities of meta-multinationals. *Global Strategy Journal, 6*(3), 211–224.
Levina, N., & Su, N (2008). Global multisourcing strategy: the emergence of a supplier portfolio in services offshoring. *Decision Sciences, 39*(3), 541–570.
Lioliou, E., Willcocks, L., & Liu, X. (2019). Researching IT multi-sourcing and opportunistic behavior in conditions of uncertainty: A case approach. *Journal of Business Research, 103*, 387–396.
Liu, H., Wei, S., Ke, W., Wei, K. K., & Hua, Z. (2016). The configuration between supply chain integration and information technology competency: A resource orchestration perspective. *Journal of Operations Management, 44*, 13–29.
McLoughlin, K., Lewis, K., Lascelles, D., & Nudurupati, S. (2021). Sustainability in supply chains: Reappraising business process management. *Production Planning & Control, 34*(1), 19–52.
McIvor, R., McCracken, R., & McHugh, M. (2011). Creating outsourced shared services arrangements: Lessons from the public sector. *European Management Journal, 29*(6), 448–461.
Mishra, R., Kr Singh, R., & Koles, B. (2021). Consumer decision-making in omnichannel retailing literature review and future research agenda. *International Journal of Consumer Studies, 45*(2), 147–174.
Mukhopadhyay, S., & Bouwman, H. (2019). Orchestration and governance in digital platform ecosystems: A literature review and trends. *Digital Policy, Regulation and Governance, 21*(4), 329–351.
Narayanan, S., Jayaraman, V., Luo, Y., & Swaminathan, J. M. (2011). The antecedents of process integration in business process outsourcing and its effect on enterprise performance. *Journal of Operations Management, 29*(1–2), 3–16.
Oshri, I., Dibbern, J., Kotlarsky, J., & Krancher, O. (2019). An information processing view on joint vendor performance in multi-sourcing: The role of the guardian. *Journal of Management Information Systems, 36*(4), 1248–1283.
Osterwalder, A., Pigneur, Y., & Tucci, C. L. (2005). Clarifying business models: Origins, present, and future of the concept. *Communication of the Association for Information Systems, 16*(1), 1–25.
Parida, V., Burström, T., Visnjic, I., & Wincent, J. (2019). Orchestrating industrial ecosystem in circular economy: A two-stage transformation model for large manufacturing companies. *Journal of Business Research, 101*, 715–725.
Parmigiani, A. (2007). Why do firms both make and buy? An investigation of concurrent sourcing. *Strategic Management Journal, 28*(3), 285–311.

Parmigiani, A., & Mitchell, W. (2009). Complementarity, capabilities, and the boundaries of the firm: The impact of within firm and interfirm expertise on concurrent sourcing of complementary components. *Strategic Management Journal, 30*(10), 1065–1091.
Peng, J., Quan, J., Zhang, G., & Dubinsky, A. J. (2016). Mediation effect of business process and supply chain management capabilities on the impact of IT on firm performance: Evidence from Chinese firms. *International Journal of Information Management, 36*(1), 89–96.
Puranam, P., Gulati, R., & Bhattacharya, S. (2013). How much to make and how much to buy? An analysis of optimal plural sourcing strategies. *Strategic Management Journal, 34*(10), 1145–1161.
Rai, A., & Sambamurthy, V. (2006). Editorial notes—the growth of interest in services management: Opportunities for information systems scholars. *Information Systems Research, 17*(4), 327–331.
Rai, A., Pavlou, P. A., Im, G., & Du, S. (2012). Interfirm IT capability profiles and communications for cocreating relational value: Evidence from the logistics industry. *MIS Quarterly*, 233–262.
Rainer, R. K., Marshall, T. E., Knapp, K. J., & Montgomery, G. H. (2007). Do information security professionals and business managers view information security issues differently? *Information Systems Security, 26*(2), 100–108.
Reijers, H. A. (2021). Business process management: The evolution of a discipline. *Computers in Industry, 126*, 103404.
Richter, P. C., & Brühl, R. (2017). Shared service centre research: A review of the past, present, and future. *European Management Journal, 35*(3), 26–38.
Roels, G. (2014). Optimal design of co-productive services: Interaction and work allocation. *Manufacturing and Service Operations Management, 16*(4), 578–594.
Rosemann, M., & vom Brocke, J. (2014). The six core elements of business process management. In *Handbook on business process management 1: Introduction, methods, and information systems* (pp. 105–122). Berlin, Heidelberg: Springer Berlin Heidelberg.
Sadiq, W., & Racca, F. (2004). *Business services orchestration: The hypertier of information technology*. Cambridge University Press, Cambridge.
Sako, M. (2006). Does trust improve business performance. *Organisational trust: A reader*, 267–294.
Sako, M., Chondrakis, G., & Vaaler, P. M. (2016). How do plural-sourcing firms make and buy? The impact of supplier portfolio design. *Organization Science, 27*(5), 1161–1182.

Sanchez, R., & Mahoney, J. T. (1996). Modularity, flexibility, and knowledge management in product and organization. *Strategic Management Journal, 17*(S2), 63–76.
Shi, X., & Liao, Z. (2013). The mediating effects of interfirm business process integration and joint teamwork on firm performance in supply chains. *Asia Pacific Journal of Management, 30*, 243–1264.
Sirmon, D. G., Hitt, M. A., & Ireland, R. D. (2007). Managing firm resources in dynamic environments to create value: Looking inside the black box. *Academy of Management Review, 32*(1), 273–292.
Sirmon, D. G., Hitt, M. A., Ireland, R. D., & Gilbert, B. A. (2011). Resource orchestration to create competitive advantage: Breadth, depth, and life cycle effects. *Journal of Management, 37*(5), 1390–1412.
Sjödin, D., Parida, V., & Visnjic, I. (2022). How can large manufacturers digitalize their business models? A framework for orchestrating industrial ecosystems. *California Management Review, 64*(3), 49–77.
Su, N., & Levina, N. (2011). Global multisourcing strategy: Integrating learning from manufacturing into IT service outsourcing. *IEEE Transactions on Engineering Management, 58*(4), 717–729.
Teece, D. J. (2014). A dynamic capabilities-based entrepreneurial theory of the multinational enterprise. *Journal of International Business Studies, 45*, 8–37.
Tian, J., Vanderstraeten, J., Matthyssens, P., & Shen, L. (2021). Developing and leveraging platforms in a traditional industry: An orchestration and co-creation perspective. *Industrial Marketing Management, 92*, 14–33.
Tiwana, A., & Kim, S. K. (2016). Concurrent IT sourcing: Mechanisms and contingent advantages. *Journal of Management Information Systems, 33*(1), 101–138.
Ulbrich, F., & Borman, M. (2012). Preventing the gradual decline of shared service centers. In *Proceedings of the Eighteenth Americas Conference on Information Systems*, Seattle, Washington, August 9–12.
Van de Rijt, J., & Santema, S. C. (2012). The best value approach in the Netherlands: A reflection on past, present and future. *Journal for the Advancement of Performance Information and Value, 4*(2), 147.
Van der Aalst, W. M. P. (2012). A decade of business process management conferences: Personal reflections on a developing discipline. In A. Barros, A. Gal, & E. Kindler (Eds.), *Business Process Management* (LNCS 7481). Springer-Verlag Berlin Heidelberg.
Van der Aalst, W. M. P., Rosemann, M., & Dumas, M. (2007). Deadline-based escalation in process-aware information systems. *Decision Support Systems, 43*(2), 492–511.

Vitasek, K., & Manrodt, K. (2012). Vested outsourcing: A flexible framework for collaborative outsourcing. *Strategic Outsourcing: An International Journal, 5*(1), 4–14.

Vom Brocke, J., Schmiedel, T., Recker, J., Trkman, P., Mertens, W., & Viaene, S. (2014). Ten principles of good business process management. *Business Process Management Journal, 20*(4), 530–548.

Westphal, P., & Sohal, A. S. (2013). Taxonomy of outsourcing decision models. *Production Planning & Control, 24*(4–5), 347–358.

Wiener, M., & Saunders, C. (2014). Force coopetition in IT multi-sourcing. *Journal of Strategic Information Systems, 23*, 210–225.

Willcocks, L. P., Lacity, M. C., & Sauer, C. (Eds.). (2017). *Outsourcing and offshoring business services*. Springer.

Wirtz, J., & Ehret, M. (2009). Creative restruction how business services drive economic evolution. *European Business Review, 21*(4), 380–394.

Wirtz, J., Tuzovic, S., & Ehret, M. (2015). Global business services: Increasing specialization and integration of the world economy as drivers of economic growth. *Journal of Service Management, 26*(4), 565–587.

Witell, L., Kowalkowski, C., Perks, H., Raddats, C., Schwabe, M., Benedettini, O., & Burton, J. (2020). Characterizing customer experience management in business markets. *Journal of Business Research, 116*, 420–430.

Yoshikuni, A. C., Dwivedi, R., Dultra-de-Lima, R. G., Parisi, C., & Oyadomari, J. C. T. (2023). Role of emerging technologies in accounting information systems for achieving strategic flexibility through decision-making performance: An exploratory study based on North American and South American firms. *Global Journal of Flexible Systems Management, 24*, 199–218.

Zhao, J., Xi, X., Wang, S., & Gong, C. (2021). Dynamic analysis of different resource allocations: Implications for resource orchestration management of strategic alliances. *Computers & Industrial Engineering, 158*. https://doi.org/10.1016/j.cie.2021.107393

4

Quantitative Research

This chapter describes the quantitative research that we conducted to examine the path relationships depicted in the conceptual research model (see Fig. 3.1). We employed Partial Least Squares Structural Equation Modelling (PLS-SEM) technique (Hair et al., 2016) to test the hypotheses and the relationships between the antecedents of business services portfolio. This approach seems to be appropriate for the research at hand. Overall, PLS-SEM offers a flexible and robust approach to test relationships and hypotheses, particularly in situations where sample size is small, and the conceptual model (see Fig. 3.1) is complex, and the research is exploratory or prediction-oriented.

4.1 Measurement Model

To establish a comprehensive list of measures and validate measurement reliability, we performed an extensive review of the current literature on plural sourcing and GBS. As such, we identify and create a list of 20 survey items in total for measuring the constructs used in the model, ranging from 2 to 5 items per construct. While all survey items used in this research were adopted from previously validated items, the wordings of

A. Plugge, S. Nikou, *Digitalisation of Global Business Services*, Technology, Work and Globalization, https://doi.org/10.1007/978-3-031-51528-6_4

some of the items were slightly modified to fit the research context. For example, to measure plural sourcing strategy, we used items from Parmigiani (2007), Janssen and Feenstra (2010) and Aier et al. (2011), or to measure orchestration of business services portfolio, we used items from studies of Ulbrich and Schulz (2014), Wirtz et al. (2015), Richter and Brühl (2017), and Maatman and Meijerink (2017).

We asked respondents to reflect on the following question "How do you personally evaluate the importance of the following statements", using five-points Likert scales. We opted for a five-point scale to prevent overwhelming respondents with an excessive number of response choices and because our research question was straightforward or pertained to a less intricate construct. Literature shows that two main criteria influencing an enterprise's business services portfolio are (a) number of business services and (b) degree of outsourcing. As per number of business services, we opted to select the four most common business services as discussed in literature (Lacity et al., 2017), namely Finance & Accounting (F&A), Information Technology (IT), Human Resources (HR), and Supply Chain Management (SCM). Addressing the degree of outsourcing, literature on plural sourcing shows three levels of outsourcing, namely low (less than 20% of the annual budget spent on outsourcing), medium (between 20% and 50% of the annual budget spent on outsourcing), and high (more than 50% of the annual budget spent on outsourcing) (Dahlberg & Lahdelma, 2007). Both the number of business services and degree of outsourcing were used as control variables.

Literature shows that other variables such as an enterprise size (Aier et al., 2011), geographical location (Ciarli et al., 2012), and level of the maturity (Lacity et al., 2017), may impact the enterprise's orchestration of business services portfolio. Therefore, in addition to the degree of outsourcing, we included the enterprise size accounted by the number of employees (small = < 10,000 and large > 10,000 employees), geographical location (1 = North and South America, 2 = Europe and Asia Pacific and Africa), and maturity level based on the year of establishment (1 = before 2006, and 2 = after 2006). In this study, these variables have been used as control variables to examine whether the proposed relationships in the model are affected by these variables.

4.2 Sampling Strategy

Based on two assumptions, we set out to collect unique and representative data from enterprises that applied a business services portfolio in the context of a plural sourcing strategy. The first assumption is that enterprises that support many types of business services both in-house and outsourced, are more likely to orchestrate their business service portfolio. Second, we assume that the degree to which business services are outsourced affect the orchestration of an enterprise's business services portfolio. In addition, we considered additional three criteria for choosing the enterprises. The first criterion was that the plural sourcing strategy must have been established in the last three years prior to data collection. Another criterion was that the enterprises' business services portfolio includes the four most common business services (F&A, HR, IT, and SCM). The last criterion was that enterprises need to be engaged with developing plural sourcing strategy and have some degree of outsourcing in their business services. The initial sampling frame comprised a commercial mailing list encompassing globally operating enterprises across diverse industries. We inquired whether they utilised business services and if they were interested in participating in a global study. By reading practitioner magazines and informal meetings with advisors, the research team was able to compose the initial list. Next, we reached out to all the enterprises by phone, which were willing to participate to explain the context of the study and to locate a knowledgeable informant. To encourage their participation, informants were promised full confidentiality of their personal information and responses. We relied on the informants' profiles for collecting data and their engagement of the plural sourcing strategy in their respective enterprise to participate in the research. As we were interested in collecting data from the most involved representatives in an enterprise, only executives (directors, vice presidents, etc.) who were actively involved in developing a plural sourcing strategy were invited to participate. In addition, we only allowed senior managers who were involved in orchestrating business services portfolio to participate in the research.

4.3 Data Collection

Following a two-stage procedure, we collected data between January 2015 and February 2019. We developed an English questionnaire and pre-tested it with fifteen potential respondents, who represented both scientists and practitioners. Attached to the survey was a short cover letter explaining the purpose of the research. While it is acknowledged that the dataset utilised in this research may be relatively old, the uniqueness associated with this dataset cannot be overlooked. We sent out 267 invites and received 121 complete responses (45% response rate). We found three main reasons for not being able to complete the survey: (i) their portfolio did not match the criteria, (ii) not being involved in establishing a plural sourcing strategy, and (iii) lack of time. Table 4.1 shows the distribution of the enterprises.

This rich dataset is rather unique, as it was collected on a global scale, representing enterprises operating internationally in different industries. We anonymised the data of participants because of confidentiality reasons. The enterprises represent ten different industries, mostly from Education, Energy & Utilities, Pharma, and Public Sector, and less from Consumer Products and Technology & Telecom (see Table 4.1 and Appendix B2). Most of the enterprises in different industries had a low (less than 20% of the annual budget) degree of outsourcing: F&A

Table 4.1 Distribution of enterprises within their industries

Industry	Firms	Percentage
Consumer Products	6	5%
Diversified Conglomerate	8	7%
Education	10	8%
Energy & Utilities	18	15%
Financial & Professional Services	9	7%
Food & Beverages	9	7%
Manufacturing & Logistics	8	7%
Pharma	15	12%
Public Sector	11	9%
Technology & Telecom	6	5%
Other	21	18%
Total	121	100%

Table 4.2 The degree of outsourcing

Degree of outsourcing	Finance & accounting		Information technology		Human resources		Supply chain management	
	Firms	%	Firms	%	Firms	%	Firms	%
Low (<20%)	69	57%	103	85%	48	40%	104	86%
Medium (20%-50%)	43	36%	13	11%	47	39%	12	10%
High (>50%)	9	7%	5	4%	26	21%	5	4%
Total	121	100%	121	100%	121	100%	121	100%

(n = 69), IT (n = 103), HR (n = 48) and SCM (n = 104). However, 26 enterprises had more than 50% of their HR outsourced, as presented in Table 4.2.

4.4 Data Analysis and Results

4.4.1 Context

Partial Least Squares Structural Equation Modelling (PLS-SEM) is employed for this evaluation. Following the recommendation provided by Gefen and Straub (2005), first the measurement model and then the structural model were assessed. We examined and evaluated the items and assessed the constructs' reliability and validity. In the first step, we accounted for the items loadings, and then examined the values of the composite reliability (CR), and the average variance extracted (AVE), as recommended by Hair et al. (2012). Except for one item, all items' loadings were consistent with the cut-off value of 0.70, see Table 4.3. The Cronbach's alpha (α) test was performed, and all values were above the cut-off value of 0.70, with lowest for orchestration of business services portfolio (0.720), and the highest for modularisation (0.901). Following the recommendation of Bagozzi and Yi (1988), and Hair et al. (2012), we examined the composite reliability (CR) values, and they were all above 0.70, see Table 4.3. Finally, the convergent validity was assessed via the AVE values with lowest for plural sourcing strategy (0.583), and 0.790 for customer orientation (Bagozzi & Yi, 1988).

Table 4.3 Descriptive statistics, internal consistency, and reliability of items

Antecedent	Items	Factor loadings	Mean	Std	α	CR	AVE
Modularised business processes	MBP-1	0.871	2.256	1.210	0.901	0.926	0.716
	MBP-2	0.849	2.287	1.294			
	MBP-3	0.844	2.482	1.541			
	MBP-4	0.799	1.933	1.333			
	MBP-5	0.865	2.317	1.285			
Customer orientation	CO-1	0.900	2.384	1.319	0.735	0.883	0.790
	CO-2	0.878	2.223	1.400			
Managing decision rights	MDR-1	0.870	2.073	1.318	0.865	0.903	0.650
	MDR-2	0.773	1.858	1.305			
	MDR-3	0.767	1.881	1.291			
	MDR-4	0.809	2.452	1.360			
	MDR-5	0.809	2.321	1.536			
IS standardisation	ISS-1	0.896	2.437	1.103	0.730	0.881	0.787
	ISS-2	0.878	1.890	1.117			
Orchestration of business services portfolio	OBSP-1	0.849	3.200	1.327	0.720	0.818	0.693
	OBSP-2	0.815	3.118	0.911			
Plural sourcing strategy	PSS-1	0.728	2.837	1.387	0.779	0.846	0.583
	PSS-2	0.612	2.737	0.880			
	PSS-3	0.842	2.850	0.963			
	PSS-4	0.848	2.766	1.338			

4.4.2 Common method bias and non-response bias test

As we collected self-report data, we assessed Common Method Bias (CMB) following Harmon's single-factor test, and a more robust method, i.e. Common Latent Factor (CLF; Podsakoff et al., 2003). The Harmon's single-factor test resulted in six factors accounting for 69% of the variance; as such no evidence of CMB issue was found in the data. In addition, the result of CLF, using the values of the chi-square difference test between the unconstrained model and a model where all paths were constrained to zero, did not show any evidence of CMB (Kock, 2015; MacKenzie & Podsakoff, 2012). As the items used to measure each construct are highly correlated and interchangeable, we used reflective constructs. Therefore, multicollinearity is not an issue of concern in this research. In addition, multicollinearity is typically a concern in multiple linear regression rather than PLS, as PLS is designed to handle collinearities between predictors more effectively. In PLS, the focus is on capturing the shared variance (constructs' latent variables) between predictors and the dependent variable. PLS regression uses latent constructs rather than individual predictors to mitigate the impact of multicollinearity. However, to assess multicollinearity in SmartPLS, we consider the following indirect methods such as Variance Inflation Factor (VIF) in the inner model (see Table 4.4). The values of VIFs were all below the threshold of 10 (in our case all below 4.4); therefore, we concluded that the data is considered free of collinearity issue, or suggesting low multicollinearity (Henseler et al., 2015).

A non-response bias test was performed in which sample framing excludes a certain type of respondents in a non-homogeneous population. In doing so, the first and last quarters of responses were compared by using a *t*-test on the average scores for the main variables of the first quartile ($n = 30$), and the last quartile ($n = 30$) of the respondents (Lau et al., 2010). The test result did not show any significant differences between the mean scores of the two groups. Following that, we examined the sample bias, using Levene's Homogeneity of Variance Test. We ran the test on several items and did not find any major differences between the groups based on the sample of firms.

For assessing discriminant validity, we followed the Fornell and Larcker (1981) criterion and examined the values of the square root of AVE for each latent variable. As recommended, the values must be greater than other correlation values among the latent variables to assure that a

Table 4.4 VIF analysis

Path relationships	VIF
Customer orientation → Modularised business processes	1.331
Costumer orientation → Orchestration of business service portfolio	1.610
Managing decision rights → Modularised business processes	1.574
Managing decision rights → Orchestration of business service portfolio	1.817
IS standardisation → Modularised business processes	1.531
IS standardisation → Orchestration of business service portfolio	1.896
Modularised business processes → Orchestration of business service portfolio	2.172
Plural sourcing → Orchestration of business service portfolio	1.376

Table 4.5 Discriminant validity: Fornell-Larcker criterion

Antecedents	MBP	CO	ISS	MDR	PSS	OBSP
Modularised business processes	**0.846**					
Customer orientation	0.749	**0.889**				
IS standardisation	0.748	0.689	**0.887**			
Managing decision rights	0.772	0.750	0.740	**0.806**		
Plural sourcing strategy	0.742	0.688	0.633	0.683	**0.764**	
Orchestration of business services portfolio	0.392	0.224	0.242	0.340	0.411	**0.832**

Table 4.6 Discriminant validity: Heterotrait-Monotrait (HTMT) criterion

Antecedent	MBP	CO	ISS	MDR	PSS	OBSP
Modularised business processes						
Customer orientation	0.808					
IS standardisation	0.715	0.840				
Managing decision rights	0.750	0.687	0.508			
Plural sourcing strategy	0.669	0.334	0.123	0.585		
Orchestration of business services portfolio	0.424	0.394	0.667	0.617	0.842	

construct in the model has not been measured through other constructs in the model (Henseler et al., 2015). As shown in Table 4.5, the square roots of AVE values in bold on the diagonal are in line with the criterion.

In addition, the discriminant validity was assessed through a more robust approach, namely Heterotrait-Monotrait (HTMT) ratio. To assess discriminant validity using HTMT, the common threshold is 0.85. If the HTMT value is less than 0.85 (Franke & Sarstedt, 2019), it indicates satisfactory discriminant validity and suggest the constructs are distinguishable from one another (Hair et al., 2017). In HTMT analysis, all values were below the threshold (see Table 4.6).

4.5 Structural Model Analysis

PLS-SEM was used to assess the path relationships proposed in the research model. PLS-SEM is a flexible and robust approach that enables testing of relationships and hypotheses, particularly in situations with small sample sizes, assumptions on multivariate normality, using of both reflective and formative constructs, complex conceptual models, and exploratory or prediction-oriented research (Henseler et al., 2015; Ringle et al., 2012). In addition, PLS-SEM allows for assessing indirect and total effects, reducing error associated with the model by assessing the relationships between multi-item constructs (Yoshikuni et al., 2023). To assess the significance of the path relationships in the model (level of 5%), we used bootstrapping and created 5000 sub-samples from the data and examined the t-statistics values. The explained variance of orchestration of business services portfolio was 52% ($R^2 = 0.516$). This means that the latent variables plural sourcing strategy, modularised business processes, and customer orientation explained nearly 52% of the variance in orchestration of business services portfolio. IS standardisation, managing decision rights and customer orientation explained 70% of the variance of modularised business processes. It should be noted that as we used PLS-SEM approach using the Smart PLS software, we cannot provide an extensive list of values corresponding to model fit data and relied only on the path coefficients and their significance (Hair et al., 2014). Nevertheless, Hooper et al. (2008) suggested using the standardised root mean square residual (SRMR ranged from 0 to 1) values for reporting the model fit data.

As recommended, the values lower than 0.08 are considered a good fit, the SRMR value in our analysis is 0.069. The path relationship between plural sourcing strategy to orchestration of business services portfolio was significant ($\beta = 0.23$, $t = 2.186$, $p < 0.05$), providing support to accept H1. The path relationship between customer orientation and orchestration of business services portfolio was significant ($\beta = 0.18$, $t = 2.088$ $p < 0.05$). Thus, H2a is supported by the data. The path between customer orientation and modularised business processes was statistically significant, thus supporting hypothesis H2b ($\beta = 0.23$, $t = 4.102$, $p < 0.001$). The results showed that the path between modularised business processes to orchestration of business services portfolio was also significant ($\beta = 0.29$, $t = 2.291$, $p < 0.05$). Therefore, the data support H3. The paths from IS standardisation to orchestration of business services portfolio and managing decision rights to orchestration of business services portfolio were not significant, thus rejecting hypotheses H4a and H5a. Nevertheless, the path relationships from IS standardisation and managing decision rights to modularised business processes were both

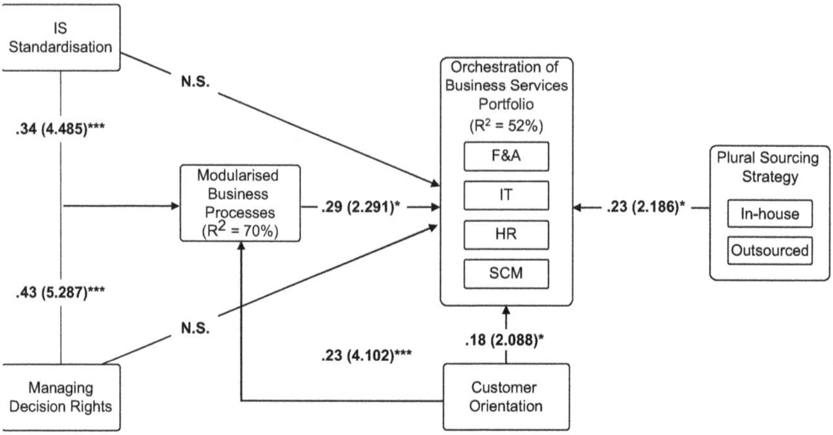

Fig. 4.1 Research model results. (Notes: *** $p < 0.001$; ** $p < 0.01$; * $p < 0.05$)

significant ($\beta = 0.34$, $t = 4.485$, $p < 0.001$; and $\beta = 0.43$, $t = 5.287$, $p < 0.001$). Thus, hypotheses 4b and 5b were supported by the data. In summary, we conclude that plural sourcing strategy, modularised business processes, and customer orientation are important antecedents that directly affect a firm's orchestration of business services portfolio, as shown in Fig. 4.1.

4.5.1 Mediation and Moderation Effects

The results of the mediation test indicate that the antecedent modularised business processes fully mediate the relationships from IS standardisation, managing decision rights, and customer orientation (partially) to orchestration of business services portfolio. The specific indirect effect value between customer orientation ➔ modularised business processes ➔ orchestration of business services portfolio was ($\beta = 0.11$, $t = 1.99$, $p < 0.05$) (see H2c). The specific indirect effect value between IS standardisation ➔ modularised business processes ➔ orchestration of business services portfolio was ($\beta = 0.10$, $t = 1.198$, $p < 0.01$), and for managing decision rights ➔ modularised business processes ➔ orchestration of business services portfolio ($\beta = 0.11$, $t = 2.078$, $p < 0.05$), (see H2d and H2e).

Given that the direct paths between IS standardisation and managing decision rights to orchestration of business services portfolio were not significant, we conclude that modularised business mediate the relationships of both antecedents with orchestration of business services portfolio (see Table 4.7). These mediation results show that modularised business processes form an essential component needed to orchestrate a firm's business services portfolio effectively.

We ran multigroup analysis using the finite mixture partial least squares (FIMIX-PLS) algorithm, see Table 4.8 (Matthews et al., 2016; Yoshikuni et al., 2023). The FIMIX-PLS algorithm can detect subpopulations by prespecifying subgroup sizes and can classify data of the inner path models estimates based on heterogeneity (Hair et al., 2017). It our analysis, two segments solution was most appropriated due to subgroup size.

Table 4.7 Mediation effect

Hypothesis	Path relationships	Specific indirect effects	VAF	Mediation
H2c	Customer orientation ➢ Modularised business processes ➢Orchestration of business services portfolio	0.11 (1.99) *	31%	Partial
H4c	IS standardisation ➢ Modularised business processes ➢ Orchestration of business services portfolio	0.10 (1.198) **	100%	Full
H5c	Managing decision rights ➢ Modularised business processes ➢ Orchestration of business services portfolio	0.11 (2.078) *	100%	Full

Table 4.8 Cross tab of FIMIXPLS segment

Observed variable	FIMIX-PLS segments			Sample % by segments		
Degree of outsourcing	1	2	Sum	1	2	Sum
Low (less than 20% of the annual budget spent on outsourcing)	59	9	68	87%	13%	56%
Medium (between 20% to 50% of the annual budget spent on outsourcing	17	2	19	89%	11%	16%
High (more than 50% of the annual budget spent on outsourcing	18	16	34	53%	47%	28%

We used enterprises' degree of outsourcing (Low = < 20%, Medium = more than 20% and less than 50%; High = >50%) to assess the moderating effect of this variable on the relationships shown in Table 4.9. The moderation test results showed that the paths from plural sourcing strategy

Table 4.9 Moderation effect

Path relationships	*β*	*T-stat*	*PLS-MGA*	Parametric test	Welch–Satterthwait test	Degree of outsourcing
Plural sourcing strategy ➔ Orchestration of business services portfolio	0.354	1.977	Sig*	Sig*	Sig*	Low
Customer orientation ➔ Orchestration of business services portfolio	-0.420	2.520	Sig**	Sig**	Sig**	Low
Customer orientation ➔ Modularised business processes	0.328	3.015	Sig***	Sig***	Sig***	Low
IS standardisation ➔ Modularised business processes	0.312	3.090	Sig***	Sig***	Sig***	Low
Managing decision rights ➔ Modularised business processes	0.301	2.410	Sig**	Sig**	Sig**	Low
Managing decision rights ➔ Modularised business processes	0.782	1.962	Sig*	Sig*	Sig*	Medium

*** Significant at 0.001 (two-tailed), ** Significant at 0.01 (two-tailed), * Significant at 0.05 (two-tailed)

and customer orientation to orchestration of business services portfolio were moderated by the organisations' degree of outsourcing. This effect suggests that for enterprises having a low degree of outsourcing, the impact of customer orientation and plural sourcing strategy is stronger than for those enterprises with a high degree of outsourcing. Interestingly, we also found moderating effects of degree of outsourcing on the relationships of customer orientation, IS standardisation, and managing decision rights with modularised business processes for enterprises with a low degree of outsourcing. This corresponds to enterprises that decide to outsource a limited part of their services to the market (low degree of outsourcing). The path between managing decision rights and modularised business processes was also significant in case of a medium degree of outsourcing.

Regarding the maturity of the enterprise, we divided the data into two groups; group 1 includes enterprises established before 2006 ($n = 47$) and group 2 includes enterprises established after 2006 ($n = 74$). The multigroup analysis (MGA) results show that the maturity of an enterprise impacts three path relationships in the model. The path between managing decision rights to modularised business processes was significant for enterprises in group 1 ($\beta = 0.46$, $t = 2.630$, $p < 0.001$). The MGA results show that the path between managing decision rights to orchestration of business services portfolio was significant only for the enterprises in group 2 ($\beta = 0.15$, $t = 1.996$, $p < 0.05$). Finally, the path between IS standardisation to modularised business processes was significant for enterprises in group 1 ($\beta = 0.10$, $t = 2.100$, $p < 0.05$).

Regarding the size of the enterprises, we divided its size into two groups according to the number of employees (group 1; small = < 10,000 ($n = 51$), and group 2: large > 10,000 employees ($n = 70$)). The MGA results show that enterprise size impacts three path relationships in the model. The paths between managing decision rights to orchestration of business services portfolio ($\beta = 0.50$, $t = 3.056$, $p < 0.001$), and customer orientation to modularise business services ($\beta = 0.61$, $t = 2.223$, $p < 0.05$) were significant for the enterprises in group 1 (small firms). The path between IS standardisation to modularised business processes was significant for enterprises in group 2 (large firms) ($\beta = 0.58$, $t = 4.826$, $p < 0.001$). This indicates that while small businesses understand the value of customer orientation, and managing both their operations and their business services, large businesses place more emphasis on using technology to modularise their business services.

Regarding the location of the enterprises, we divided enterprises into group 1 (North America, and South America, n = 56), and group 2 (Europe, Asia Pacific, and Africa, n = 65). The MGA results show that the enterprises' geographical location impacts three path relationships in the model. The path between managing decision rights to orchestration of business services portfolio was significant only for the enterprises located in group 2 ($\beta = 0.38$, $t = 2.054$, $p < 0.05$). The path between customer orientation to modularised business processes was significant for enterprises located in Europe, Asia Pacific, and Africa ($\beta = 0.78$, $t = 5.617$, $p < 0.001$). In addition, the path between plural sourcing strategy to orchestration of business services portfolio was significant for enterprises located in group 1 ($\beta = 0.38$, $t = 2.054$, $p < 0.05$). Finally, the geographical location of the enterprises impacts the path between IS standardisation to modularised business processes for enterprises located in group 1 ($\beta = 0.32$, $t = 2.352$, $p < 0.01$).

4.6 Discussion

Our findings show that the antecedents plural sourcing strategy, customer orientation, and modularised business processes have a direct and significant effect on enterprises' orchestration of business services portfolio. The results of the present research go beyond the findings of Sako et al. (2016), who found that supplier portfolio design affects plural sourcing from a transaction cost perspective. We extend this finding by focusing on enterprises' orchestration of business services portfolio that include the provisioning of internal as well as external business services by applying an ROT lens. Based on the findings, it can be argued that a business services portfolio orchestrates the production of in-house and outsourced business services.

The research findings suggest that the antecedent modularised business processes directly influence the orchestration of business services portfolio positively, and as such, contributes to creating business process flexibility (Van der Aalst, 2012). The results show that the modularised business processes is essential to support enterprises in accomplishing business services portfolio flexibility in a plural sourcing context. In addition, the results show that IS standardisation and managing decision rights indirectly impact the enterprises' orchestration of business service portfolio through modularised business processes acts as a mediator. The SEM results show that customer orientation has both direct and indirect effect on the dependent variable, i.e. orchestration of business services portfolio. The outcome of the study demonstrates that an enterprise's plural sourcing strategy, modularised business processes, and customer orientation are perceived to be critical antecedents to establish a business services portfolio. In the present study, IS standardisation and managing decision rights do not influence a business services portfolio directly but only indirectly.

4.7 Conclusions

This chapter addresses main objective 2: *Theoretically develop and empirically validate a business services portfolio model and its corresponding antecedents.*

Within the context of a plural sourcing strategy, the five identified antecedents were discussed more in-depth. By studying relevant literature, we proposed eight important relationships between the antecedents under study to orchestration of business services portfolio. In addition, we argue that the role of modularised business processes may act as a moderator between the antecedents and a business services portfolio. As a result, we developed three additional hypotheses. The various relationships as proposed were translated into a conceptual research model that shows the expected path relationships. As a next step, we examined the path relationships by employing Partial Least Squares Structural Equation Modelling (SEM) technique (Hair et al., 2016). Our analysis provides evidence and support for the following hypotheses: H1, H2a, H2b, H3, H4a, and H4b. However, in contrast to our expectations, hypotheses H4a and H5a were rejected in the proposed conceptual model.

In addition, this chapter addresses the objective 3: *Show how business processes act as a mediator towards a business services portfolio.*

Our survey on GBS drivers (see Table 2.2) addresses the role of business process excellence as enterprises in most industries acknowledge its importance. An exception is organisations that correspond to Education and Public Sector. As discussed, scholars underpin the importance of business processes to support a business services portfolio. Hence, we decided to conduct mediation and moderation tests to find evidence for the role and importance of the business processes. The results of the mediation test indicate that the antecedent modularised business processes fully mediate the relationships from IS standardisation, managing decision rights, and customer orientation (partially) to orchestration of business services portfolio. As a next step, we used enterprises' degree of outsourcing as a control variable to assess the moderating effect of the antecedent modularised business processes. Five significant path relationships were identified in the case of a low degree of outsourcing in practice. In other words, we found five paths where the low degree of outsourcing has a moderating effect. However, the path relationship (e.g. managing decision rights to modularised business processes) was identified in case enterprises apply a medium degree of outsourcing. By analysing mediation and moderation effects, we answer main objective 3.

References

Aier, S., Bucher, T., & Winter, R. (2011). Critical success factors of service orientation in information systems engineering. *Business & Information Systems Engineering, 3*(2), 77–88.

Bagozzi, R. P., & Yi, Y. (1988). On the evaluation of structural equation models. *Journal of the Academy of Marketing Science, 16*(1), 74–94.

Ciarli, T., Meliciani, V., & Savona, M. (2012). Knowledge dynamics, structural change and the geography of business services. *Journal of Economic Surveys, 26*(3), 445–467.

Dahlberg, T., & Lahdelma, P. (2007). IT Governance Maturity and IT Outsourcing Degree: An Exploratory Study. In *Proceedings of the 39th annual Hawaii International Conference on System Sciences,* paper 236a.

Fornell, C., & Larcker, D. F. (1981). Evaluating structural equation models with unobservable variables and measurement error. *Journal of Marketing Research, 18*(1), 39–50.

Franke, G., & Sarstedt, M. (2019). Heuristics versus statistics in discriminant validity testing: A comparison of four procedures. *Internet Research, 29*(3), 430–447.
Gefen, D., & Straub, D. (2005). A practical guide to factorial validity using PLS-Graph: Tutorial and annotated example. *Communication of the Association for Information Systems, 16*(5), 91–109.
Hair, J., Hollingsworth, C. L., Randolph, A. B., & Chong, A. Y. L. (2017). An updated and expanded assessment of PLS-SEM in information systems research. *Industrial Management & Data Systems, 117*(3), 442–458.
Hair, J. F., Hult, G. T. M., Ringle, C., & Sarstedt, M. (2016). *A primer on partial least squares structural equation modeling (PLS-SEM)*. Sage Publications.
Hair, J. F., Sarstedt, M., Hopkins, L., & Kuppelwieser, V. G. (2014). Partial least squares structural equation modeling (PLS-SEM): An emerging tool in business research. *European Business Review, 26*(2), 106–121.
Hair, J. F., Sarstedt, M., Ringle, C. M., & Mena, J. A. (2012). An assessment of the use of partial least squares structural equation modeling in marketing research. *Journal of the Academy of Marketing Science, 40*(3), 414–433.
Henseler, J., Ringle, C. M., & Sarstedt, M. (2015). A new criterion for assessing discriminant validity in variance-based structural equation modeling. *Journal of the Academy of Marketing Science, 43*(1), 115–135.
Hooper, D., Coughlan, J., & Mullen, M. R. (2008). Structural equation modelling: Guidelines for determining model fit. *The Electronic Journal of Business Research Methods, 6*(1), 53–60.
Janssen, M., & Feenstra, R. (2010). Service portfolios for supply chain composition: Creating business network interoperability and agility. *International Journal of Computer Integrated Manufacturing, 23*(8–9), 747–757.
Kock, N. (2015). Common method bias in PLS-SEM: A full collinearity assessment approach. *International Journal of e-Collaboration, 11*(4), 1–10.
Lacity, M. C., Khan, S. A., & Yan, A. (2017). Review of the empirical business services sourcing literature: An update and future directions. In *Outsourcing and offshoring business services* (pp. 499–651). Palgrave Macmillan.
Lau, A. K. W., Tang, E., & Yam, R. C. M. (2010). Effects of suppliers and customer integration on product innovation and performance: Empirical evidence in Hong Kong manufacturers. *Journal of Production Innovation Management, 27*(5), 761–777.
Maatman, M., & Meijerink, J. (2017). Why sharing is synergy: The role of decentralized control mechanisms and centralized HR capabilities in creating HR shared service value. *Personnel Review, 46*(7), 1297–1317.

MacKenzie, S. B., & Podsakoff, P. M. (2012). Common method bias in marketing: Causes, mechanisms, and procedural remedies. *Journal of Retailing, 88*(4), 542–555.

Matthews, L. M., Sarstedt, M., Hair, J. F., & Ringle, C. M. (2016). Identifying and treating unobserved heterogeneity with FIMIX-PLS: Part II—A case study. *European Business Review, 28*(2), 208–224.

Parmigiani, A. (2007). Why do firms both make and buy? An investigation of concurrent sourcing. *Strategic Management Journal, 28*(3), 285–311.

Podsakoff, P. M., MacKenzie, S. B., Lee, J. Y., & Podsakoff, N. P. (2003). Common method biases in behavioral research: A critical review of the literature and recommended remedies. *Journal of Applied Psychology, 88*(5), 879–903.

Richter, P. C., & Brühl, R. (2017). Shared service centre research: A review of the past, present, and future. *European Management Journal, 35*(3), 26–38.

Ringle, C. M., Sarstedt, M., & Straub, D. W. (2012). Editor's comments: A critical look at the use of PLS-SEM in MIS Quarterly. *MIS Quarterly, 36*(1), iii–xiv.

Sako, M., Chondrakis, G., & Vaaler, P. M. (2016). How do plural-sourcing firms make and buy? The impact of supplier portfolio design. *Organization Science, 27*(5), 1161–1182.

Ulbrich, F., & Schulz, V. (2014). Seven challenges management must overcome when implementing IT-shared services. *Strategic Outsourcing: An International Journal, 7*(2), 94–106.

Van der Aalst, W. M. P. (2012). A decade of business process management conferences: Personal reflections on a developing discipline. In A. Barros, A. Gal, & E. Kindler (Eds.), *Business Process Management* (LNCS 7481). Springer-Verlag Berlin Heidelberg.

Wirtz, J., Tuzovic, S., & Ehret, M. (2015). Global business services: Increasing specialization and integration of the world economy as drivers of economic growth. *Journal of Service Management., 26*(4), 565–587.

Yoshikuni, A. C., Dwivedi, R., Dultra-de-Lima, R. G., Parisi, C., & Oyadomari, J. C. T. (2023). Role of emerging technologies in accounting information systems for achieving strategic flexibility through decision-making performance: An exploratory study based on North American and South American firms. *Global Journal of Flexible Systems Management, 24*, 199–218.

5

Configurational Thinking Approach

In the present chapter, our investigative focus shifts towards a nuanced exploration of the determinants shaping the orchestration of a business service portfolio by applying fuzzy-set Qualitative Comparative Analysis (fsQCA). This methodology is renowned for its capacity to elucidate complex causal configurations within complex systems. Our methodological rationale for adopting fsQCA resides in its inherent suitability for accommodating the intricacies inherent in our research objectives. This allows us to create a deeper understanding and comprehension of the conditional interplays driving business service portfolio orchestration.

Drawing upon the same dataset previously subjected to the rigorous scrutiny of Partial Least Squares Structural Equation Modelling (PLS-SEM) in Chap. 3, our deliberate selection of fsQCA as the analytical tool is rooted in a deliberate intent to obtain complementary insights. This dual-method approach enables us to discern convergences and divergences between the findings obtained through the two distinct yet complementary methodologies. As such, we foster a comprehensive understanding of the multifaceted conditions underpinning the phenomenon under investigation. In essence, this chapter serves as a pivotal juncture wherein we harness the distinct attributes of fsQCA and

A. Plugge, S. Nikou, *Digitalisation of Global Business Services*, Technology, Work and Globalization, https://doi.org/10.1007/978-3-031-51528-6_5

PLS-SEM to uncover a more holistic understanding of the complex interrelationships shaping business service portfolio orchestration. By synergistically leveraging the strengths of these methodologies, we aim to transcend the limitations of any single analytical approach and thereby advance a more robust comprehension of the multiple interdependent determinants. Consequently, we govern this pivotal facet of organisational dynamics, i.e. orchestration of business services portfolio.

5.1 Research Methodology

Literature shows only four studies specifically addressed business services configurations, of which two studies used qualitative research to explore seven antecedents to describe business services configurations (Schulz et al., 2009; Schulz & Brenner, 2010). The third and fourth study applied a quantitative approach and used cluster analysis to obtain business services configurations (Aksin & Mansini, 2008; Richter, 2021). The results of these four studies provide relevant insights and perspectives on business services configurations. However, the antecedents studied in those studies vary (e.g. service charges, external market view, contract form, centre concept, operational capabilities). Because of the inconsistent predictions and empirical results, enterprises are uncertain about how to understand the combination of antecedents that lead to the desired outcome, which is orchestration of business services portfolio. Therefore, we aim to fill this literature gap by examining the relationship between antecedents of and their combined effect on orchestration of business services portfolio through configurational thinking theory, fuzzy-set Qualitative Comparative Analysis (FsQCA: Ragin, 2008). This method is based on set theory and provides a mean to identify the combination of conditions that lead to the outcome of interest. For example, a successful business services implementation and its impact on, e.g. an enterprise's business model. The configurational thinking method is an emerging alternative to conventional methods, which enables not only to understand the complexity of organisational phenomena and causal complexity, but also to find pattern of combinations of multiple independent variables that together lead to a dependent variable (Fiss, 2011; Misangyi et al., 2017).

5.1.1 A Configurational Approach

Configuration thinking theories view phenomena as clusters of interconnected elements that must be simultaneously understood and viewed as a holistic and integrated pattern (El Sawy et al., 2010). Such theories consider the relationship between individual conditions (variables). Configuration theory is well suited as an inquiring approach to study the complexity of business services environments, such as mutual causality, fuzzy boundaries, and discontinuities (Meyer et al., 1993; Fiss, 2011). This method has been applied in various disciplines such as OM research (Mikalef et al., 2015). Miller (1981, p. 5) demonstrated that "instead of looking at a few variables or at linear associations among such variables, the focus should be on finding the frequency of the recurring clusters of attributes or gestalts". Given the gap identified in the business services literature into account, it could be suggested that a more rigorous approach is required to examine the interdependencies of factors (conditions in terms of FsQCA) contributing to the orchestration of business services portfolio. By means of a more advanced data analysis method, more insights can be gained, which can explain the inconsistent findings in previous research (Legewie, 2013). As such, a more fine-grained approach such as fsQCA can be seen as one of the most appropriate methods to understand the causal complexity of the organisational phenomena (Rihoux & Ragin, 2009).

This methodological choice is inspired based on three objectives, (i) conjunction, which refers to the interdependency of multiple conditions leading to the same outcome (Schneider & Wagemann, 2012), (ii) equifinality, that refers to the possibility of multiple pathways (different causal recipes) leading to the same outcome (Fiss, 2011) and (iii) asymmetry, which means that conditions found to have a causal relationship in one configuration may be unrelated or even inversely related in another configuration (Meyer et al., 1993, p. 1178).

5.1.2 Measurement Model, Sample Selection and Data Collection

To ensure the reliability of the measurement and to have a comprehensive list of measures, all survey items for each condition (factor) used in this study were selected from previously validated measures (see Sect. 4.1). A description of the sampling strategy is described in Sect. 5.2. To select the most appropriate enterprises, we used the same data set and corresponding criteria as discussed in Chap. 3 (quantitative study).

5.2 Analysis

5.2.1 Calibration

The first step is the calibration of the raw measurements into fuzzy membership scores ranging from 0 to 1, where 0 indicates fully out, or no set membership, and 1 indicates fully in or full set membership (Ragin, 2008). The entire set of the indicators were reflectively measured using five-points Likert scales. There are two common approaches for calibration, direct, and indirect calibration. In direct calibration, three anchors will be used to identify the degree of membership for each condition (Woodside, 2014). To calibrate these measures, three qualitative anchors were specified for the calibration. A fuzzy score = 0.95 was assigned for full membership, fuzzy score = 0.05 for full non-membership, and fuzzy score = 0.50 for cross-over point. As fsQCA is sensitive to analyse the cases with exact 0.50 score membership (Ragin, 2009), we followed the approach recommended by Fiss (2011) and Pappas et al. (2020), and added a constant value (i.e. 0.001) to cross-over values. However, this addition does not affect the results but guarantees that none of the cases is dropped in fsQCA.

5.2.2 Necessity and Sufficiency Analysis

The next stage is to conduct a necessity analysis to see if there are any conditions in the dataset that can be recognised as being required for the desired outcome to occur, i.e. orchestration of business services portfolio (measured with 4 items). This entails that the membership score of the outcome is consistently lower than the membership score of the causal condition under consideration. The consistency value will be used to see if a condition is necessary for the outcome to occur. A value higher than 0.90 indicates the existence of an important relationship (Schneider & Wagemann, 2012). The results of the analysis showed that all condition had the values below the threshold value (see Table 5.1). While this initial test offers useful insights, a sufficiency analysis which is the last step of fsQCA analysis needs to be performed to gain additional insights about the interdependencies between the antecedents of orchestration of business services portfolio. However, before running the sufficiency analysis, a truth table of 2^k rows was constructed, where k is the number of conditions, and each row indicates a possible combination.

5.2.3 Truth-table

After calibration and the necessity analysis the truth-table was constructed. As there are five conditions (i.e. modularised business processes, plural sourcing strategy, IS standardisation, customer orientation, and managing decision rights) leading to orchestration of business services

Table 5.1 Necessity Analysis (outcome condition = orchestration of business services portfolio)

Condition	Consistency	Coverage
Size of the enterprise	0.57 (0.48)	0.42 (0.48)
Modularised business processes	0.76 (0.70)	0.56 (0.56)
Plural sourcing strategy	0.74 (0.75)	0.59 (0.54)
IS standardisation	0.73 (0.67)	0.59 (0.59)
Customer orientation	0.74 (0.71)	0.55 (0.57)
Managing decision rights	0.74 (0.71)	0.58 (0.56)

Note: The value for the negation of a condition is shown in parentheses

portfolio, the truth-table will contain $2^5 = 32$ rows, one for each logically possible combination of five presence/absence conditions. Based on the recommendation provided by Ragin (2008), the consistency value of each row (configuration) should be 0.75 or higher. Consistency refers to the extent to which a combination of causal conditions in the constructed truth-table is sufficient to lead to the desired outcome. However, in our study, a more conservative approach was considered and the value of 0.85 was set for the consistency cut-off. A consistency value, according to Schneider and Wagemann (2012), is comparable to the significance level in traditional regression and correlational approaches. After construction of the truth-table, configurations that did not adhere to the cut-off rule were removed from further analysis. To ensure that the minimum number of empirical cases exist for the configuration assessment, a frequency cut-off point is established, and the recommended frequency threshold is 1, when the total number of cases in the analysis is relatively small (Ragin, 2008). However, a more conservative threshold must be selected when the total N is large (Ragin, 2009).

5.2.4 Solution Sets

In the final step of the fsQCA analysis (the sufficiency analysis), three solution sets of consistent and sufficient configurations of causal combinations are produced. By using the minimisation technique on truth-table results, the fsQCA analysis generates three types of solutions: (a) parsimonious, (b) intermediate, and (c) complex solutions. A solution refers to a combination of conditions supported by a high number of cases and is produced through a logical procedure known as the Quine-McCluskey minimisation technique (Ragin, 2008). While complex solutions include all possible configurations when logical operations are applied, parsimonious solutions include all possible configurations by applying all simplifying conditions without any evaluation of their plausibility (Delgosha et al., 2021; Rihoux & Ragin, 2009). In this research, complex solutions have been used to illustrate the results (Mendel & Korjani, 2012; Rihoux & Ragin, 2009; Delgosha et al., 2021). In each solution a condition is either a core condition or a peripheral condition

(Fiss, 2011), core conditions appear both in the parsimonious and intermediate solutions, and peripheral conditions appear only in the intermediate solutions. In this study, the fsQCA 3.0, and R 3.6.1 software with the QCA package version 3.5 were used.

5.3 Results

5.3.1 Illustration of the fsQCA Results

When reporting the results, the following notations will be used to illustrate the results in the tables. Black circles (●) indicate the presence of a condition, and blank circles (O) indicate its absence. Blank spaces indicate "do not care" or the causal condition may be either absent or present (Ragin & Fiss, 2008). Large circles present core conditions, and small circles present peripheral conditions. Additionally, in further analysis, the size of enterprises was used to gain a more thorough understanding of the data and how different configurations of conditions lead to orchestration of business services portfolio. When the size of the enterprises is included in the analysis, it is operationalised as a crisp variable, using black circles (●) to denote "large" enterprise and blank circles (O) to denote "small" enterprise.

5.3.2 Analysis of Sufficiency for Global Business Services Implementation

For orchestration of business services portfolio, when the size of the enterprises was not considered in the analysis, the fsQCA analysis generated seven solutions (see Table 5.2). Solution 1 indicates that the presence of IS standardisation (ISS) and customer orientation (CO), and the absence of plural sourcing strategy (PSS) together lead to the outcome of interest, i.e. orchestration of business services portfolio (OBSP). Regarding the raw coverage, this solution has the third highest value (0.397). Solution 2 indicates that the presence of ISS, and managing decision-rights (MDR), and the absence of PSS together lead to the

Table 5.2 Intermediate solutions, without size of the firms

Solution	MBP	PSS	ISS	CO	MDR	Raw Coverage	Unique Coverage	Consistency
1		○	●	●		0.397	0.005	0.810
2		○	●		⬤	0.374	0.006	0.851
3	⬤			○	●	0.370	0.009	0.976
4	●			●	○	0.631	0.009	0.937
5	○	●		○	○	0.305	0.007	0.864
6	○	●		●	●	0.610	0.008	0.983
7	●	○		●		0.381	0.003	0.965
Overall solution consistency			0.862					
Overall solution coverage			0.649					

Note: MBP = Modularised business processes; PSS = Plural sourcing strategy; ISS = IS standardisation; CO = Customer orientation; MDR = Managing decision rights

outcome of interest. In this solution, MDR is a core condition. Solution 3 indicates the presence of two conditions, MBP, MDR, and the absence of CO together lead to the OBSP. In this solution, MBP is a core condition. Solution 4 indicates that the presence of MBP and CO, and the absence of MDR lead to the outcome of interest. This solution has the highest raw coverage value amongst all seven configurations. Solution 5 indicates the presence of PSS and the absence of three conditions, MBP, CO and MDR combined lead to the occurrence of OBSP. Solution 6 indicates the presence of three conditions, PSS, CO, and MDR, and the absence of MBP lead to OBSP. This solution had the highest consistency value (0.983). Finally, solution 7 indicates the presence of MBP and CO, and the absence of PSS are sufficient conditions for the outcome to occur. Based on configuration of conditions in these seven solutions, it can be concluded that when the size of the enterprises is not considered in the analysis, the presence or the absence of four conditions: MBP, PSS, CO, and MDR play important role for the outcome to occur.

The raw coverage values in these seven solutions were between 0.305 and 0.631. The consistency values (the extent to which a given combination is a sufficient condition for the outcome), was above 0.81 for all configurations, which is higher than the cut-off value of 0.75 (Ragin,

Table 5.3 Solutions and their corresponding cases

Solution	Cases (enterprises under study)
S1: ~PSS_F*ISS_F*CO_F	51, 29, 97, 93, 5, 57, 61, 82
S2: ~PSS_F*ISS_F*MDR_F	65, 29, 97, 31, 81, 5, 57, 61, 82
S3: MPB_F*~CO_F*MDR_F	98, 31, 81, 86, 102, 4, 22
S4: MPB_F*CO_F*~MDR_F	15, 50, 93, 6, 59, 10, 11, 26, 115
S5: PSS_F*~MPB_F*~CO_F*~MDR_F	39, 46, 66, 45
S6: PSS_F*~MPB_F*CO_F*MDR_F	3, 103, 89, 105
S7: ~PSS_F*MPB_F*CO_F	15, 50, 67, 119, 93, 5, 57, 61, 82

Note: Tilde shows the absence of conditions

2008). Finally, the overall solution consistency is 0.862 and the overall solution coverage (the proportion of cases in terms of fuzzy membership value that can be described by at least one configuration in a solution set) is 0.649, indicating that these seven solutions cover almost nearly 65% of the cases. Table 5.3 shows detailed information about the configurations and the cases that belong to a particular solution. It should be noted that a case can be part of more than one solution.

Aksin and Mansini (2008) and (Knol et al., 2014), have found that the size of an enterprise has an impact on implementing business services. As such, the *size of enterprises* (small enterprises = < 10.000 fte and large enterprises > 10.000 fte), was included as a separate condition in the analysis. Interestingly, the findings revealed different configurations compared to the findings without the enterprise size. The fsQCA findings generated seven solutions (see Table 5.4) and in six solutions, the size of the enterprises plays an important role.

Solution 1 indicates that the presence of modularised business processes (MBP), plural sourcing strategy (PSS), IS standardisation (ISS), and the absence of managing decision rights (MDR) lead to the outcome of interest, orchestration of business services portfolio (OBSP). This solution applies only to small enterprises. In this solution, MBP is a core condition. Solution 2 indicates the presence of customer orientation (CO) and the absence of three conditions, MBP, PSS and ISS combined lead to the OBSP. This solution applies to large enterprises. Solution 3 which is applicable only to large enterprises indicates four conditions: namely, MBP, PSS, ISS and MDR lead to OBSP. Solution 4 indicates the presence of MBP, ISS, CO, and MDR for large-size enterprises lead to

Table 5.4 Intermediate solutions, with size of the firms

Solution	SIZ	MBP	PSS	ISS	CO	MDR	Raw Coverage	Unique Coverage	Consistency
1	○	⬤	●	●		○	0.158	0.005	0.881
2	●	○	○	○	●		0.284	0.036	0.834
3	●	●	●	●		●	0.303	0.015	0.823
4	●	●		●	●	●	0.315	0.017	0.803
5		●	●	○	●	●	0.333	0.041	0.904
6	○	○	●	○	○	●	0.118	0.025	0.899
7	●	⬤	●	●	●		0.306	0.002	0.844
Overall solution consistency				0.877					
Overall solution coverage				0.617					

Note: SIZ = Size; Note: MBP = Modularised business processes; OBSP = Orchestration of business services portfolio; ISS = IS standardisation; CO = Customer orientation; MDR = Managing decision rights; Size (Small = ○; Large = ●)

OBSP. Solution 5 indicates the presence of four conditions, MBP, PSS, CO, and MDR, and the absence of ISS lead to OBSP, this solution applies to both small- and large-size enterprises. This configuration has the highest values both for consistency (0.904) and for coverage (0.333). Solution 6 indicates the absence of four conditions, MBP, ISS, CO, and MDR, and the presence of PSS lead to OBSP. This solution is applicable only for small-size enterprises. Finally, solution seven indicates that the presence of MBP, PSS, ISS, and CO lead to OBSP for large-size enterprises. In this solution, MBP is a core condition. All in all, it can be concluded that the enterprise size plays a role in configurations leading to OBSP. In addition, we noticed that multiple causal conditions lead to the same outcome (OBSP). In other words, the use of fsQCA enabled us to account for equifinality when the same outcome results from different conditions (or their combinations), which provides complementary explanations and additional understanding for mixed or non-results derived from correlational methods. Moreover, the use of configurational thinking method enabled us to account for asymmetric relations across interdependent conditions. In other words, we were able to account for asymmetric relations between conditions (antecedents) and outcomes when the conditions (and their reasoning) for the presence of an outcome may differ from its absence.

Table 5.5 Solutions and their corresponding cases

Solution	Cases (Enterprises under study)
S1: ~Size_F*PSS_F*MPB_F*ISS_F*~MDR_F	13, 60, 64, 26, 115
S2: Size_F*~PSS_F*~MPB_F*~ISS_F*CO_F	96, 117, 30, 49, 62, 78
S3: Size_F*PSS_F*MPB_F*ISS_F*MDR_F	4, 22, 1, 20, 34, 40, 68, 72, 84, 85, 87, 88, 109, 110, 116, 120
S4: Size_F*MPB_F*ISS_F*CO_F*MDR_F	5, 61, 82, 1, 20, 34, 40, 68, 72, 84, 85, 87, 88, 109, 110, 116, 120
S5: PSS_F*MPB_F*~ISS_F*CO_F*MDR_F	19, 48, 63, 12, 27
S6: ~Size_F*PSS_F*~MPB_F*~ISS_F*~CO_F*~MDR_F	39, 46
S7: Size_F*PSS_F*MPB_F*ISS_F*CO_F	1, 10, 11, 20, 34, 40, 68, 72, 84, 85, 87, 88, 109, 110, 116, 120

Note: Tilde shows the absence of conditions

The raw coverage is between 0.118 and 0.333 and the consistency values in all seven solutions are equal or above (0.803) recommended threshold. The overall solution consistency is 0.877, and the overall solution coverage is 0.617, indicating that these seven solutions explain almost 62% of the cases (sample). As expected, modularised business processes and plural sourcing strategy are important conditions for the outcome OBSP. The presence of these conditions is observed in several solutions. Table 5.5 shows information about the configurations and the cases that correspond to a particular solution.

5.4 Discussion

This research shows that different configurations (combination of causal conditions) lead to OBSP, supporting their contingent nature. The findings demonstrate that all business services conditions (e.g. modularised business processes, customer orientation, and IS standardisation) in addition to plural sourcing strategy are perceived to be essential for orchestration of business services portfolio, and that the interdependencies among these conditions (antecedents) is paramount. By applying fsQCA three objectives are obtained. First, the fsQCA results showed that there can be different configurations that lead to the same outcome (in this research

OBSP), this phenomenon is known as *equifinality*. Second, as fsQCA looks for the effect of combinations of conditions (present or absent), the results showed that each configuration can contain different combinations of causal conditions (asymmetric relations). Third, based on a calibration process, the importance of the authors theoretical or substantive knowledge was emphasised. As such, domain knowledge is required to carefully transform the empirical data into measures of set membership. For instance, by adding a control variable such as enterprise size. These three objectives allow the authors to claim that the fsQCA is especially useful for explaining complex phenomena like business services and how to orchestrate it in plural sourcing context, and how different conditions (antecedents) and control variables such as size of the enterprises produce different impacts. Next, we discuss the theoretical and practical implications of the results.

5.5 Theoretical Implications

This research shows that antecedents influencing orchestration of business services portfolio depends on the various business services configurations, which provide evidence to use context-aware research approaches. More specifically, continuously adapting a modularised business processes based on customer orientation and IS standardisation is essential. As such, business services should not be viewed as static arrangements but rather as dynamic arrangements since the effect of combinations of conditions may change. Based on the results of this research, three key implications were identified.

First, the premise of prior research was to identify individual antecedents of orchestration of business services, studying the direct relationship between them (e.g. Niehaves & Krause, 2010; Richter & Brühl, 2017). Since the combination of distinct conditions builds multiple configurations of orchestration of business services, this research confirms that previous research methods like qualitative studies (Schulz et al., 2009), and cluster analysis (Akin & Mansini, 2008) may not be appropriate to provide a comprehensive view in how conditions combined lead to the outcome of interest. As far as we are aware, this is one of the first studies on plural sourcing strategy context that uses an fsQCA analysis and provides evidence to determine business services configurations. As such sufficient, yet complementary, evidence is provided to support the premise that alternative combinations of conditions might be equally beneficial in achieving business services orchestration. Importantly, when determining business services orchestration, not only the antecedents of business services should be viewed. We also must consider the role that plural sourcing strategy plays to identify relevant solutions. The findings of this research go beyond the use of traditional regression analysis and cluster analysis as the fsQCA results identified how different conditions work together and lead to the outcome of interest. By means of a more advanced data analysis method, it can be assumed that fsQCA is a prerequisite to determine configurations leading to orchestration of business services portfolio.

Second, by investigating business services configurations based on salient conditions within a context of a larger number of cases (Richter & Brühl, 2017, p. 10), this paper contributes to business services research. When including the size of the enterprises as a separate condition (see Table 5.4), the results indicate that modularised business processes, PSS and ISS are perceived to be a dominant condition due to their presence or absence in all solutions. This finding supports previous research of Ulbrich and Schulz (2014), who showed that business services portfolio is a severe management challenge when implementing IT oriented business services. In addition, the role of customer orientation (CO) and managing decision rights (MDR) varies when comparing the fsQCA solutions with and without the enterprise size. This can be explained as an enterprise having to identify customers' demand and their governing mechanism first before building a business services portfolio (Janssen & Joha, 2006). Thus, both conditions can be considered as resource integrators of value creation, providing standardised services with no or a limited degree of customisation. These new insights go beyond the findings of Richter and Brühl (2017) and Richter (2021), on global business services literature.

Third, addressing IS standardisation (ISS), it can be noticed that this condition is present in two of seven solutions (see Table 5.2). This is consistent with literature (Aksin & Mansini, 2008; El Sawy et al., 2010;

Miskon et al., 2012) in which IS standardisation is identified as an important element. Interestingly, when the size of enterprises was included in the analysis (see Table 5.4), the presence of this condition increases to four out of seven configurations. However, this outcome was not expected as previous service operations research underpinned the importance of IS standardisation. An explanation can be found in the way this research was structured as well as the applied approach, i.e. the fsQCA. It appears that, when the size of the enterprises is not considered in the analysis, the limited role of ISS is compensated by an increase of plural sourcing strategy, customer orientation, and managing decision rights.

5.6 Practical Implications

This study has two practical implications for enterprises and practitioners. First, seven distinctive solutions (see Table 5.4) were found when the enterprise size is considered. The results of this research reveal that antecedents that influence business services orchestration are dependent on the business services configuration. Consequently, insights in business services configurations are important for managers to know which antecedents contribute to orchestration of business services portfolio specifically. When enterprises pay more attention to IS standardised services, they decrease the level of "service customisation" and as such, maximise business services efficiency. Second, the findings suggest that an enterprise's executive management should pay a close attention to invest in establishing a business services organisation, which continuously improves business services, customer management and the governance mechanism to maintain their relationships with customers. Even though the type of business services organisation may vary, the findings suggest that regular evaluations regarding changing customer needs (e.g. customer orientation) allow executive management to adopt business services as they are in the position to foster organisational responsiveness.

5.7 Conclusions

Given the prevalence of the variety of business services and the potential benefits associated with the internal and external resource management, determining different configurations leading to orchestration of business services remains a critical issue for enterprises' competitiveness. Based on a unique dataset that includes 121 international private companies and public administrations firms from different geographies with different sizes, we enhance our comprehension of the antecedents of OBSP by employing the configurational thinking approach (fsQCA), offering a complementary perspective to our analysis conducted in Chap. 3 using the PLS-SEM method. The new insights shed light on combined effect and interdependencies of business services conditions. The results of this research enable to better understand the causal complexity and interdependencies and combined effects between five essential business services conditions (e.g. modularised business processes, IS standardisation, managing decision rights, customer orientation, and plural sourcing strategy). Because fsQCA is case-oriented and set-theoretic in nature, it is an appropriate method for exploring and identifying important causal relationships between business services conditions and its orchestration. When considering the enterprise size, in total, seven solutions were identified providing support for the equifinality principle. An essential finding of the current research is that orchestration of business services does not mainly rely on a single well-developed resource (e.g. IS standardisation).

There is no academic study, to the best of the authors' knowledge, that examines orchestration of business services based on salient conditions using a configurational thinking approach. Compared to most of the academic research, this study provides relatively novel insights by means of applying fsQCA and its impact on an enterprise's business model.

References

Aksin, Z., & Mansini, A. (2008). Successful strategies for internal outsourcing and offshoring of business services: An empirical investigation. *Journal of Operations Management, 26*(2), 239–256.

Delgosha, M. S., Saheb, T., & Hajiheydari, N. (2021). Modelling the asymmetrical relationships between digitalization and sustainable competitiveness: A cross-country configurational analysis. *Information Systems Frontiers, 23*, 1317–1337.
El Sawy, O. A., Malhotra, A., Park, Y., & Pavlou, P. A. (2010). Research commentary—Seeking the configurations of digital ecodynamics: It takes three to Tango. *Information Systems Research, 21*(4), 835–848.
Fiss, P. C. (2011). Building better causal theories: A fuzzy set approach to typologies in organisation research. *Academy of Management Journal, 54*(2), 393–420.
Janssen, M., & Joha, A. (2006). Motives for establishing shared service centers in public administrations. *International Journal of Information Management, 26*(2), 102–115.
Knol, A., Janssen, M., & Sol, H. (2014). A taxonomy of management challenges for developing shared services arrangements. *European Management Journal, 32*(1), 91–103.
Legewie, N. (2013). An introduction to applied data analysis with qualitative comparative analysis. In Forum Qualitative Sozialforschung/Forum. *Qualitative Social Research, 14*(3), 1–45.
Mendel, J. M., & Korjani, M. M. (2012). Charles Ragin's fuzzy set qualitative comparative analysis (fsQCA) used for linguistic summarizations. *Information Science, 202*, 1–23.
Meyer, A. D., Tsui, A. S., & Hinings, C. R. (1993). Configurational approaches to organisational analysis. *Academy of Management Journal, 36*(6), 175–1195.
Mikalef, P., Pateli, A., Batenburg, R. S., & Wetering, R.v.d. (2015). Purchasing alignment under multiple contingencies: A configuration theory approach. *Industrial Management & Data Systems, 115*(4), 625–645.
Miller, D. (1981). Toward a new contingency approach: The search for organizational gestalts. *Journal of Management Studies, 18*(1), 1–26.
Misangyi, V. F., Greckhamer, T., Furnari, S., Fiss, P. C., Crilly, D., & Aguilera, R. V. (2017). Embracing causal complexity: The emergence of a neo-configurational perspective. *Journal of Management, 43*(1), 255–282.
Miskon, S., Bandara, W., Gable, G., & Fielt, E. (2012). Success factors for ICT shared services in the higher education sector. *Journal of Information Technology Research, 5*(3), 1–24.
Niehaves, B., & Krause, A. (2010). Shared Service strategies in local government: A multiple case study exploration. *Transforming Government. People, Process and Policy, 4*(3), 266–279.

Pappas, I. O., Papavlasopoulou, S., Mikalef, P., & Giannakos, M. N. (2020). Identifying the combinations of motivations and emotions for creating satisfied users in SNSs: An fsQCA approach. *International Journal of Information Management, 53*, 102128.
Ragin, C. C. (2008). *Redesigning social inquiry: Fuzzy set and beyond*. University of Chicago Press.
Ragin, C. C. (2009). Qualitative comparative analysis using fuzzy sets (fsQCA). In B. Rihoux & C. C. Ragin (Eds.), *Applied social research methods: Configurational comparative methods: Qualitative comparative analysis (QCA) and related techniques, 51* (pp. 87–122). SAGE Publications, Inc.
Ragin, C. C., & Fiss, P. (2008). Net effects versus configurations: An empirical demonstration. In C. C. Ragin (Ed.), *Redesigning social inquiry: Fuzzy sets and beyond* (pp. 190–212). University of Chicago Press.
Richter, P. (2021). Shared services: Configurations, dynamics and performance. *Baltic Journal of Management, 16*(4), 501–518.
Richter, P. C., & Brühl, R. (2017). Shared service centre research: A review of the past, present, and future. *European Management Journal, 35*(3), 26–38.
Rihoux, B., & Ragin, C. C. (2009). *Configurational comparative methods: Qualitative Comparative Analysis (QCA) and related techniques*. Sage Publications.
Schneider, C. Q., & Wagemann, C. (2012). *Set-theoretic methods for the social sciences: A guide to qualitative comparative analysis*. Cambridge University Press.
Schulz, V., & Brenner, W. (2010). Characteristics of shared service centres. *Transforming Government. People, Process and Policy, 4*(3), 210–219.
Schulz, V., Hochstein, A., Uebernickel, F., & Brenner, W. (2009). Categorization of shared service centers: Insights from the IT services industry. In *13th Pacific Asia Conference on Information Systems: IT Services in a Global Environment*, PACIS 2009.
Ulbrich, F., & Schulz, V. (2014). Seven challenges management must overcome when implementing IT-shared services. *Strategic Outsourcing: An International Journal, 7*(2), 94–106.
Woodside, A. G. (2014). Embrace-perform-model: Complexity theory, contrarian case analysis, and multiple realities. *Journal of Business Research, 67*(12), 2495–2503.

6

Case Study 1: Logistic Service Provider

6.1 Context of the Case Study

The logistic service provider specifically operates in Belgium, the Netherlands, and Luxemburg (BeNeLux), offering simple, smart and sustainable logistic solutions. During the COVID-19 pandemic lockdown, customers and employees have been influenced, as they had to adapt to a situation in which uncertainty is the norm. The logistic service provider was able to continue their services, including the delivery of parcels and mail, and a variety of logistic solutions. During this period, the logistic service provider was able to create a connection between the physical and digital world by changing their way of working by investing in digital solutions. Therefore, this strategy supported their ambition to become a leading logistic and parcel service provider.

To illustrate some figures, the logistic service provider runs 35 mail and parcel sorting centres and around 4000 outlets in external shops, supported by approximately 40,000 employees in total. Some examples of their services include parcel services, fulfilment solutions, flora and city logistics, health logistic, cargo, and data solutions. The log istic service provider's business strategy illustrates their ambition to strengthen their competitive position in the market by accelerating their digital

A. Plugge, S. Nikou, *Digitalisation of Global Business Services*, Technology, Work and Globalization, https://doi.org/10.1007/978-3-031-51528-6_6

transformation journey. As such, they intend to build further on their digital platform, connecting customers and solutions by means of smart digital journeys. The ongoing digitalisation introduced several opportunities. For instance, the use of IT and data enables the enterprise to support customers in tailoring their solutions, such as offering multiple delivery time-frame options. The logistic service provider embraces the developments in technology as their operations department has been affected. For instance, the use of data will provide the opportunity to manage demand peaks, provide demand and supply forecasts, and, as such, optimise operations.

6.2 Financial Shared Service Centre

The unit of analysis of our study is the logistic service provider's Financial Shared Service Centre (FSSC), which was established in three phases.

1. **Phase 1: Set up period (2001–2006)**

The FSSC was established in the period 2001–2006, originating from accounting departments, which were distributed in the BeNeLux. There were more than 40 departments, with each having between four to ten employees. The logistic service provider gradually migrated to one location for financial services and another one for providing commercial services. The main objective to initiate the FSSC was to centralise and standardise financial services and in doing so, the aim was to achieve cost savings and improved quality, as well as meeting the reporting standards. This initiative allowed them to ensure the continuity of financial services. Accordingly, financial business processes and outcomes had become more predictable, which resulted in improved controls and decreased the auditing costs. During the migration period resistance occurred to some degree as employees in the business had the impression that the original situation to provide financial services was far better. However, the migration period was completed by introducing dedicated client-focus teams to support customers and increase the added value of the FSSC.

To support the objective to achieve cost reduction, the FSSC started to act as a customer-oriented organisation providing financial services that were based on Service Level Agreements (SLAs), and a fixed amount of Full Time Equivalents (FTEs). To provide a service-oriented view, employees were trained and educated in bridging the gap between demand and supply and instructed to focus on delivering services. The first results showed a decrease on transaction costs that were the result of an increase in quality and professionalism. At the same time, discussions were initiated whether the financial services should be "supply-driven (push) or demand-driven (pull)". Financial services were predominantly provided on the principle of standardisation with some room for customised solutions (e.g. business specific) taking relevant processes and IT-architecture into account.

2. **Phase 2: Scope extension period (2007–2013)**

The second phase can be characterised as a gradual FSSC growth model, as the logistic service provider introduced operational accounting services (such as AP and General Ledger). Next, the FSSC applied a full SSC approach for all accounting services, including billing and functional support. Five years after the centralisation of financial services, process-focus teams were established to underpin the importance of standardised business processes. This was supported by applying LEAN management and continuous improvements. Specific attention was paid to train employees and strengthen their competences, for instance, by introducing Lean belts. During this period, the FSSC investigated the opportunity to offer financial services to external companies.

From a digitalisation perspective, the FSSC started to develop roadmaps to plan data and digital initiatives. Next, they introduced a service catalogue in which financial services were offered based on SLA's. Subsequently, the FSSC changed their cost model by transforming an FTE model into a fixed price model, and finally to a fixed fee per financial service. During this period all customers were supported by means of a single ERP system as corresponding processes were already automated, for example invoice handling. The FSSC focused on creating value-adding services, while routine-based activities were automated by means of digital technologies. Overall, the design, governance and sourcing decisions were driven by the logistic service provider's business dynamics.

3. **Phase 3: Digitalisation period (2014…)**

Today, the FSSC consists of 110 FTE, and supports various business units, including e-commerce services, and data solutions. The FSSC supports 30 reporting units, 250,000 customers, handling 250,000 supplier invoices and 1,400,000 customer invoices. The main strategy of the FSSC is to preserve applying digitalisation and further professionalisation of teams and processes. The main strategy is based on five pillars. At the start, the FSSC raised the slogan "Digital First" to underpin their ambition to focus on digitalisation. Second, to become a digital native, their financial processes need to support digitalisation, and as such they will allow them to develop data-driven solutions. Third, their aim is to intensify the collaboration with business departments as digitalisation is considered to support an end-to-end business process supported by technology. Fourth, agility of employees is the key to achieving the digital ambitions set by the company, meaning that employees will be affected by digitalising financial services. Finally, the FSSC's objective is to become the one and the only financial entity that supports the organisation as a whole. This means that financial dispersed activities (e.g. per business unit), will be operated by the FSSC to contribute to create additional value. To support the company's strategy, the FSSC stated six principles to achieve their goal: (1) centralise, (2) eliminate, (3) simplify, (4) standardise, (5) automate/digitise, (6) robotise. To underpin this ambition, the FSSC focuses on various digital initiatives. Some examples include the transformation to become a full cloud organisation. Other initiatives are data science groups (e.g. data mining projects), combining data, analytics and RPA 2.0 solutions. Importantly, various developments will influence this ambition. Specifically, changing law and legislation may impact their business, such as International Financial Reporting Standards (IFRS).

In the coming years, the theme environment, social, and governance (ESG) will be even more important as it is expected to influence the enterprise. An example is the obligation to comply with ESG reporting demands (e.g. CSRD, EUtaxonomy), which will influence business processes and corresponding reporting. Digital payment solutions, cyber-security and online-fraud are expected to affect the financial services too. Consequently, the FSSC has to cater for these developments and develop strategies to overcome potential challenges.

6.2.1 Plural Sourcing Strategy

With regard to a plural sourcing strategy, the logistic service provider's strategy is twofold. First, a strategic decision has been made to organise finance related digital initiatives within the FSSC. Importantly, by organising these activities internally the FSSC remains "in control", while IT and digital solutions are organised within the FSSC. Examples of IT and digital solutions as coordinated by the FSSC are the implementation of Robotic Process Automation (RPA), process mining and task mining solutions, machine learning solutions, and data science. The rationale is to encourage the alignment between business departments (business units) and the FSSC as digital financial services initiatives are closely related to business processes. As such, both business process opportunity development and solution acceptance are improved. The innovative digital team is rather small (4 FTE), and aims to understand how digital technologies work, exploring advantages and creating insights to benefit from. These activities are conducted in close collaboration with other FSSC representatives. Second, mainstream IT solutions are provided by the logistic service provider's centralised IT department. The IT department applies a plural sourcing strategy by integrating both in-house and outsourced services. Examples of a plural sourcing strategy include SAP and Salesforce solutions that are managed in a collaborative setting with the suppliers. Other examples of outsourced services, which are contracted and organised by the central IT department, are workplace solutions, cloud and network infrastructure. In addition, various Software as a Service (SaaS) applications are bought from the market, such as an automated in-voice verification application (DokuWeb).

In practice, the digital FSSC team intensively collaborates with the IT department as the IT architecture has to ensure a coherent IT landscape including digital solutions. For example, each RPA process is validated by IT architects to investigate the impact on the landscape and added value. The approach is to automating processes first by means of SAP and Salesforce solutions. If this is not feasible, then RPA comes into play. When new SAP or Salesforce releases are implemented, the IT and digital FSSC team collaboratively discuss the potential effects to minimise operational risks.

One of the interviewees mentioned that: "*Various implementation strategies are applied. For example, SAP releases are based on a structural approach. As such, RPA solutions can be tested upfront to avoid unwanted effects on outages. Salesforce changes, on the other hand, are handled in an Agile way of working. In sprints of two weeks functionality is added in a new go live version. As a result, RPA effects cannot be tested fully during the sprint period. Consequently, we experience process related effects after the go live date*" (Source: RPA developer).

6.2.2 Business Services Portfolio

The FSSC established a business services portfolio that comprises six business services: (1) Commercial BackOffice, (2) Purchase to Pay, (3) Billing to Cash, (4) Record to Report, (5) Functional Support, and (6) Process, Digital and Compliance. It was found that the quality of services (portfolio) has improved when the FSSC started to implement digital solutions. At the same time, operational costs have decreased due to a reduction of employees, but mainly as a result of reduced re-work and decreased lead times.

As one of the interviewees mentioned: "*Recently in co-operation with the Insights-department we implemented a solution that automatically reads invoices by means of an AI application that uses algorithms. The AI application is able to transform unstructured data into structured data and supports our portfolio of various financial services. Interestingly, if we can develop and maintain such a solution ourselves, we don't need other parties for extra support. So, the question on the table is: how can we develop and organise solutions ourselves?*" (Source: Manager Process & Change management).

The business services portfolio as a whole did not change, but the way in which financial services are provided has changed as multiple manual tasks have been automated. The digitalisation journey resulted in an intensive collaboration between representatives of the FSSC, IT department and data science team by co-exploring and co-developing digital solutions. For example, in 2016, the Accounts Payable team consisted of 35 FTE, which decreased to 13 FTE over time, due to the digitalisation of Accounts Payable tasks. By using RPA solutions, the FSSC was able to decrease the number of FTEs by 12 by means of skipping unfulfilled vacancies and using natural progression. The introduction of RPA for instance also required new roles and positions such as RPA developer, Data Process Specialist and RPA Business Analyst. Often challenges are identified regarding to the data that is used as part of financial transactions. Importantly, the business services portfolio may change in the near future; for instance, as a result of merger and acquisitions or new requirements of ESG, which requires financial reporting services. Therefore, the strategy of the FSSC department is to standardise and digitalise financial processes to create economy of scale and increase the implementation of new financial-oriented business services. Consequently, the FSSC is able to create a solid base to implement new administrations and new requirements around ESG.

6.2.3 Modularised Business Processes

Based on the FSSC strategy to standardise business services, the interview results show that the employees' satisfaction has increased as process lead times decreased. Using employee input, the FSSC further standardised their financial business processes. Although business processes are automated to a large degree by the logistic service provider's ERP platforms, such as SAP, a next step was to robotise the "last mile". In practice multiple routine-based activities had to be executed that could not be fulfilled by the company's SAP platform or the other IT solutions. Hence, the FSSC automated these activities, such as invoice bookings and conducting prebooking tasks up to € 500, by implementing the bots and an invoice-classification-solution via Machine Learning (ML). As a result, employees only need to focus on exceptions handling like repairing invoice-differences.

As one of the interviewees mentioned: "*We do not do any kind of data entry anymore, we just focus on exceptions handling. Of all our 110 FTEs approximately 20 of them support the maintenance of the financial systems and digital solutions directly (e.g. SAP, RPA, process mining, machine learning), 60 FTEs provide classical financial business services, 20 FTE's on commercial services and the remaining number of FTE (10) work on process improvements and data and digital solutions*" (Source: Manager FSSC).

Specifically, end-to-end business processes, such as Procure-2-Pay comprises various sub-processes, which are often interdependent. Consequently, the end-to-end business process is perceived to be very complex. Addressing phase 3 (digitalisation period), it was found that the degree of sub-process complexity is decreased by digitalising corresponding process steps. In addition, it was noticed that the value of the FSSC increased as a result of digitalisation. The value is expressed by an increased understanding of FSSC employees of end-to-end business processes. The process steps can be analysed even better while process improvement suggestions are applied. This will lead to fact-based evidence, such as the indication of the number of (un)solved financial cases per week or month. The challenge, however, is the availability and connectivity of correct data and to prepare process related data as often multiple sources are required for the execution of process mining. An example is a financial invoice task that requires a specific ID number of the invoice, the required tasks (e.g. prebooking tasks), and the proposed execution time. We find that historical data is not always available which may hinder the execution of robotised process tasks. To address the importance of digital initiatives FSSC management proactively informed their employees by inviting them to co-develop solutions. This initiative decreased the degree of uncertainty that comes with digitalisation. Employees were able to share their knowledge and experience which resulted in an increase of FSSC satisfaction scores and increased openness for digital initiatives.

The interviews revealed that process mining is applied to further optimise business process tasks as for instance invoice issues could be solved rapidly (see Fig. 6.1). It was found that the outcomes of previous process mining pilots showed a quick learning curve in applying business process improvements. By simplifying business process tasks, the degree of robotisation can be increased. As such, FSSC employees focus on specified tasks like exceptions handling.

As one of the interviewees mentioned: "*We conducted a pilot based on PAFNow to optimise complaints handling with regard to the invoice process. Complaints are usually stored in our Salesforce platform; we analyse the complaints and if needed initiate a payment request. Our back-office colleagues*

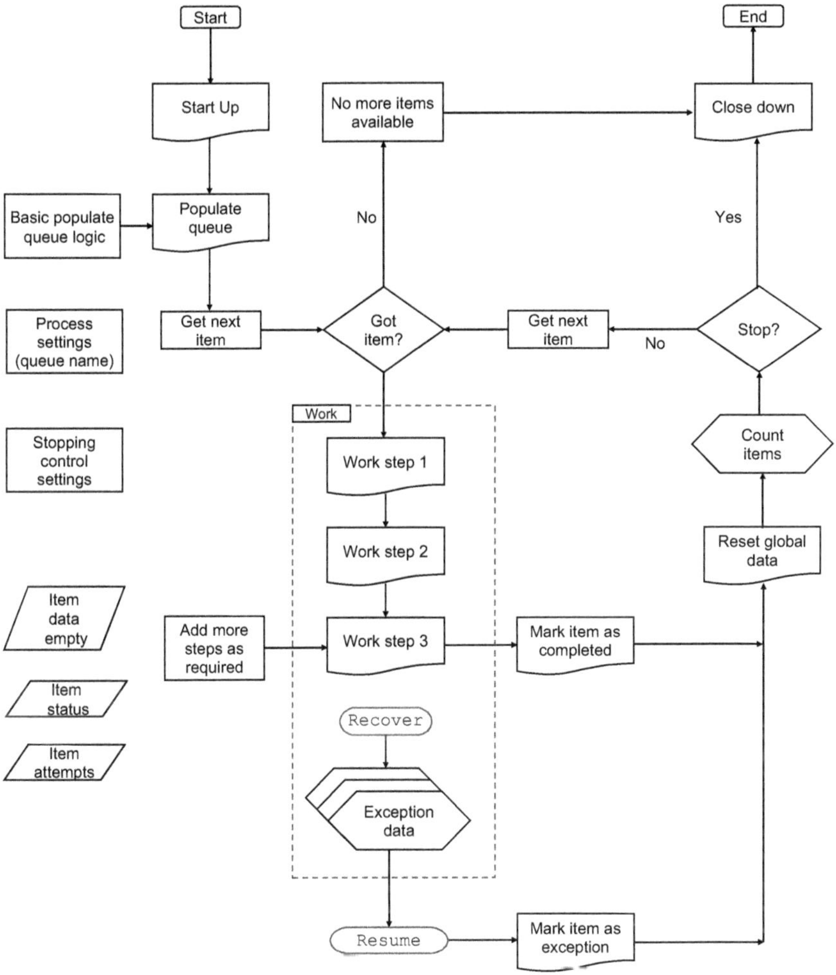

Fig. 6.1 Example of a process mining flow

will check on missing information and, if needed, conduct an additional analysis. As a result of the process mining pilot, we changed the process script to apply improvements. For example, we added additional rows in the application to overcome digital ping-pong effects (who is responsible). The process mining outcomes are directly visualised on a dashboard to keep track on future events" (Source: Manager Process & Change Management).

In addition, it was found that the logistic service provider also pioneers with task mining to explore how employees handle process related tasks in practice. The goal of the pilot is to improve task efficiencies by streamlining the most efficient way in which process related tasks can be executed.

One of the interviewees mentioned that: "*We started a task mining pilot to explore how employees handle tasks as part of a (sub)process and to identify the order in which tasks are conducted. We want to see how activities are performed and based on the pilot insights improve the execution. Our aim is to identify wat type of task mining activities can be automated by RPA. The pilot is based on UIPath Task mining. We see task mining as a valuable addition to process mining*" (Source: RPA developer).

6.2.4 Customer Orientation

The analysis of the interviews shows that the financial business services as provided by the FSSC are rather straight forward (e.g. Purchase2Pay, Billing2Cash, Record2Report). However, the authors identified various portfolio effects. Examples include new smaller administrations based on merger and acquisitions, limited degree of remaining commercial activities and the rise of non-financial reporting (for instance ESG). The interaction between the FSSC, and their customers, both internal and external, is limited due to soundly implemented processes. Hence, internal business departments do not raise the need for service level reports anymore. On the other hand, there is a need to align operational tasks on a day-to-day basis, increase quality review alignment meetings, and discuss major developments (e.g. forecasting). From a customer orientation point of view, we find examples that FSSC employees develop new solutions to further digitalise financial services. For example, we find that the FSSC's digital team collaborates with the IT department to explore how digital ML features decrease the complexity of Purchase2Pay services. As a result, the FSSC is able to develop seamless services. The aim is to support customers to work independent of time and place.

Based on discussions with customers, the interviewees addressed the importance of setting up a business case for new digital solutions. Often interesting ideas are shared and discussed with internal departments to improve financial services by means of digitalisation. Importantly, a pilot has been conducted in practice. However, the final step is to conduct a business case, both qualitative and quantitative. For example, some process mining solutions are very expensive due to license costs, while the benefits are limited from a cost perspective. These costs also include the integration with supplier systems that are outsourced to the market. As the FSSC is not able to fully finance the process mining tool itself other departments of the logistic service provider have to contribute to the investment.

6.2.5 IS Standardisation

The FSSC focuses on a digital and data-driven strategy in which end-to-end business processes forms the starting point. The sub-processes are explored from a digitalisation's perspective to identify benefits. The aim of the FSSC is not to replace the employees by digital solutions, but rather focusing on the process optimalisation and creating added value for the customers. To sketch the IT landscape (see Fig. 6.2), the FSSC uses a standardised digital platform based on the service provider UiPath on top of existing core platforms like SAP and Salesforce. The digital platform supports three organisational entities, namely, Finance, HR, and IT. A digital orchestrator, which is part of the UiPath platform manages the use of robots. The RPA bots are integrated in the UiPath platform, and include seven bots for Finance and HR, supporting approximately 60 financial processes. Multiple RPA bots for various financial processes are developed based on an RPA framework and architecture while applying best practices. The digital platform offers the opportunity to "scale up or scale down" the number of bots dynamically. An advantage of the platform is that it provides automated transactional evidence. This is used for internal and external audits resulting in less manual governance related tasks.

As one of the interviewees mentioned put it: "*To illustrate our digital landscape, we first started with the financial processes that are supported by our SAP platform. Next, we implemented RPA bots that are integrated with*

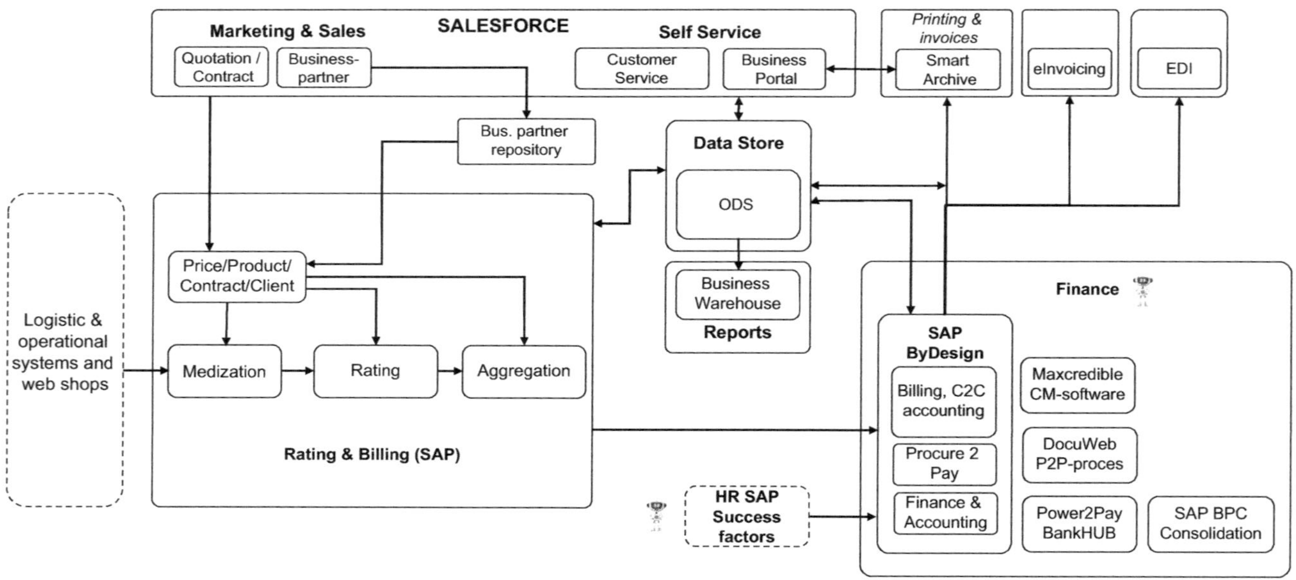

Fig. 6.2 High-level overview of the IT landscape

the DokuWeb application that collects input for automated controls (VAT checks) and purchase numbers. As a next step, RPA bots are fully integrated with the SAP platform to support a seamless eInvoice process. As a final step, transactions are automatically verified and when agreed, executed by the SAP platform. Only in case exceptions occur, employees have to step in" (Source: CFO BU Customer excellence & Digital).

Other interviewees mentioned: "*Today we offer a service that is based on cooperation between chatbots and RPA processes to support internal and external customer contact. When we pioneer in exploring new solutions we aim to focus on value. What are the benefits? As some solutions, like process mining tools are expensive, we sometimes use simple tools to understand their contribution to the business. For example, does a tool contribute to a one-time-right principle of does the tool decrease frictions in customer processes*" (Source: Manager Accounts Payable FSSC).

The effect of implementing digital solutions is identified in the field of digital transactions. Due to the pandemic, employees, working from home, were not able to cope with the invoices that were physically sent by mail. The FSSC asked external customers, who were not used to electronic invoices to send digital invoices. In parallel a digital solution based on RPA and ML to automate the transaction invoice process was implemented. As an indication, before the pandemic, the FSSC handled 12.000 invoices per month, which increased rapidly during the pandemic. Right now, the FSSC processes 400 invoices per month due to digitalisation.

As one of the interviewees mentioned: "*As an effect of the pandemic we noticed that FSSC employees had to spend much more time on handling emails that included supplier invoices, which resulted in additional verification tasks. We developed a solution in which ML is used to automatically check email boxes (three times a day) and process the invoices to the right inbox of the invoice verification tool. The technology was already available; however, the pandemic accelerated that improvement*" (Source: CFO BU Customer excellence & Digital).

Importantly, the FSSC pays attention to the quality of applying digital solutions. An example was found in the context of financial data. The success of the use of digital solutions is dependent on the availability and accuracy of financial data. Due to the importance and value of data, the

FSSC invested in a data-driven strategy. Next, they plan to create a coherent digital approach, aiming at increasing the degree of success.

6.2.6 Managing Decision Rights

Addressing the antecedent managing decision rights, a distinction should be made between two perspectives. First, managing decision rights, relates to digitalising business process steps by means of RPA, ML and AI related solutions. The interview results show that predictive type of decisions have been digitalised, for instance, as part of RPA and ML solutions. Managing decision rights that correspond to more routine-based and uniformed process steps can be robotised easily.

As one of the interviewees mentioned: "*Digital decision rights, is automated in our tooling like RPA and ML. For example, automated invoice bookings are executed by bots that includes decision making. So, the code review is very important. Especially if you want to robotise more precious processes. The question is who is responsible for the code review to automate the separation of duties as we have to meet quality and compliance standards*" (Source: RPA Developer).

Importantly, we found some examples in which decision-making process steps are much more difficult to automate. For example, more adhoc related decision making may require multiple options that involve various decision makers. Handling multiple options at the same time that spans various decision-making units is more difficult to automate. Another example relates to fraud detection. To comply with governance policies and rules, the FSSC needs to execute various checks and balances. When "ghost invoices" are identified multiple decisions have to be executed by an RPA bot (e.g. check the supplier number, check unique source data), which in practice is undoable.

As one of the interviewees mentioned: "*In practice, we experienced that a bot is not able to execute process steps that require checks from three independent source systems, including all exceptions that may occur. We noticed that such tasks are still too complex to configure in the bot. In these cases, we decided to apply these steps manually, which underpins the value of human effort*" (Source: RPA Developer).

Managing decision rights is also related to the organisational structure in which digitalised solutions are provided. The business units determine the degree of required governance rules and mechanisms due to accountability. The FSSC is responsible for various financial business services including their digital solutions (e.g. digital team) while mainstream solutions like SAP and Salesforce are supported by the IT department. Data that is stored in core platforms, like SAP and Salesforce is leading, while RPA, ML and dashboard solutions use the data stored in core platforms (for instance, data lakes).

As one of the interviewees mentioned put it: "*This is a real struggle. Who is responsible for the data that is used to support financial business services? Is it the IT department maintaining the SAP platform, or the FSSC department (e.g. digital team) as we are responsible to run the financial services. Or is it the infrastructure team as they are responsible for the original financial data sources. To create clarity currently we develop a data taxonomy, including governance related responsibilities within our organisation*" (Source: Data Specialist).

6.3 Analysis

6.3.1 Resource Orchestration Theory

From a resource orchestration theory perspective, we find that senior management focuses on establishing sound end-to-end (E2E) financial business processes to support their services. Based on E2E processes, resources are deployed in two core entities: (1) a digital team as part of the FSSC that build and maintain solutions like RPA, machine learning (in corporation with the central Insights-team) and process mining/task mining, and (2) the IT department that is responsible for running and maintaining (cloud) platform services. Due to this distinction, each entity is able to apply their specific skills and expertise. By creating this federative type of structure, senior management is able to generate synergetic effects. To achieve these effects, senior management has developed two important mechanisms to create coherent IT solutions. As a first step, management decided that insights from both the FSSC digital team and the IT department must be shared internally to a broader community. Consequently, employees from both organisational entities proactively share digital solution insights with various departments, including HR and logistics. The goal is to show the benefits that digital solutions bring to the table for business and staff departments. For example, how RPA, ML and process mining solutions simplifies process related tasks and avoid manual routine-based work. By providing demos and organising interactive sessions opportunities are identified that may provide future benefits. As a second step, senior management decided to implement joint meetings on a regular basis in which the FSSC digital team as well as the IT department collaborate. A management decision that we find is that the IT department, more specifically, IT architecture, is responsible for orchestrating the IT landscape as a whole. This include FSSC supported digital solutions (RPA, ML), internal IT, and external IT applications, and infrastructure provided by suppliers. The decision to establish joint meetings is consistent with the finding of Capaldo (2014), who argued that "interorganisational coordination is achieved through social mechanisms, that are, governance mechanisms are based on social relationships and networks", (p. 687). During the joint meetings, the focus is to share relevant insights, analyse the effects of new digital technologies, and ultimately develop new integrated technical solutions.

As one of the interviewees put it: "*We decided that IT architecture is responsible to manage a coherent IT landscape including digital solutions, such as RPA and process mining. Each RPA process is validated by IT architects to check the impact on the landscape, added value and coherence with our platforms like Salesforce and SAP. We intensively collaborate, for example, with the consultants of the regular IT teams to inform them about changes that may occur when new releases of Salesforce or SAP are implemented. The FSSC's digital team is involved in release test activities to ensure a sound performance and we are jointly involved in quarterly Product Increment (PI) events to develop new digital solutions*" (Source: Manager Accounts Payable FSSC).

The decision to appoint the IT department as an internal orchestrator is motivated by the strategic sourcing decision to partially outsource IT activities, such as the SAP platform. As the IT department's senior management is responsible for orchestrating the internal as well as the outsourced resources, it is essential to create a coherent view. To provide E2E financial processes, the IT department is able to ensure that the chain of internal (e.g. FSSC digital team, IT departments) and external resources are orchestrated in a coherent way. In doing so, digital solutions and platforms support financial services that are bundled into a business services portfolio. This finding is consistent with Handley and Benton (2013) and Sako et al. (2016) who found that a business services portfolio that is based on a plural sourcing strategy must be orchestrated carefully to ensure a sound performance.

From the perspective of ROT, the results of the analysis demonstrate that senior management acknowledge the importance of capabilities, such as developing skills and experience in the field of data analyses. In fact, it was found that new employees are hired who have extensive experience to improve the data quality (e.g. accuracy, correctness, completeness). Senior management have the opinion that the mindset of new employees is at least as important as data skills and adjusted the job descriptions to bundle various skills. The knowledge and experience to measure and report data evidence still has to be developed. Consequently, the combination of data skills and mindset is essential to deal with uncertainty.

To leverage skills and expertise, FSSC senior management organises townhall meetings and open-door meetings, both individual and group meetings, with the aim to share the actual insights. The management have invited business-related employees to create awareness in how technology may contribute to daily work. In a similar vein, the management has initiated videos and demos to inspire employees to start innovations. We find that knowledge sharing has become an important element in providing knowledge-intensive services, which financial services are. This is consistent with literature (Zhang, 2018) in which the authors argue that knowledge sharing contributes to successful implementation of an organisation's business strategy. As knowledge sharing within a service-oriented strategy is considered to be complex, the study findings shed light on how enterprises develop mechanisms (townhall meetings, awareness sessions, videos and demos) that may overcome uncertainty. Hence, enterprises should invest in building knowledge sharing mechanisms to support the exchange of information (Rai et al., 2012). This corresponds to FSSC management that involved their employees in co-developing digital solutions.

6.3.2 Boundary Resources

The results of the analysis show that the digital team within the FSSC is responsible to design, build, implement and maintain various digital solutions, including RPA, ML, AI, process mining and task mining. In parallel, the IT department is responsible for the implementation of new platform functionalities by means of new releases. While platform owners like SAP and Salesforce have control over their service system, the IT department is able to stimulate generativity by introducing new functionalities. The latter corresponds to the concept of boundary resources in which the IT department encourage innovation while the platform owner secures the platform. In this regard, Ghazawneh and Henfridsson (2015) suggest boundary resources as key resources that resolve the paradox of the simultaneous control and generativity. They argue that the platform owner can be characterised as the primary designer of boundary resources, while third party developers are recipients of these boundary resources. Our analyses, however, reveal that the IT department acts as a developer as they develop and implement new functionalities. Our insights go beyond the findings of Ghazawneh and Henfridsson (2015), as development roles can also be sourced within an enterprise. Importantly, this result in new challenges as the IT department acts as a developer while maintaining the end-to-end IT landscape at the same time. This corresponds to the findings of Eaton et al. (2015) in which the authors argue that platform dynamics can be conceptualised in terms of distributed actors that collectively tune boundary resources.

Hence, the IT department has to sustain the internal relationships with the end users that are needed to explore new ideas and foster capability development (Cenamor & Frishammar, 2021). In addition, they need to leverage and ensure the quality of existing IT solutions, which corresponds to exploiting existing products and services (Hein et al., 2020). If the IT department is unaware of how to balance exploitation and exploration, this may hinder their role within the enterprise. This challenge corresponds to the concept of organisational ambidexterity (OA) in which the IT department must balance both exploration and exploitation (Gibson & Birkinshaw, 2004; Gupta et al., 2006).

According to Vargo and Akaka (2012), resources are essential components of value creation. We find that the integration of resources (e.g. SAP, Salesforce, RPA, ML) was complicated due to the fact that various actors in the ecosystem operate from dispersed locations (logistic service provider locations, cloud solutions). Importantly, all actors have to align operational tasks, share new developments and commonly agree on which functionality must be provided by which actor. As such, the enterprise lacks a focus on resource complementarity, an issue discussed previously by Wieland et al. (2012). Because coordination and delivery locations are divided within the enterprise, the orchestration of digital platforms and solutions increase the degree of plural sourcing complexity. The data analysis shows that the various parties (e.g. FSSC digital team, IT department, external platform owners) all have to contribute to integrate their resources, which, if not orchestrated effectively, may result in service underperformance.

The results of the analysis also reveal that the IT department decided to build and implement a digital integration platform that interconnects all digital solutions. More specifically, the integration platform has built in digital solutions to support RPA and ML functionality. A second functionality of the platform is to integrate various digital platforms and solutions. In doing so, the IT department is able to orchestrate all digital solutions through a variety of distributed boundary resources facilitating automated coordination of activities at arm's length. Specifically, the IT department implemented an integration platform that acts as a digital orchestrator, to manage boundary resources by means of Application Programming Interfaces (APIs). Our insights show that the integration platform supports development activities (e.g. scale up and scale down RPA bots) as well as ensure the maintenance of SAP and Salesforce. The analysis of the interviews reveals that the IT department acts as a boundary spanner towards their environment. This is consistent with previous research (Organ, 1971) in which a boundary spanner acts as change agent to exchange information between multiple organisational entities. Hence, the IT department as boundary spanner is responsible for changing attitudes and perceptions, as shown by the examples in which the IT department addresses the need for knowledge sharing. The integration platform can be perceived as a mechanism to exchange information between various organisational entities. The mechanism of implementing an integration platform prevents the enterprise ecosystem for barriers that may hinder the exchange of information and data.

Based on our findings, it can be argued that a platform that provides an integration solution and digital functionality at the same time will contribute to faster innovation trajectories compared to non-digital systems. Our insights on applying a hybrid digital platform shed some light on a fundamental research issue as how digital platforms actually emerge (De Reuver et al., 2018, p. 130). In our case study, the logistic service provider decided to implement this solution to cater for rapid changing circumstances and as such, deal with enterprise dynamics. This decision was made from a strategic position as the logistic service provider had to enable the provisioning of financial services for internal and external users. This strategy shows that the integration platform was designed and implemented consciously and was not an accidental result. By applying an integrated platform, the logistic service provider creates digital flexibility as boundary resources may change over time. As such, the enterprise is able to survive in the long run.

6.4 Conclusion

In this chapter, we studied the enterprise of a logistic service provider by focusing on how financial business services are managed and developed by the FSSC. More specifically, we studied the antecedents as described in our research model (see Chap. 4).

With regard to the business services portfolio, we found that the type of services did not change. However, based on the FSSC's customer orientation view we found multiple examples in which the FSSC, business departments and IT department explored and implemented digital technologies that were used to improve business services. Next, we found evidence that the FSSC's focus to digitalise financial business processes resulted in a decrease of business services implementation effort. In addition, we found that the IT department, which applied a plural sourcing strategy, addressed the importance to standardise digital platforms. As a result, IS standardisation contributed to a decrease of business services implementation effort. When addressing managing decision rights, we only found that routine-based tasks were automated. Both the FSSC and IT department are involved in the orchestration of the antecedents in scope. To orchestrate financial business services, senior management's decision to appoint the IT department as orchestrator enabled them to coordinate the relationships between boundary resource actors. Consequently, the IT department is able to support the exchange of knowledge and information between various boundary resources. We may conclude that the FSSC's digital strategy is operationalised by means of the orchestration of the integration platform by "connecting the dots" between various digital solutions.

To summarise, we found evidence that the FSSC paid attention to all antecedents as part of our research model. We may conclude that IS standardisation can be perceived as an essential antecedent. This finding is consistent with the outcomes of the fsQCA analysis where IS standardisation is considered to be an essential condition in four out of seven solutions.

References

Capaldo, A. (2014). Network governance: A cross-level study of social mechanisms, knowledge benefits, and strategic outcomes in joint-design alliances. *Industrial Marketing Management, 43*(4), 685–703.

Cenamor, J., & Frishammar, J. (2021). Openness in platform ecosystems: Innovation strategies for complementary products. *Research Policy, 50*(1), 104148.

De Reuver, M., Sørensen, C., & Basole, R. C. (2018). The digital platform: A research agenda. *Journal of Information Technology, 33*(2), 124–135.

Eaton, B. D., Elaluf-Calderwood, S., Sørensen, C., & Yoo, Y. (2015). Distributed tuning of boundary resources: The case of Apple's IOS service system. *MIS Quarterly: Special Issue on Service Innovation in a Digital Age, 39*(1), 217–243.

Ghazawneh, A., & Henfridsson, O. (2015). A paradigmatic analysis of digital application marketplaces. *Journal of Information Technology, 30*(3), 198–208.
Gibson, C. B., & Birkinshaw, J. (2004). The antecedents, consequences, and mediating role of organizational ambidexterity. *Academy of Management Journal, 47*(2), 209–226.
Gupta, A. K., Smith, K. G., & Shalley, C. E. (2006). The interplay between exploration and exploitation. *Academy of Management Journal, 49*(4), 693–706.
Handley, S. M., & Benton, W. C. (2013). The influence of task- and location-specific complexity on the control and coordination costs in global outsourcing relationships. *Journal of Operations Management, 31*(3), 109–128.
Hein, A., Schreieck, M., Riasanow, T., et al. (2020). Digital platform ecosystems. *Electronic Markets, 30*, 87–98.
Organ, D. W. (1971). Linking pins between organizations and environment. *Business Horizons, 14*, 73–80.
Rai, A., Keil, M., Hornyak, R., & Wullenweber, K. (2012). Hybrid relational-contractual governance for business process outsourcing. *Journal of Management Information Systems, 29*(2), 213–256.
Sako, M., Chondrakis, G., & Vaaler, P. M. (2016). How do plural-sourcing firms make and buy? The impact of supplier portfolio design. *Organization Science, 27*(5), 1161–1182.
Vargo, S. L., & Akaka, M. A. (2012). Value cocreation and service systems (re) formation: A service ecosystems view. *Service Science, 4*(3), 208–217.
Wieland, H., Polese, F., & Vargo, S. L. (2012). Toward a service (eco)systems perspective on value creation. *International Journal of Service Science, Management, Engineering, and Technology, 3*(3), 12–25.
Zhang, Z. (2018). Organizational culture and knowledge sharing: Design of incentives and business processes. *Business Process Management Journal, 24*(2), 384–399.

7

Case Study 2: Employment Agency

In this chapter we describe the second case study, which is a global operating employment agency. We first outline the context of the employment agency. Next, we describe how the agency established their Financial Shared Service Centre (FSSC). Then, the antecedents that are part of our research will be elaborated. As a final step, the analyses of the findings and concluding remarks will be presented.

7.1 Context of the Case Study

The employment agency is a global operating full-service HR service provider founded in 1960. The enterprise's main goal is to support as many people as possible in realising their true potential throughout their working life. Their services range from staffing, recruitment process outsourcing, career development, online talent acquisition, re-integration, outplacement, and payroll services up to strategic HR consultancy and full-service recruitment solutions in various industries. The enterprise consists of multiple labels in which each has a specific expertise to support the services as addressed. In 2021 the enterprise, which includes more than 40,000 corporate employees, helped more than two million

A. Plugge, S. Nikou, *Digitalisation of Global Business Services*, Technology, Work and Globalization, https://doi.org/10.1007/978-3-031-51528-6_7

people find a job and advised 200,000 clients on their HR needs. A key principle of the enterprise is to use data and technology to support their consultants across almost 5000 locations in almost 40 international markets. The combination of technology and building relationships makes their offer quite unique. The enterprise's core values illustrate that HR related services are embedded in sharing knowledge and creating trust while focusing on corporate social responsibility. As described by the interviewees, the enterprise culture can be characterised as customer-centric and adaptive.

The enterprise is affected by various societal, and technology-driven trends, which have influenced their employment services offerings. In addition, the globalisation, social media, retirement waves and talent scarcity, to name a few, have a significant effect in supporting people to find another job. At the same time, an important trend is observed, which is the role of governments in various countries that is decreasing when it comes to employment and personal work-related circumstances. As an effect of the COVID-19 pandemic, the enterprise experienced a significant backdrop in jobs as multiple firms had to decrease the number of employees (great resignation). Currently, the enterprise experiences a changing behaviour amongst job seekers in Europe. In particular, youngsters are very much influenced by social media and have a broad choice in selecting jobs. The enterprises conducted a work monitor study, which shows that employees in various types of companies are open to switching to another job when an interesting opportunity occurs. This trend influences the dynamics in the market and increases the urgency for companies to attract and retain scarce personnel.

In order to handle talent shortage challenges effectively, timing has become essential in finding and matching talent. The employment agency has to provide job opportunities "on the spot" to attract job seekers and mediates (negotiates) with clients to come to an agreement. When the enterprise is not able to respond to job seekers, they switch to other agencies immediately. Hence, timing and response times have become even more important than before in the pandemic situation.

7.2 Financial Shared Service Centre

The unit of analysis of the current study is the enterprise's FSSC, which provides services to both internal departments and external clients. The enterprise's FSSC acts as a centralised hub in providing financial services in which technology plays an essential role. The FSSC aims to automate manual tasks as much as possible, like employee and contingent talent assignments, timesheets, and invoices, supported by automated tools and intelligent analytics. In doing so, financial-related processes are automated, and accessible for end users (e.g. internal departments, external clients) by means of an HR portal (e.g. web and app). The FSSC services include financial onboarding, payroll, benefit administration, scheduling, and analytics amongst others. As a result, end users benefit by spending less time on administration, less paperwork, error free billing, and reduction of financial administrative processes by simplifying approval processes for time data.

The FSSC divides their tasks amongst two teams. The first team focuses on financial services, such as Procure-To-Pay Automation (P2P), and invoicing. These activities can be characterised as predictive, standardised, and routine-based. The second team focuses on operational services, in which employees specifically handle exceptions as an outcome of automated tasks by means of digital solutions such as Robotic Process Automation (RPA), Machine Learning (ML), and Artificial Intelligence (AI). As an example, the financial services team coordinates the P2P process that includes invoices, which were originally handled manually. During the past years, these types of activities have been fully digitalised by means of RPA solutions. As P2P activities are rather straightforward and standardised, it was rather easy to seemingly automate these activities. The operations team is responsible for exceptions handling and quality control. As a result, P2P process activities are fulfilled as efficiently as possible.

As one of the interviewees mentioned: "*Originally, we had 15 FTE to support the P2P process, today we have 7 FTE in place, while the lead times to provide tasks are decreased. This was a gradual development as we transformed from manual to automated tasks. Today, we focus on E2E financial process chains, for instance spend analytics on a global level that is a scalable solution. We automated the last mile by adjusting existing platforms such as RPA and OCR*" (Source: Product owner Process & RPA).

Currently, the enterprise as a whole is transforming into a digital enterprise by means of harmonising the enterprise's IT landscape. Consequently, the FSSC and IT department are jointly working on future digital financial services and, in doing so, they have been better able to match clients and job seekers needs. The FSSC aims at digitalising the financial services as much as possible. Digital solutions that support financial processes are organised within the FSSC, such as RPA, process mining and task mining. From an organisational perspective, the FSSC implements the agile principle of "*tribes*". By means of themes, such as legal, law, legislation, tribe participants develop new digital solutions. Next, they study the impact of future services and proofs of concepts and share lessons learned in which product owners coordinate activities. Consequently, the current IT and digital landscape is changing rapidly due to the overall digital transformation programme.

In this regard, one of the interviewees mentioned that: "*We organised RPA solutions closely related to the business. The challenge is to link automation to our business strategy and identify how digital solutions contribute to creating business value and benefits. At a strategic level this is quite a challenge as we also do not know what our business strategy looks like in five years. We use a reversed engineering approach and start with applying technological opportunities and learn on the spot. To some degree we fear digital solutions as we do not know their effect on aspects like jobs, privacy, organisation, and governance. From an IT view, this is much more clear. We aim at being a full digital enterprise which must be reflected in the capillaries of our organisation*" (Source: IT director).

Impact of Digitalisation on Employees

At the start, FSSC employees had the impression that RPA bots became a threat to replace their work. As the FSSC gradually changed over time and was impacted by fierce market competition, increase of job seekers, and new technologies, the employees did not experienced automation as a threat anymore. As both market conditions changed and internal employees experienced an increased work pressure, digital solutions were embraced internally. The analysis of the content of the interviews shows that the degree of digitalisation needs to be increased to keep up pace with dynamic market conditions. This is mainly due to the short lead times to match clients and talent. Today, this matching process is expressed in hours and not days. By digitalising FSSC processes and corresponding tasks, employees are able to support the hiring of new internal talent more efficiently. The interviews revealed that some employees were not able to cope with these changes and left the enterprise as the pressure to provide tasks was perceived to be out of their comfort zone. As an effect of the rise of digital solutions, the retention rate of employees may increase. In turn, this causes a challenge as the FSSC financial services support both internal business units and external client organisations and job seekers. This may influence the quality and volume of the financial services provided by the FSSC in the long term.

One of the interviewees mentioned that: "*From an external view, the retention rate amongst temporary workers is extreme high. Our aim is to achieve a higher degree of bonding with temporarily workers, which positively affects their stay at client organisations. A low retention rate means a significant business value for our clients. Therefore, we have to develop and introduce new functions like ambassadors and trainers to create a nice environment and even locations, this could be attractive for the youngsters. Internally, we notice that some FSSC employees struggle with digitalisation, which is still is a low percentage. We use dashboards to monitor our internal retention rate. The challenge is to find out what types of skills are required to develop new strategies to retain our own employees. As we are closely aligned with primary business services, we have to develop these strategies and create business driven insights*" (Source: Business director).

Today, the FSSC noticed a new challenge due to the raise of digital solutions. Employees only face the output of automated transactions that refer to exceptions, or, in other words, what goes wrong. This affects employees' behaviour as the impression could lead to the idea that employees caused these exceptions. This idea results in a reduced level of job satisfaction, which requires attention from an enterprise cultural perspective. Importantly, applying digital solutions requires a more holistic view on handling financial business services as processes need to be studied from an end-to-end (E2E) perspective. As an example, we find that it is easier to hire employees with process knowledge and experience while having limited experience with digital solutions (RPA). The FSSC experienced that digital solutions can be learned more quickly compared to understanding complex E2E financial processes.

As an example, the administrative E2E matching process includes the following steps: find a candidate, search and match, hire a candidate, onboarding, and placement at a client organisation. The FSSC studied both perspectives and learned that the process approach is more successful in speeding up the digitalisation journey. In parallel, we find that the FSSC invested in the digital education of their employees to make them tech savvy; for instance, some employees are trained to become data specialists. All employees working with RPA solutions and process mining solutions were trained and learned various programming languages to adjust platforms and processes.

In the near future the FSSC expects that new competitors will appear as multiple financial services can be automated, and corresponding processes digitalised. To stay relevant and competitive, the FSSC develops new digital solutions in collaboration with Google, such as AI matching and execution of financial services to job seekers and clients. The rise of digital driven business services may even result in adjusting the enterprise's current business model by introducing Human Resource Outsourcing services, Recruitment Process Outsourcing services and Finance and Accounting Outsourcing services to create added value. Due to the rise of digitalising financial services, the enterprise representatives who were interviewed expect that exceptions will remain, which results in providing more customised type of financial services. As such, it is expected that the FSSC will transform from providing standardised services (operational excellence based on automated solutions) to customised services (operational excellence based on exceptions handling).

As one of the interviewees mentioned: "*Our development of dashboards shows that an employee's digital colleague handles x jobs per hour successfully (take the robot out of the human). In the near future, we expect that pop-ups on an employees' screen generated by bots will proactively collaborate with human colleagues in fulfilling financial tasks. This will result in a new type of people-centric coaches who will guide the interaction between humans and bots*" (Source: Principal staff manager Business Services).

7.2.1 Plural Sourcing Strategy

The employment agency as a whole includes multiple Operating Companies (OpCo's) that originally decided to implement and operate IT and digital systems and applications independently from other OpCo's. Since the enterprise focus had changed, deciding to apply a more holistic view on E2E business processes, each OpCo faces interdependency challenges with other OpCo's. To cater for changing circumstances, such as law and legislation, the enterprise initiated a digital transformation strategy and plan to harmonise the IT and digital landscape. Examples include Customer Relationship Management (CRM), Enterprise Resource Planning (ERP) and tracking systems. To bundle scarce resources and knowledge, Centres of Excellence were established at a local country level that provides support in case of specific digital challenges. In addition, a global operating model has been implemented to support the harmonisation approach while standardisation of IT systems and applications is used as a leading design principle.

From a plural sourcing strategy view, main platforms and applications (e.g. ERP, CRM) are outsourced to the market and based on a SaaS delivery model like treasury systems and payment systems. Some functionalities can be fine-tuned by the IT department. The IT department established an in-house team to customise digital solutions to support large-size OpCo's. IT infrastructure and cloud network related functionalities are fully outsourced to IT service providers, such as Amazon Web Services and Google.

IT and digital solutions within the enterprise are organised from a federative point of view. Traditionally, mainstream type of IT solutions (e.g. ERP, CRM) are organised from a centralised perspective as the IT department is better capable to cater for changing conditions, and, as such, create flexibility. Digital solutions like RPA and ML are organised within, and maintained by, the FSSC. This is an explicit choice as the FSSC is closely aligned with business departments, and as such able to validate if new digital solutions work in practice. Importantly, we observed that FSSC and the IT department jointly work on planning activities to create a heartbeat when implementing applications of new functionalities. The mechanism of joint planning will accelerate the digitalisation of financial services and decreases operational risks. The enterprise under study applies a strict rule that new IT and digital solutions are business case driven. This means that solutions are studied from various perspectives to examine their impact such as quality of service, quantity of transactions, finance, law and regulations, security, privacy, and architecture. The aim is to achieve a coherent view between all these aspects before a decision is made to invest and implement a solution. As an example, the FSSC includes an RPA team (12 FTE), who co-develop digital solutions with IT architects, who are organised in the IT department. When a business case for a new digital solution is positively validated, the IT department focus is on integrating the RPA solution with the IT landscape.

One of the interviewees mentioned that: "*Robotisation, for instance, is used in case of positioning talent at our external clients. We do this for more than 200 external clients currently supported by local teams. In the mid-term, about 3 to 5 years, we will transform towards a global digital platform. Robotisation will support multiple functionalities from rerouting data and information up to full onboarding of job seekers by means of bots. These bots are connected to our digital mainstream platforms*" (Source: Business director).

7.2.2 Business Services Portfolio

Based on the interview results, we find that the financial services portfolio has not been automated any further. The portfolio consists of regular financial services and includes accounts payable and payroll, that support typical functionalities like time sheets, personnel files, salary sheets, and bank accounts. We find that the financial services of the FSSC in scope are automated to a large extend by means of portals and digital solutions such as RPA and ML that are interconnected with existing platforms like ERP and CRM. From a content perspective, changing law and regulations influence the type of services and as such, financial services need to be adjusted regularly.

7.2.3 Modularised Business Processes

To fulfil an essential role in the market of matching talent, business processes have been standardised to achieve business goals and as such a high market share. The FSSC aims at realising a 0% error rate based on the optimised business processes that are ultimately digitalised. With regard to the administrative organisation that matches job seekers and clients, digitalised business processes are all standardised (i.e. hiring, development, and onboarding). As a result, a digital backbone of core business processes is established that accelerates the provisioning of business services. Core business processes are closely related to financial business processes that support various administrative processes.

One of the interviewees mentioned that: "*We apply multiple RPA solutions to fulfil financial process related tasks. For instance, for checking cost codes on a daily basis, run Chamber of Commerce checks, and execute close-out orders automatically. The ambition is to increase the added value of digital solutions and make manual work less attractive. The precondition to deal with automation is to implement uniform and standardised business processes*" (Source: Principal staff manager Business Services).

In Fig. 7.1, the high-level P2P process is illustrated that provides insight in essential process steps.

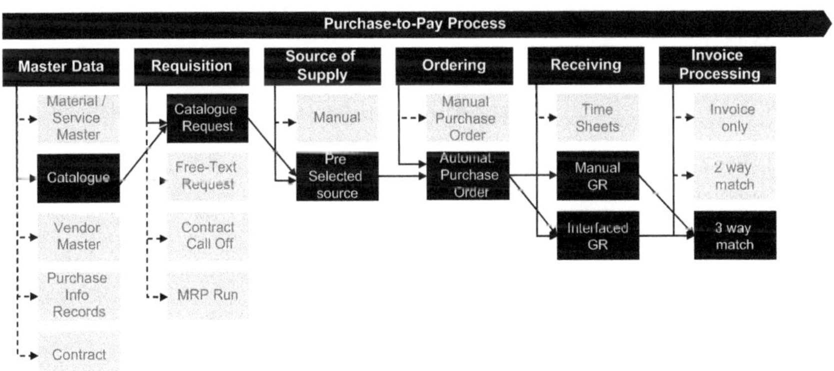

Fig. 7.1 P2P process (high-level)

In addition, the digitalisation of financial business processes; for instance, by means of RPA and process mining, provides insights to increase the optimalisation of sub-processes. Based on the interview results, we find that FSSC employees adjust these sub-processes as a result of digital initiatives. To manage interdependencies between digitalised sub-processes, the FSSC decided to coordinate financial processes from an E2E perspective to achieve coherence. More importantly, enterprise guidance shows that business units remain accountable for coordinating E2E business processes. In case of large and complex E2E processes, the FSSC established process owners who are responsible for managing the chain from declarations up to costs per hour of employees. By using E2E financial processes as a guiding principle, the FSSC developed integrated digital solutions that may create challenges, as multiple sub-processes are interwoven and, as such, need to interact. Therefore, the digital transformation journey has to provide answers for these challenges.

One of the interviewees mentioned that: "*For the screening of employees we designed process flows that were implemented in practice. As a result of changes in regulations we noticed that sometimes process mining tools have become too slow to handle dynamics. Right now, bots do all the work as part of P2P processes, and we just have one hour left for exceptions handling. A reason not to apply process mining tools is that the logging of data must be exchanged with other toolsets. As log files do not correspond yet, we decided not to use process mining tools in this field*" (Source: Product owner Process & RPA).

In Fig. 7.2, the process steps with regard to purchase orders are shown, which are automated in the enterprise under study by means of RPA.

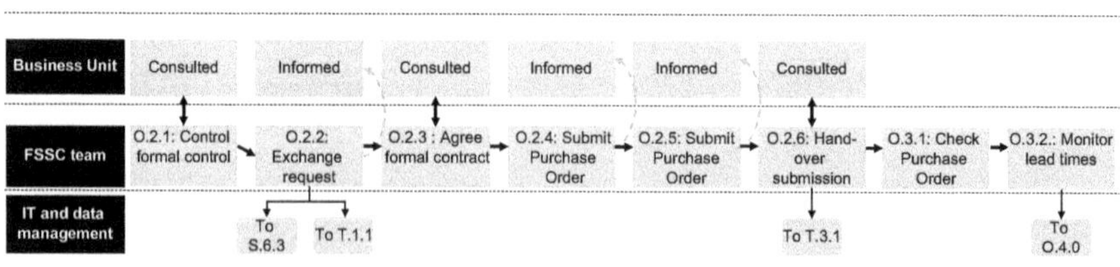

Fig. 7.2 Detailed P2P purchase order steps explained

7.2.4 Customer Orientation

The interview results reveal that FSSC employees and business representatives are continuously aligned to match business needs and digital solutions. To explore new opportunities, various proofs of concepts are initiated to reduce routine-oriented tasks (RPA, ML), improve business process efficiencies like process mining and task mining, and better forecast talents needs by means of AI based predictive analysis. As the FSSC has experience with business process thinking and digital solutions, they are organised at arms-length from business units. The collaboration between FSSC and business increased the degree of trust.

7.2.5 IS Standardisation

From an IT and digital perspective, we find that the FSSC designed a roadmap for future digital solutions. The roadmap was developed by using various design principles in which two were specifically addressed, (a) a uniform data model, and (b) a global information model. These principles are used as inputs for the digital transformation journey as strategically decided by the enterprise.

One of the interviewees mentioned that: "*We are in the middle of a digital transformation journey. The goal is to make work more attractive by reducing routine type of work and simplify business processes and tasks. Do more with less employees. From an external view the impact of corporate social responsibility and ESG affects our business as we have to adjust financial processes and show the evidence that we are transparent regarding labour conditions. Changing client demands shows that we have to provide information of the educational level of recruited staff automatically by using portals. So, the transformation journey aims to provide frictionless business services to internal and external users*" (Source: IT director).

The interview results show that architecture is key in designing and implementing a sound IT and digital landscape and will drive the digitalisation journey. IT services are standardised as much as possible to achieve agility, while the modularisation of functionality offers opportunities to cater for business needs. The IT landscape is divided into two domains: (a) front-office solutions to support financial services predominantly supported by salesforce, and (b) mid-office and back-office solutions supported by JD Edwards. The IT department maintains ERP and CRM platforms that are widely used within the enterprise. These platforms comprise various functionalities that are modularised by design; however, difficult to unpack. The latter becomes an important challenge as changing conditions like regulations require platform modifications. Various data sources that correspond to ERP platforms are interconnected to multiple data lakes as a vehicle to collect and store data.

The first step of digitalisation is to design the process flows and next automate these steps. Interviewees argued that a lot of time savings can be achieved by executing both steps. A second step that was taken was to visualise the outcome of financial business process steps by means of digital dashboards. The main digital functionality is based on RPA solutions. In addition, process mining solutions are used to develop scalable financial process designs as they show the contribute to the added value of digital solutions.

One of the interviewees mentioned that: "*Now we have a process analyst working for 6 weeks to design a complete process flow. As a next step we use task mining to identify tasks at an end-user level to further improve the effectiveness of executing process tasks. However, we are not sure if we focus on an end-user level if we comply with privacy rules and regulations. The technology is in place, but privacy regulations may hinder the implementation of task mining solutions. In short, the organisation is not ready yet*" (Source: Product owner Process & RPA).

By analysing the interview data, we find that various digital tools and solutions are in place to support financial services in various areas like credit risk assessments and automated entry of files into business intelligence (BI) tooling. Besides the role of RPA, the FSSC uses intelligent document processing to automatically read documents and translate unstructured data into structured data. This application is based on ML and AI principles. Various other types of ML and AI solutions are tested to monitor and analyse financial processes and conduct compliance checks.

One of the interviewees mentioned that: "*Our data science architects and data engineers support AI solutions. We experiment with ethical AI solutions which is still in an early phase. We follow governmental regulations strictly as we want to avoid ethical profiling. An example is the Google AI as matchmaker between searching for a job and finding a job. Right now, the AI is not that developed to avoid ethical profiling. As such, we only apply AI for business financial related tasks. The future will focus on AI as predictive analysis solution. The condition is that data must be structured, complete and accurate*" (Source: Product owner Process & RPA).

In addition, external websites are supported by chatbot functionality to support talent who search job opportunities. We find that both FSSC and the IT department have decided to invest in hyper automation in which all of the above technologies are integrated. To study hyper automation opportunities, a collaboration with Garter has been established to continuously scan new opportunities to digitalise processes and tasks. It is expected that in the next three to five years, the existing IT and digital solutions will merge into one single platform that also act as an integrator.

To create a coherent digital landscape that supports mainstream ERP and CRM systems, micro-services, data lake solutions and fragmented digital solutions, the IT department have decided to implement an integrated platform. The current integration platform of the enterprise is based on the UiPath platform that provides multiple functionalities ranging from bots, chatbots, process mining, task mining, and process orchestration tasks. The IT department implemented two types of integration platforms to separate the support of enterprise business units and external client organisations. As such, the IT department designed a loosely coupled digital landscape. By applying an integrated approach, the enterprise avoids fragmented digital solutions that are unable to exchange data and, as such, may hinder operational performance. Changes in the integration platform are based on an agile approach (e.g. epics, stories) that fits with the aim to create scalable digital landscape. The results of the interview reveal that the IT department is responsible for orchestrating the digital landscape and integrating various in-house and outsourced systems and platforms. From an architectural view, the integration approach is based on API configurations that exchange information between the individual systems and platforms. An illustration of the digital landscape is depicted in Fig. 7.3.

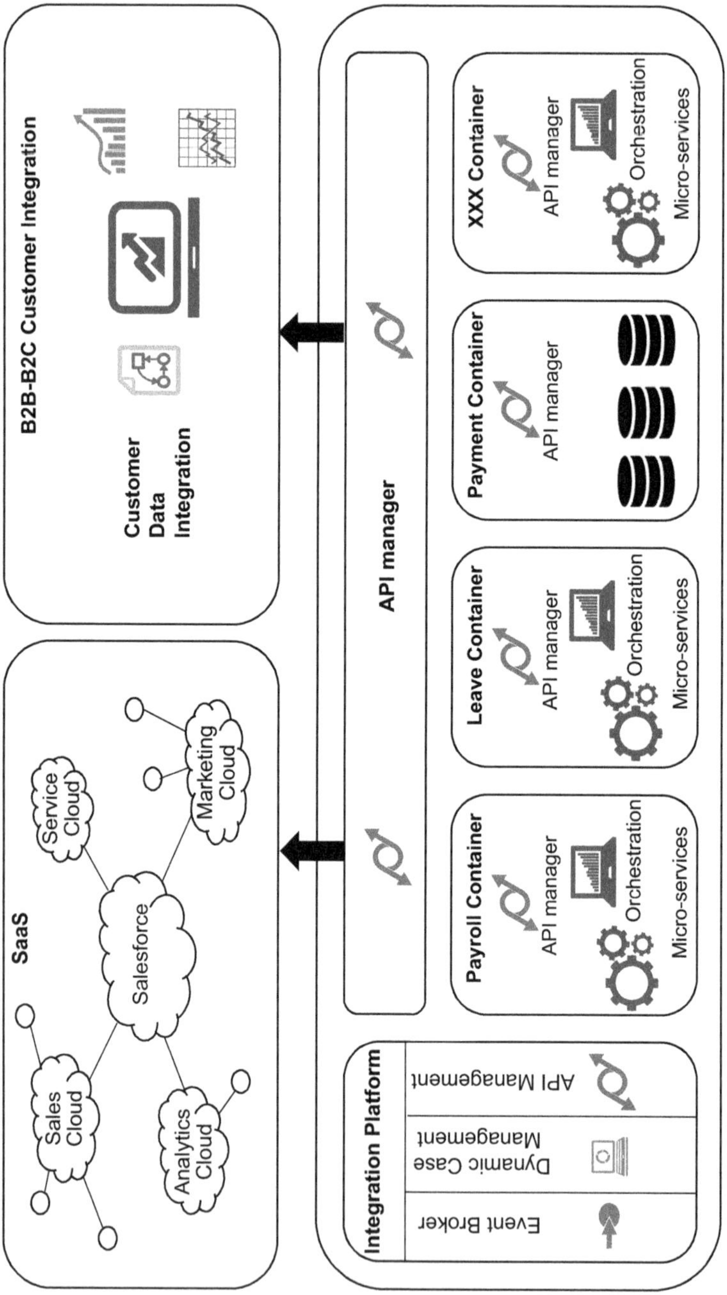

Fig. 7.3 Example of the digital landscape including APIs and micro-services

7.2.6 Managing Decision Rights

We find that decision rights are embedded in the IT architectural guidelines and implemented in the IT department's way of working. For instance, decision rights standards are distributed by a digital tool to the FSSC and business units. From a practical perspective, decision rights can be automated in case of routine-based process steps, in other words, when simple Yes or No decisions are requested. In a similar vein, FSSC has developed a planning tool based on an AI solution themselves, which creates a planning overview to fulfil financial tasks. Managing decision rights as part of agreed governance rules are automated in the tool, while employees (humans) conduct a final check. The same goes for a business unit task to hire external talent in which AI solutions will automatically onboard external job seekers. These examples show that routine-based and predictive types of decisions are automated. However, the authors could not find any examples in which decision rights are automated in case of dynamic circumstances.

7.3 Analysis

7.3.1 Resource Orchestration Theory

As a consequence, the agency's plural sourcing strategy, and its senior management's focus is to bundle internal and external resources effectively. Our analysis shows that at an operational level the IT department acts as an orchestrator for external service providers as well as to the FSSC. Outsourced ERP platforms and cloud services like Salesforce and JD Edwards, Amazon Web Services, and Google, are bundled with in-house IT services to create a coherent IT and digital landscape.

Our analysis demonstrates that the enterprise under study has a broad experience with the digitalisation of business services. As a result, their digital landscape has extended over time as various fragmented solutions were implemented. Consequently, the complexity to maintain a fragmented digital landscape has increased as dependencies between digital solutions need to be coordinated. As multi-sourced arrangements are perceived to be the dominant modus operandi of firms' governance mechanisms may support the coordination of multi-sourcing arrangements (Plugge & Janssen, 2014). In particular, we find that the coordination mechanism "standardisation" is used in practice to decrease interdependence complexity. Standardisation corresponds to the flow type of dependency that relates to an activity that produces a resource that is used by another activity (Malone & Crowston, 1990). For instance, RPA, ML, and ERP resources provided by suppliers are used by the IT department's resources to support the provisioning of financial business services. To avoid indistinctness with regard to interdependencies between an increasing number of parties, the "standardisation" limits coordination problems within the external ecosystem. To support standardisation, senior management decided to opt for an integration strategy that supports openness as design principle. This is reflected by their API strategy, which is illustrated in the digital landscape architecture, and can be seen as a less complex subtype of digital infrastructure with specific control arrangements (Hanseth & Lyytinen, 2010). Senior management's decision to apply standardisation and openness as design principles allows the enterprise under study to redesign their business processes by reusing and combining web services (Fremantle et al., 2002).

It was found that senior management consciously modularised financial business processes to create E2E oversight. In summary, it can be concluded that the case study analysis provides evidence that E2E processes are modularised by means of enabling information systems, e.g. micro-services. This is supported by research of Van der Aalst (2012), in which the author argues that a firm's management aims to synchronise their business services portfolio via dynamic orchestration of their business processes, and, as such, is better able to adapt to changing conditions. As a result, modular independent services contribute to focus on a firm's core capabilities (Bharadwaj et al., 2013).

It was found that the initiated digital transformation programme at the enterprise under study aims to reduce the degree of complexity that contributes to a digital landscape bundling internal and external resources. This is consistent with findings of Sirmon et al. (2007) in which the authors posit that the ROT is one of the most important competencies a firm can internalise. The outcome of our analysis also shows that senior management has decided to structure in-house and outsourced resources by means of integration platforms to achieve a frictionless landscape. In doing so, the degree of digital landscape complexity has been reduced. We suggest that the implementation of integrated platforms contributes to the transformation and disruptive impact of the enterprise under study and as such, affecting the business environment as a whole, which is consistent with the findings of Parker et al. (2016). In addition, the analysis reveals that the IT department acts as an internal orchestrator to bundle resources, taking FSSC's goals and digital solutions into account. As a result of the collaboration between the IT department and FSSC, it could be observed that the internal conflicts about mutual responsibilities have been mitigated. This is consistent with the concept of dynamic capabilities (Teece, 2014) in which resource orchestration is essential to mitigate internal conflicts and improving the resources' complementarities.

7.3.2 Boundary Resources

The findings of this study show that establishing integrated platforms based on micro-services support modularised processes effectively. The findings of this study operationalise the study of De Reuver et al. (2018), in which the authors argue that the transformation from monolithic systems to micro-services support flexible means for inter-organisational relations through a variety of distributed boundary resources. We find that integration platforms interconnect with other systems and platforms by means of boundary resources, e.g. APIs, which facilitates highly distributed and automated coordination of activities at arm's length. Research on digital platform ecosystems (DPE), and corresponding technologies shows that a platform owner, which in our case is UiPath, aims to secure its control over the platform (Panico & Cennamo, 2022). Complementors, which in our case study correspond to the IT department, create complementary products, often called complements, that can be used by platform users e.g. FSSC employees and end users. It is through boundary resources like APIs that the IT department resolves the paradoxical tension between the generativity, and control of the integrated platform. The study findings correspond to the idea of tuning (Eaton et al., 2015) by demonstrating how boundary resources change over time, applying an agile approach. This study shows that in the context of a complex digital landscape with digital technologies, the IT department make sense of the technology, which in turn may affect other platform owners' processes and functionalities.

Since various systems and platforms are operated in-house and outsourced, we argue that the orchestration of integrated platforms does not only include the coordination of the enterprise digital landscape. It also orchestrates the dependencies towards and between multiple external suppliers. The decision of the enterprise to establish cooperating business services that are loosely coupled corresponds to the concept of service orientation (Cherbakov et al., 2005), in which applications span multiple information systems. By creating business services that are enabled by modularised technical solutions, the employment agency is better able to create business value in service relationships (Arsanjani, 2002). We argue that applying a service-oriented way of thinking leverages technology in a response to bundling internal and external resources.

The analysis demonstrates that the introduction of new digital solutions that support financial services to both internal employees and external client organisations orchestrated by integrated platforms contribute to implementation success of financial business services. Modularised financial processes coordinated from an E2E approach simplify the implementation complexity. Hence, it can be suggested that modularisation supported by a digital integration approach can be perceived as a strategy to overcome organisational barriers between silo-based internal business units.

One of the interviewees mentioned that: "*We are confident that the use of integration platforms will increase the implementation success of financial services as current challenges, such as suboptimal technologies or focus on sub-processes, will be solved. As such, the digitalisation of financial services will support multiple business departments at the same time*" (Source IT director).

7.4 Conclusion

In this chapter, we studied the enterprise of an employment agency by focusing on how financial business services are managed and developed by the FSSC. More specifically, we studied the antecedents as described in our research model (see Chap. 4).

We found that the FSSC standardised their financial business process and addressed the importance of digitalising financial sub-processes. This corresponds to the antecedent of modularised business processes. By applying an IS standardisation approach, the FSSC and IT department explored and implemented a range of digital technologies and platforms. The decision to standardise IS can be seen as a prerequisite to further digitalise business services. As a result, the implementation effort of business services decreased. This effect was entered by the FSSC's need to improve the quality of financial business services (customer orientation). The research results further revealed that only routine-based decision rights were digitalised by means of digital tools. We may conclude that the business services portfolio became fully digitalised although the type of services did not change. In addition, we conclude that the IT department acts as an orchestrator that bundles internal and external business services by means of boundary resources. Senior management's strategy to foster the collaboration between the FSSC and IT department resulted in faster digital innovations. Consequently, financial business services were managed from a holistic view to avoid operational issues.

To summarise, we found evidence that the FSSC paid attention to all antecedents as part of our research model. We may conclude that modularised business processes can be seen as an essential antecedent in which they act as a mediator for IS standardisation specifically. This finding is consistent with the outcomes of the fsQCA analysis where IS standardisation is an essential condition in four out of seven solutions.

References

Arsanjani, A. (2002). Developing and integrating enterprise components and services. *Communications of the ACM, 45*(10), 30–34.

Bharadwaj, A., El Sawy, O. A., Pavlou, P. A., & Venkatraman, N. (2013). Digital Business Strategy: Toward a next generation of insights. *MIS Quarterly, 37*(2), 471–482.

Cherbakov, L., Galambos, G., Harishankar, R., Kalyana, S., & Rackham, G. (2005). Impact of service orientation at the business level. *IBM Systems Journal, 44*(4), 653–668.

De Reuver, M., Sørensen, C., & Basole, R. C. (2018). The digital platform: A research agenda. *Journal of Information Management, 33*(2), 124–135.

Eaton, B., Elaluf-Calderwood, S., Sørensen, C., & Yoo, Y. (2015). Distributed tuning of boundary resources: The case of Apple's iOS service system. *MIS Quarterly, 39*(1), 217–244.

Fremantle, P., Weerawarana, S., & Khalaf, R. (2002). Enterprise services: Examining the emerging files of web services and how it is integrated into existing enterprise infrastructures. *Communications of the ACM, 45*(10), 77–82.

Hanseth, O., & Lyytinen, K. (2010). Design theory for dynamic complexity in information infrastructures: The case of building Internet. *Journal of Information Technology, 25*(1), 1–19.

Malone, T. W., & Crowston, K. (1990). What is coordination theory and how can it help design cooperative work systems? In *Proceedings of the 1990 ACM conference on Computer supported cooperative work* (pp. 357–370).

Panico, C., & Cennamo, C. (2022). User preferences and strategic interactions in platform ecosystems. *Strategic Management Journal, 43*(3), 507–529.

Parker, G. G., Van Alstyne, M. W., & Choudary, S. P. (2016). *Platform revolution: How networked markets are transforming the economy and how to make them work for you*. WW Norton & Co.

Plugge, A. G., & Janssen, W. F. W. A. H. (2014). Governance of multivendor outsourcing arrangements: A coordination and resource dependency view. In I. Oshri, J. Kotlarsky, & L. P. Willcocks (Eds.), *Governing sourcing relationships, LNBIP 195* (pp. 78–97). Springer. https://doi.org/10.1007/978-3-319-11367-8_6

Sirmon, D. G., Hitt, M. A., & Ireland, R. D. (2007). Managing firm resources in dynamic environments to create value: Looking inside the black box. *Academy of Management Review, 32*(1), 273–292.
Teece, D. J. (2014). A dynamic capabilities-based entrepreneurial theory of the multinational enterprise. *Journal of International Business Studies, 45*, 8–37.
Van der Aalst, W. M. P. (2012). A decade of business process management conferences: Personal reflections on a developing discipline. In A. Barros, A. Gal, & E. Kindler (Eds.), *Business process management, LNCS 7481*. Springer.

8

Case Study 3: Construction and Building Company

8.1 Context of the Case Study

The enterprise is a global operating construction and development organisation, which has been in operation for over 100 years. The construction unit is the enterprise's largest division with over 1.740 employees at the time of writing this chapter (2023). At the construction unit, the primary focus is on the acquisition and execution of integrated projects related to infrastructure, residential, commercial, utility, and industrial sectors. The unit possess specialised knowledge in several ears, such as car park construction, road construction, integrated tunnelling, offshore wind farm development, and foundation solutions. Additional expertise also includes the transformation, renovation, and restoration of buildings through modular construction and concrete solutions. Its purpose is to build a safe and sustainable living environment characterised by health, comfort, and well-being. To achieve this, the company has four overarching ambitions, including operational excellence, employer of choice, value creation, and sustainable development. The company focuses on its employee value proposition, fostering a culture of performance, and operational excellence to remain an employer of choice. They want to have a qualified workforce, stimulate productivity and employability, and

A. Plugge, S. Nikou, *Digitalisation of Global Business Services*, Technology, Work and Globalization, https://doi.org/10.1007/978-3-031-51528-6_8

create a healthy and welcoming work environment. The enterprise emphasises on the importance of quality and control of processes to deliver the best value for clients.

The enterprise is renowned for its expertise in engineering, building, and managing complex projects that range from residential and commercial buildings to infrastructure and energy-related developments. The headquarters is in the Netherlands, and projects are located both within the Netherlands and beyond, including the United States, Canada, and the Middle East. The enterprise's vision is to create a safe and sustainable living environment that prioritises the health, comfort, and well-being of its clients and the community. The company is committed to using sustainable building practices and materials that promote energy efficiency, reduce waste, and limit the impact on the environment. Their dedicated and skilled team of professionals is responsible for ensuring that its projects meet the highest standards of safety, quality, and innovation. They bring a wealth of experience and expertise to each project, providing customised solutions that meet the unique needs and requirements of each client. The sustainable development strategies of the company focus on reducing its negative impact on the environment and promoting biodiversity. It invests in renewable energy and uses sustainable materials. The company also aims to take care of its employees by offering competitive compensation, individual care, and personal growth opportunities.

In addition to its construction and development services, the enterprise also offers a range of specialised services, including engineering, project management, and consultancy. The company prides itself on its ability to provide end-to-end solutions for complex projects, from the initial design phase to the final delivery and maintenance of the completed structure. The company has received numerous awards and recognition for its work, including the Dutch Building Award and the BREEAM Award for sustainable building practices (ESG). They are committed to promote diversity and inclusion in the workplace, as evidenced by its participation and its ongoing efforts to create a safe and inclusive work environment for all employees.

8.2 Financial Shared Service Centre

The unit of analysis of our study is the construction company's FSSC. The FSSC is a centralised unit within a company that provides financial services, such as accounting, payroll, and accounts payable to multiple business units or subsidiaries. The purpose of establishing an FSSC is to streamline and standardise financial processes across the organisation, reduce costs, and improve efficiency and quality of financial services. In general, the FSSC operates by consolidating the financial functions of various business units or subsidiaries into one centralised location. This can involve standardising accounting policies, procedures, and systems across the organisation, as well as automating processes wherever possible. The FSSC is staffed by finance professionals who are responsible for providing financial services to the rest of the organisation and their contractors, such as processing transactions, generating financial reports, and providing financial analysis.

One of the interviewees mentioned that "*The invoices is the main part of our business at the moment. There are about 200,000 invoices that we need to process each year and that goes with the so-called purchase to pay cycle. So, for each invoice, you need to have a purchase order. You need to have a receipt for the goods and services receipt and in between, the company tried with procurement to find a solution how to control all the spendings and obligation that has been entered into the system. So, in that respect, all of those transactions will we try to digitalise that, and it took a while, but we are almost there*" (Source: Manager Administration).

The specific practices and processes used by an FSSC can vary depending on the company and industry. In the case of this construction company, their FSSC may operate in a similar way, providing centralised financial services to different business units or subsidiaries within the company. However, the exact practices and processes used would depend on the specific needs and requirements of the enterprise.

Regarding the implementation of the FSSC, one of the interviewees mentioned that "*The shared service centre is the financial shared service centre, right? So, the impact on the whole company was at the time that people did not believe that we would need a shared service centre. All the business units were like independent entities, and they found that there was no need for the shared service centre*" (Source: Manager Business Consultancy).

The same interviewee mentioned that after five years since starting the project "*Now we are coming down to standardisation and harmonisation of the different transactions and processes. We are using a central application to process incoming invoices from suppliers. Not outgoing invoices, because that is an autonomous situation for the business because they know more than us what to invoice and if there is a problem, clients can approach them for explanations directly*" (Source: Manager Administration).

In general, some of the benefits of implementing an FSSC may include:

- Standardisation and consistency of financial processes across the organisation.
- Improved efficiency and speed of financial transactions and reporting.
- Reduced costs through economies of scale and automation.
- Improved accuracy and quality of financial data and reporting.
- Enhanced ability to provide financial analysis and insights to the organisation as a whole.

With respect to internal challenges regarding the implementation of the FSSC, one of the interviewees mentioned that "*In that respect also, we have our own existing stuff who always needs an upgrade in our refreshment in what we are doing in the shared service centre. What we have done so far is to organise once in a week, a one-hour question. Employees can call in while experts are ready to answer any questions they have. So, in the beginning there were a lot of people calling in. Now, it is like, one or two people only calling*" (Source: Manager Business Consultancy).

Overall, it was found that the FSSC can be an effective way to streamline and optimise the enterprise's financial processes, reduce costs, and improve overall financial performance.

- **Impact of digitalisation on employees**

Digitalisation refers to the process of using digital technologies to transform business processes and operations. This can involve automating tasks, adopting, and implementing new digital tools and digital platforms, and leveraging data and analytics to improve decision making. As such, digitalisation can have a significant impact on employees in various ways. For example, digitalisation can introduce changes in job roles and responsibilities through implementation of new digital tools and processes. Employees may need to adapt to new ways of working and learn new skills to perform their jobs effectively. By introducing new digital tools in the enterprise, some job roles may become obsolete, while new roles may emerge, requiring employees to acquire new knowledge and expertise. In addition, digitalisation can increase efficiency and productivity. For instance, digitalisation can help streamline and automate tasks, allowing employees to focus on more high-value tasks that require critical thinking and creativity. This can lead to increased efficiency and productivity and may result in job satisfaction for employees who prefer challenging work.

Digitalisation and introducing new digital technologies can improve collaboration and communication. As an example, digitalisation can enable employees to work more collaboratively and communicate more efficiently across units, locations, and time zones. This can improve employee engagement, promote knowledge-sharing, and enhance the overall work culture. Our research has shown that sharing knowledge has become a crucial component when delivering knowledge-based services such as financial services. This aligns with the findings of Wang and Hou (2015) and Zhang (2018), where the authors argued that knowledge sharing is instrumental in achieving an organisation's business strategy.

Regarding the digitalisation impact, one of the interviewees mentioned that "*So in that sense, digital technologies just have to achieve a goal. And I do not think there is any much more to it than that, it is a tool to align your processes because when working with digital tools, you need to have clear input or uniform inputs. In that sense, it also helps to get your processes organised in a better way. But really a strategic ambition is to be the number one digital company*" (Source: Manager Administration).

In addition, the same interviewee mentioned that "*RPA for example, is really hot at the moment. We get opportunities to start exploring new tools like RPA and AI, and when we have a feeling that it could contribute to our company, we invite our IT steering committee to give a judgment. We further explore such tools and then we asked the business to come up with some business cases. In the end, it will be like a business case driven decision, on a case-by-case basis*" (Source Manager Administration).

Other impact of digitalisation on the company's workforce can facilitate the balance between work and life. In this regard, digitalisation can allow for more flexible working arrangements, such as remote work, which can improve work-life balance for employees. It can also reduce the need for employees to commute to work, which can lead to reduced stress and improved well-being. One of the interviewees mentioned that "*There are still a lot of hurdles that we need to take. We are working with people. For instance, if somebody leaves the company, and a new person comes in, we must make sure that the onboarding is OK. If the business unit does not have anybody who can do the onboarding, this person will be a swimming around for one or two months not knowing who to approach and what to do*" (Source: Manager Business Consultancy).

In addition to the challenges discussed above, one of the interviewees noted an important problem with the digital technology integration and implementation at the case company. He mentioned that "*If invoices cannot be matched with a purchase order or the receipt of the purchase order, the invoice cannot be processed, which means that the invoice cannot be paid. We are finding ourselves frequently in an old-produced situation where invoices are overdue. Suppliers are complaining about their payments and often saying that we are stopping the delivery*" (Source Manager Business Consultancy).

Finally, the impact of digitalisation on the enterprise's workforces may relate to job security. While digitalisation can improve efficiency and productivity, it can also result in job displacement, particularly for employees whose job roles become obsolete due to automation. The enterprise may need to invest in upskilling and reskilling programmes and workshops to help employees adapt to new roles or acquire new skills and digital competence to remain relevant in the job market.

8.2.1 Plural Sourcing Strategy

The plural sourcing strategy involves engaging multiple suppliers to provide goods or services, rather than relying on a single supplier. The goal of the plural sourcing strategy of the enterprise under study is to diversify risk, increase competition, and ultimately achieve better value for all stakeholders involved in the processes and all operations. For example, the enterprise contracted multiple suppliers for different materials such as steel, cement, or timber (supply chain management). One of the benefits of plural sourcing includes diversification of risk. By engaging multiple suppliers, the company is able to mitigate the risk of relying on a single supplier for critical materials and services. This can help ensure continuity of supply and reduce the impact of supply chain disruptions. Plural sourcing also can provide additional benefits such as increased competition. By engaging multiple suppliers, the company can create a competitive environment, encouraging suppliers to offer better pricing and quality to win business. It can also provide a better access to specialised expertise. With successful and strategical implementation of plural sourcing, the enterprise can engage with multiple suppliers, which allows them to tap into specialised expertise and knowledge that might not be available from a single supplier.

8.2.2 Business Service Portfolio

It is reported that, based on interviews conducted, the enterprise under investigation has not yet fully automated its financial services portfolio. However, they have strategic plans to incorporate more digital tools in the future. The portfolio includes traditional financial services such as bill payment systems, accounts payable, and payroll, which provide support for tasks such as paying the bills, salary sheets, and bank accounts. According to the interview findings, the financial services offered by the FSSC have largely been automated using portals and digital solutions such as Robotic Process Automation (RPA) and Machine Learning (ML).

8.2.3 Modularised Business Processes

The enterprise has implemented digital technologies to improve their business processes. Some of the potential benefits of digital technologies include (1) improved efficiency, where digital technologies can help streamline processes and reduce the time and resources required to complete tasks. It can also (2) enhance collaboration, such that with the use of digital tools, different teams and stakeholders can easily share knowledge and information, and collaborate on projects, leading to better outcomes. It can also (3) allow better risk management and help identify and mitigate risks early in the project lifecycle, reducing the likelihood of delays and cost overruns. It is important to note that the specific impact of digital technologies on the enterprise's business processes would depend on the types of tools and solutions they have implemented or plan to do so, as well as how these tools are integrated into their operations.

Regarding implementation of digital tools such as RPA and supporting financial business processes that support various administrative processes, one of the interviewees mentioned that "*For instance, the number of steps that needs to be taken. Currently I am pretty sure that it can be decreased by 50%. So, the process will be shorter. In that respect, it will allow the operations people, to add more control points in what they are doing, or it will increase the customer satisfaction in servicing the customers and not waiting for, let's say, information that still needs to be processed. So, all of that will be made shorter and of course efficiency will go higher. This is at least the expectation*" (Source Manager Administration).

8.2.4 Customer Orientation

The interview analysis revealed that the FSSC aims to align enterprise's objectives and their relationships with customers. It was found that FSSC demands management from the customer perspective. One of the interviewees mentioned that "*Our customer is interested in the service levels based on both quality and quantity. So how we meet these service levels is basically indifferent to them*". The same interviewee continued by indicating that "*And our internal customers, they just want an invoice to be booked on the right course centre on time and paid on time. So, they do not get phone calls or angry suppliers on the construction side. If we do that fully manually or fully automated, it is basically indifferent to them. The only thing is of course there is a cost related to it*" (Source Manager Business Consultancy).

One of our interviewees commented on how intelligent automation affects the demand management of FSSC from a customer perspective or orientation, when we asked for their views. He mentioned that "*Management is confronted to the facts when the complaints come in from suppliers and customers, then it will be reported on board level. Then, management will have to look at it. And this is where we are now. They are looking at it and they see that there is not only a financial issue, but also operational. Satisfaction of people just doing their job, I am pretty sure that is the most important thing that you need*". He continued by stating that "*Because good people are very scarce to find. We need to do anything that can make them happy in their job and that is not only financial, but also taking away all the frustration that is going along with the job and that is where automation comes in. So that would help them a lot as well*" *(Source Manager Administration)*.

8.2.5 IS Standardisation

The enterprise has divided the theme of digitalisation and innovation into three major topics: (1) data, digitalisation, and analytics, (2) automation and robotics, and (3) advanced building methods. The core focus of the enterprise regarding the data, digitalisation and analytics is to upgrade existing technical systems, such as document management and Building Information Modelling (BIM) collaboration tools, and to transform them into a common data environment. The enterprise is also streamlining data flows and visualising data through dashboarding to provide better insight into business operations and increase responsiveness and decision making. They strive to develop the QS2Field application for safety and quality inspections, which is being used to standardise registrations and create a single source of information that will enable them to learn and adjust faster. It can be used on desktops, laptops, tablets, and mobile phones. Additionally, the enterprise is introducing a centralised information platform (*KnowMan*) to make knowledge accessible for all employees. Regarding data, digitalisation and analytics, the enterprise strategy is to upgrade their existing technical systems and move towards a common data environment. This involves moving all on-premises data sources to the cloud, including next-generation administrative systems and data analytics, to increase data accessibility, security, collaboration, and automation to support business processes.

Addressing automation and robotics, the enterprise strategy is to automate and streamline processes through robotics and advanced building methods. They invest in automation and robotics technologies to improve efficiency and productivity in construction processes. This includes using drones and other automated tools to reduce the amount of manual labour required on construction sites. They also explore advanced building methods, such as modular construction and 3D printing, to further improve efficiency and productivity. Modular construction involves building individual components of a structure offsite and then assembling them onsite. This reduces construction time and labour costs. 3D printing allows for the creation of complex shapes and structures, which can be produced quickly and at a lower cost than traditional construction methods.

Regarding advanced building methods, the focus and objective of the enterprise is to use advanced building methods such as Building Information Modelling (BIM) and digital twin processes to increase efficiency, improve quality, and enhance collaboration throughout the construction process. They piloted 4D and 5D software in 2022 in one its projects. This enabled them to control the time-to-cost dimension and identify how progress monitoring added value to their project reporting. They also use point clouds for as-build comparisons, helping them reduce failure costs, and aim to further develop innovative ideas, such as using visualisation to enhance feasibility and safety. The enterprise plans to improve the quality of metadata in models, bring 3D models on-site through personal smart devices, and use data for progress monitoring. They aim to have a progress and cost dashboard operational for one of their projects in 2023.

8.2.6 Managing Decision Rights

Digitalisation refers to the use of technologies such as AI, ML, and RPA to automate tasks and processes that were previously performed manually. This can help to improve efficiency, reduce errors, and free up human resources for more complex tasks. In the case of the enterprise under study, digitalisation could have several impacts on the decision rights that correspond to financial services. For example, it can improve project management, such that automated decision rights can help with project planning and scheduling, resource allocation, and risk management. This could support the enterprise to better manage their projects, ensuring that they are delivered on time, within budget, and to the required quality standards.

Digitalisation would have an impact on the decision rights of the FSSC such that it can help to improve and enhance quality control. With the use of AI and ML algorithms, the FSSC could automate decisions to monitor construction materials and equipment, as well as the inspection of construction sites. This could help to identify and resolve issues more quickly, improving quality control and reducing the risk of defects or safety issues. In addition, it can help to increase efficiency in administrative tasks. For example, RPA can be used to automate routine decisions such as invoice processing and contract management tasks. This could help to reduce the workload of administrative staff and free up their time for more strategic tasks. Automating decision rights can help to improve customer experience. By automating processes such as project tracking and communication with clients, the enterprise could provide a more seamless and transparent experience for their customers. This may improve customer satisfaction and loyalty.

However, it should be noted that automated decision making can introduce potential risks and challenges. As such, it is important for the FSSC to ensure that the benefits of automation outweigh any potential drawbacks, and that they have appropriate measures in place to mitigate risks such as data security and job displacement. Overall, digitalisation has the potential to impact the decision rights of services, helping them to improve efficiency, quality, and customer experience. When we asked "how does of digitalisation (intelligent automation) would have an impact on the decision rights of the FSSCs? One of the interviewees mentioned that "*I think the automated decisions of financial processes will lead to improved efficiency; I mean efficiency is the keyword.*" Another mentioned that "*You reach maybe more controls compliance type of topics. It will help to face out certain steps, eliminate human steps. So, in that sense, it can definitely improve controls, I am sure*" (Source Manager Business Consultancy).

8.3 Analysis

8.3.1 Resource Orchestration Theory

Due to the implementation of digital technologies and tools, the enterprise's senior management focus is to bundle the internal and the external resources effectively. The orchestration of internal and external resources can be investigated under theoretical lens of institutional theory (Figueiredo & Pinto, 2021), or resource orchestration theory (Kumar et al., 2022; Maatman & Bondarouk, 2014). With regard to resource configurations, the enterprise has a diverse range of resources, including skilled personnel, construction equipment, and expertise in various areas such as civil engineering and sustainable building. They also have a strong brand and reputation for delivering high-quality projects. However, they may face challenges in coordinating and integrating these resources effectively. Regarding resource deployment, a decentralised structure is used including various business units and projects operating independently. This may provide flexibility and agility in responding to customer needs, but it may also result in redundancy and inefficiencies in resource deployment. The enterprise may need to develop more standardised processes and procedures to optimise resource deployment across the organisation. They may benefit from improving their resource orchestration capabilities. This could involve better alignment of resources with the organisation's strategic goals, as well as more effective coordination and collaboration across different business units and functions. Adopting digitalisation, as discussed in the previous section, could also help to improve resource orchestration by streamlining processes and freeing up human resources for more value-adding activities.

In addition, the enterprise may improve resource optimisation by leveraging data analytics and technology (Grover et al., 2018; Okanga &

Groenewald, 2019), to better understand resource utilisation and identify opportunities for improvement. This may involve implementing systems for tracking and analysing data on equipment usage, labour productivity, and project costs. The enterprise could also invest in upskilling their workforce to enable them to take on more complex and higher-value tasks. Overall, the case company has a strong set of resources, both internal and external but they may need to work on improving their resource orchestration capabilities to fully leverage these resources and sustain their competitive advantage.

8.3.2 Boundary Resources

Integration platforms, also known as boundary resources, can increase the implementation of financial business services at the FSSC under study by providing a centralised location for information and data to be shared between different systems and stakeholders. This can help to streamline processes, reduce errors, and increase efficiency. Based on our analysis we find that the FSSC uses boundary resources to help facilitate their financial business services by integrating their financial systems with their project management systems. This allows them to better manage their financial resources, including budgeting, forecasting, and reporting, and to track financial performance more easily across multiple projects. By using integration platforms or boundary resources, the enterprise as a whole may increase the implementation success of their financial business services. In addition, they are able to improve collaboration, communication, and data sharing between different systems and stakeholders. The FSSC recognised the importance of digital solutions in supporting their financial business services both for internal employees and for external clients. However, the FSSC should aim to integrate digital platforms that orchestrate different financial systems, including budgeting, forecasting, and reporting. These integrated platforms help to streamline and optimise the financial services, which in turn can improve efficiency, accuracy, and reduce costs.

One key aspect of boundary resources and the digital solutions is their ability to support internal employees in managing financial data and processes. For example, the enterprise's project managers can access real-time data on project budgets, cash flows, and forecasts, enabling them to make more informed decisions about resource allocation and cost management. By having a centralised and integrated platform, employees across the company can have access to the same information, ensuring consistency and reducing errors. In addition to supporting internal employees, the case company's digital solutions should aim to help support financial services for external client organisations. For instance, they should strive to offer digital solutions that enable clients to monitor project progress, costs, and other financial data in real-time. This not only provides transparency for the client, but it also helps to build trust and increase satisfaction with enterprise's services.

Overall, the use of digital solutions and integrated platforms helps the enterprise to optimise their financial business services and provide more value to their clients. By having a centralised platform, financial business processes can be streamlined and ensure consistency across different systems and stakeholders. Additionally, the use of digital solutions can provide greater transparency and data-driven decision-making capabilities for both internal employees and external clients.

8.4 Conclusion

In this chapter, we studied the enterprise of a construction and building company by focusing on how financial business services are managed and developed by the FSSC. More specifically, we studied the antecedents as described in our research model (see Chap. 4).

We find that the FSSC has not fully digitalised its business processes, although the FSSC explores and invests in digital technologies. Regarding decision making as part of financial business processes we find that the FSSC is in its early days to automate decision rights. Although we found some examples of the antecedent customer orientation the FSSC lacks a strong emphasis to improve their financial business services. When addressing IS standardisation we conclude that the use of digital platforms and applications contributes to the implementation of business services. Consequently, digital technologies can help streamline business processes and reduce the time and resources required to complete business services tasks. Based on the findings we may conclude that the business services portfolio is partially digitalised although the type of services did not change. We find that the FSSC's and IT department's main goal is to develop orchestration capabilities to effective coordinate internal and external resources. To support their orchestration capability future digital integration platforms will support orchestration tasks more easily. This will reduce lead times of digitalised financial services. In doing so, the FSSC is better able to solve existing challenges throughout its business operations. To summarise, we found evidence that the FSSC partially paid attention to the antecedents as part of our research model. We may conclude that business processes and IS standardisation can be seen as essential antecedents as part of orchestration tasks. In particular, the importance of IS standardisation fits with the findings of the fsQCA analysis where IS standardisation is considered to be an essential condition (four out of seven solutions).

References

Figueiredo, A. S., & Pinto, L. H. (2021). Robotizing shared service centres: Key challenges and outcomes. *Journal of Service Theory and Practice, 31*(1), 157–178.

Grover, V., Chiang, R. H., Liang, T. P., & Zhang, D. (2018). Creating strategic business value from big data analytics: A research framework. *Journal of Management Information Systems, 35*(2), 388–423.

Kumar, M., Pullman, M., Bouzdine-Chameeva, T., & Sanchez Rodrigues, V. (2022). The role of the hub-firm in developing innovation capabilities: Considering the French wine industry cluster from a resource orchestration lens. *International Journal of Operations & Production Management, 42*(4), 526–551.

Maatman, M., & Bondarouk, T. (2014). Value creation by transactional shared service centers: mapping capabilities. In *Shared services as a new organizational form* (Advanced Series in Management) (Vol. 13, pp. 153–174). Emerald Group Publishing Limited.

Okanga, B., & Groenewald, D. (2019). Optimising enterprise resource planning system to leverage a firm's absorptive and adaptive capabilities. *South African Journal of Information Management, 21*(1), 1–15.

Wang, W. T., & Hou, Y. P. (2015). Motivations of employees' knowledge sharing behaviours: A self-determination perspective. *Information and Organization, 25*(1), 1–26.

Zhang, Z. (2018). Organizational culture and knowledge sharing: Design of incentives and business processes. *Business Process Management Journal, 24*(2), 384–399.

9

Case Study 4: Financial Services Provider

In this chapter, we describe the fourth case study, which is a global operating service provider specialised in financial services. We first sketch out the context of the service provider, and next, describe how they established the delivery of financial business services (FSSC). Then, we elaborate on the antecedents that are part of our research. As a final step, we analyse the findings and summarise our conclusions.

9.1 Context of the Case Study

The financial services provider operates on a global level and offers both business process and IT services to their customers. Their areas of expertise include digital, engineering and cloud services that include traditional, transformational, and future needs. The provider acts in all commonly known industries such as banking, manufacturing, telecommunication, energy and utilities and public sector. From a technology perspective, they established strategic alliances with technology suppliers who are perceived as market leaders in their respectable fields of expertise (i.e. Microsoft, Oracle, Salesforce, SAP, Google Cloud, Blue Prism etc.). An important ambition of the service provider is to support their

A. Plugge, S. Nikou, *Digitalisation of Global Business Services*, Technology, Work and Globalization, https://doi.org/10.1007/978-3-031-51528-6_9

customers to become a sustainable enterprise arguing that businesses are using technology to achieve an equitable workplace. The service provider acknowledges that they are committed to focus on long-term value creation for all stakeholders and incorporates Environmental, Social, and Governance (ESG) practices to underpin a sustainable present and future. In doing so, they focus and aim to contribute to the United Nations Sustainable Development Goals (SDGs).

Importantly, the financial services provider has established a commendable reputation in the market regarding transformations, including customers business models, service portfolio, technology, and digitalisation. They provide services on a global level that are supported by delivery centres located in the United States, Europe, and Asia-Pacific. In particular, the service provider aims to innovate customers businesses by establishing innovation hubs. These innovation hubs are staffed with representatives of their customers, their own organisation and start-ups and scale-ups. By creating a business ecosystem supported by state-of-the-art technologies, all stakeholders are able to create value for their own organisation and to the ecosystem as a whole.

As the provider's strategy is to fulfil a best-in-class position in the market they acquired a banking license in one of their geographies. Their objective to acquire a banking license is twofold. First, they want to understand financial services in-depth and next suggest improvements to increase the quality of existing services. In doing so, the provider has an in-depth understanding of all relevant financial activities which is helpful to advise their customers. Second, based on an in-depth understanding of financial services in-house digital solutions can be developed and implemented to decrease the cost level of existing services while increasing their quality. By embracing digitalisation new services can be developed and integrated with their business services portfolio.

One of the interviewees mentioned that "*When providing digital solutions our customers benefit from new solutions, such as financial calculations, that leads to more empowered customer stakeholders. In addition, as we develop and test digital solutions in-house, we know which one of them makes sense in a customer context. By digitalisation we as a provider are able to launch new financial services quicker than before. An advantage of digitisation is that it offers the opportunity to create real time experiences for end users*" (Source: Senior Vice President Europe).

In the context of the provider's strategic vision, we find that they apply an ecosystem strategy with both their customers and other service providers. Their ecosystem vision is based on the principle of an open network that allows multiple providers and their customers to collaborate in improving existing financial services and designing new ones. As an example, insurance firms collaborate with technical suppliers to support households in solving technical issues. The provider under study took the initiate to develop digital financial services (e.g. digital supported insurance policies, refunds) based on the input of various technical suppliers, which in the end increases customers satisfaction. This approach is related to the provider's strategy to build innovations hubs or innovation studio's that allows customers, suppliers and third parties to focus on digitalised services.

9.2 Financial Shared Service Centre

The service provider under study provides end-to-end digital service offerings that are organised as a financial shared service centre (FSSC). The FSSC provide financial services to their customers in which they embrace digital disruptions to change existing business models. For example, collaboration with Fintech start-ups to rethink financial operating models by creating banking simplification, transparency, and customer experience, and implementing regulatory directives to support financial services. To achieve these goals, the financial services provider invests in financial-oriented start-ups and application modernisation. Their aim is to enable their customers to become a technology platform organisation providing financial services. Their finance delivery team comprise of various capabilities including financial experts, digital and automation subject matter experts and data analysts to support financial transformations. From a financial perspective, they provide services in the field of Order To Cash (O2C), Procure To Pay (P2P), Record To Report (R2R), performance management and transformation. In the context of digital technologies, they support Artificial Intelligence (AI), Machine

Learning (ML), computer vision techniques and integration with Robotic Process Automation (RPA) type of solutions.

Impact of Digitalisation on Employees

When providing services to their customers the financial services provider is faced with continuous changes both from a financial services perspective and from a digital technology perspective. This impacts the knowledge and experience of their employees as they have to adapt regularly. For instance, in the field of understanding radical type of digital technologies. The financial service provider invests in training and education of their employees continuously as a mechanism to stay relevant in their field. From a practical view, employees need to keep up the pace of learning and explore the value of digital technologies. Today, education, skills, and experience in the context of emerging digital technologies, like digital platforms, is even more relevant. In particular, customers' demands that the financial services provider becomes accountable when providing financial services that are grounded on digital technologies. Therefore, training is an equal responsibility of the provider and their employees.

One of the interviewees argued that "*if you do not have the skills, you are out as it not about experience anymore. The technology changes so rapidly and becomes so complex that even skilled colleagues are severely challenged. To counter this challenge, we focus on the foundations: how to operate (governance), do we have the process in scope and how to we train our experts to remain skilled resources*" (Source: Delivery manager).

To ensure that employees are well trained the provider established an internal capability and competency unit in which new digital technologies are shared, explored, and educated. To support employees in their education journey, the financial services provider applies various mechanisms. As an example, we find that a certain percentage of their time needs to be reserved for training and education. In doing so, the provider ensures that employees upskill their capabilities. Besides joining obliged education programmes employees are encouraged to explore digital focus areas that reflect their passion. The rationale behind this mechanism is that employees who are motivated intrinsically perform better in practice. We find that employees are incentivised when joining education and training programmes. They are rewarded from a recognition perspective;

for instance, by publishing their names and expertise in internal and external magazines, such as achieving certain technology related certificates. This mechanism addresses employees' intrinsic motivation and passion of using technologies.

One of the interviewees mentioned that "*Change is always constant! An important asset of our company is our capability to embrace new technologies as they support our financial services. We pay a lot of attention and effort to educate our employees in order to support them in their daily work. This is recognised by our customers as they acknowledge the up-to-date skills of for instance our engineers, delivery managers and subject matter experts in providing financial services*" (Source: Delivery manager).

From a similar view, the financial services provider offers their employees to switch to other type of technologies and fields and as such, encourage them to stay motivated. Based on the interviews we find that applying these mechanisms mitigate the retention risk of employees. One of the interviewees mentioned that "*We noticed that attention to education and training mitigate the risk of attrition. In the past we had a high degree of infant attrition, meaning that a significant number of employees left the firm within 12 months. By focusing on the personal motivation of our employees we noticed that the infant attrition rate reduced. This is a positive outcome that benefits our firm and customers*" (Source: Director financial services).

In addition, well-trained employees such as technical engineers, and digital technology experts contribute to the performance of the provider in supporting their customers. The goal of the financial service provider is to achieve 80% of motivated employees that as a result, provide value-added services to customers.

9.2.1 Plural Sourcing Strategy

From a strategic perspective we find that the financial services provider built all their financial services in-house. The rationale to provide services in-house is grounded in their expertise to develop and implement qualitative financial services to their customers. We find that the provider applied a plural sourcing strategy in the field of information technology specifically. To achieve their financial services goals the provider under study established plural sourcing partnerships with multiple technology suppliers to design and develop financial services that are build in-house. Examples correspond to ERP suppliers like SAP, Oracle, and Microsoft, and digital technology suppliers like Aris, Blue Prism, Celonis, and UiPath. This strategy supports their aim to provide digital solutions, and by integration financial and digitalised services the provider is able to support their customers with attractive and relevant services.

9.2.2 Business Services Portfolio

When addressing the providers financial business services portfolio, we find that digitalisation has a significant effect on customers' demand on the use of existing financial services. Customers demand that financial services are based on digital technologies to respond on customers request swiftly. Although financial services like Procure To Pay (P2P) and Order To Cash (O2C) are predominantly supported by Enterprise Resource Management (ERP) systems, such as SAP, Oracle, and Microsoft, still some manual tasks need to be conducted. Examples are collecting additional data and verifying customers background checks. By automating current manual tasks, the financial services provider's business portfolio is digitalised further.

One of the interviewees mentioned that "*The impact of digitalisation on our service portfolio is 100%. For instance, during the Covid period our customers' end users worked at home but still have to conduct financial tasks. Our portfolio supports these tasks independent of an end user's location. We supported our financial customers by digitalising their branch offices and developed digital kiosks and point of sales systems within an office that can be used by a customer's customers. This shows that existing services were digitalised while new digital services have been introduced, which in the end all affect our financial services portfolio*" (Source: Director financial services).

Based on the interviews we find that the benefits of increased digitalisation of the services portfolio are twofold. First, customers benefit from a digitalised services portfolio as costs optimalisations can be measured explicitly. Due to inefficiencies in their existing IT landscape, such a replacing manual tasks by digital tools and applying extreme automation financial services costs are decreased. The provider under study uses the term 'automation to the bone' to apply continuous monitoring and improvements in their services portfolio to achieve this goal explicitly. The second benefit corresponds to the provider's organisation by integrating digital technologies (e.g. cloud hypervisors, low-code platforms) to build and provide financial services to their customers. Interviews reveal that technical engineers are in the lead to explore the added value of digital technologies. When relevant, they reach out internally to financial services teams to discuss business relevance. This digital experience driven approach is supported by developing frameworks and models to accelerate the introduction of digital financial services.

9.2.3 Modularised Business Processes

Interviews shows that business processes are essential in providing financial business services to customers. As mentioned previously, ERP systems rely heavily on automated business processes. Interviews show, however, that customer ERP systems have been customised over time to support their financial services effectively. This approach increased the complexity to manage and extend ERP systems and their automated business processes. We find that business processes have been modularised specifically to automate sub-processes. As such, modularisation is perceived to be a prerequisite to digitalise financial business services. As the degree of existing digitalised customer business processes may vary the provider under study developed three key business process strategies to support their customers. First, in case customers use their ERP systems from a systems of record view they do not affect the ERP core model. In this case, the provider opts the strategy not to modernise the legacy systems but extend ERP systems with digital technologies (e.g. RPA, ML) and automate "last mile" financial business processes. Second, in situations where a customer ERP landscape cannot be adjusted the provider use a modernisation strategy to start from scratch. This radical form of innovation means that a new ERP environment is build including highly automated business processes by means of digital technologies. Consequently, modularised business processes form the fundament to automate business processes. Such a new ERP environment includes RPA and ML bots and provides the opportunity to optimise business processes by means of process mining tools. A third strategy is based on an incremental approach to modernise the ERP landscape. An example corresponds to develop and implement a billing application that is connected to the existing ERP system and avoid manual labour tasks.

One of the interviewees mentioned that "*The strategy to embrace digitalisation is related to the lead time and complexity to digitalise supporting financial business processes. For sure, financial business processes can be automated further, which take lesser time to conduct the same activities. As an example, in the past we needed three months to approve financial tasks, now by building an app we need seven days*" (Source: Digital solution architect).

The three strategies, all affect customers financial business processes although the impact may vary depending on the type of strategy. The decision to choose a specific strategy is based on a risk analysis and timing. A key finding is; however, that financial business process and digital technologies are interdependent and as a result, effect customers financial services directly. An example of digitalised financial business processes reflects a customer's on-boarding process to welcome new clients.

One of the interviewees explained this change "*As the first on-boarding process step is to check the degree of efficient, it originally took 7 to 8 working days. This was caused by conducting multiple manual checks and balances. As we automated the on-boarding process and related sub-processes we were able to skip all manual tasks that resulted in an execution of maximal 2 hours. We introduced an automated workflow based on our digital platform to avoid redundant tasks and as a result, optimised the on-boarding business process. We continuously monitor this process to identify additional process improvements*" (Source: Director financial services).

Based on provider's documentation, we find that digital technologies are used to conduct a deep dive in the business process logic as a mean to streamline business processes.

9.2.4 Customer Orientation

One view on how the provider pays attention to customer orientation is the role of their contact centre that handles customer requests. At operational level the provider analyses all incoming requests and provide feedback to the respective customers proactively. Based on the feedback the provider discusses the need to adapt existing financial services or introduce new ones.

One of the interviewees mentioned that "*We support a global financial institution around the globe. Based on numerus end users service requests our contact centre analyses their root causes and bundle the outcomes in a small report. Next, our service delivery managers start to discuss the data analysis with the customer at central level. Often the customer does not have a clue about the number and type of all their end users' requests. By feeding them with relevant data we verify if we have to change the financial services or not. In the near future we develop proactive analysis tools to support the customer even better*" (Source: Delivery manager).

We find that digital technologies are also used to explore opportunities. For example, with regard to data monetarisation, we found that data can only be used effectively in case of data coherence. Relationships between data monitoring, data analytics, and data reporting must be coherent to identify opportunities to improve financial services, such as financial bond products and insurance products.

9.2.5 IS Standardisation

The financial services provider acknowledges the opportunities that digital technologies may contribute when combining them with financial services. Their digitalisation strategy is based on three pillars. The first pillar corresponds to their global emerging technology team, which reports to the global Chief Technology Officer (CTO) directly. This emerging technology team, which collaborates with technology suppliers, is based on existing plural sourcing partnerships. This team fulfils the role of an explorative entity by understanding how an emergent technology actually works. Examples are the metaverse, crypto and contact computing. In case, an emerging technology is found to be relevant, it is discussed with the financial services organisation as part of the business process outsourcing department that forms the second pillar of the digitalisation strategy. The collaboration between the emerging technology team and financial services organisation aims to experiment emerging technologies in the context of financial services. The focus of conducting experiments is to test how the functionality of a new digital technology contributes to financial services.

One of the interviewees mentioned that "*It is interesting to explore if it makes sense to use blockchain technology to support a customer's insurance policies. To test its relevance, we build use cases first and as a next step, test blockchain technology. Another example is to experiment if a customer can do business in a customer's metaverse environment. We check how to log on to the metaverse and see the customer's various product offerings all without going to a physical bank. When valuable, the financial services teams include the emerging technology into their existing financial services or create new ones (e.g. payment services, retail banking, life insurances, clearing tasks)*" (Source: Digital solution architect).

The third pillar focuses on adapting financial services by means of emerging technologies and next adjusting the financial services portfolio. In doing so, customers may benefit from emerging technologies in the context of financial services. Based on interviews, we find that the provider is organised internally by establishing virtual teams. This approach encourages collaboration between various disciplines, such as the emerging technology entity and financial services organisation, and helps to understand digitalisation effects in customer organisations. By working in an agile way, new digital solutions are accelerated by onboarding financial services in a customer organisation.

To support certain type of financial services, ERP systems and digital technologies are integrated that supports an end-to-end business process analysis. We find examples like workplace services and chat bots that are based on an AI engine. The interviews show that the provider opts to use various emerging digital technologies rather than applying a full integration platform, which is also capable to analyse the data. To support financial business services the provider established various data platforms. These platforms are used to support multiple digital technologies by connecting technology suppliers. In doing so, the provider bundles internal and external resources effectively. An example of a data platform framework is illustrated in Fig. 9.1.

One of the interviewees mentioned that "*We use different options to exchange data. One way is to use digital technologies the other is to apply an*

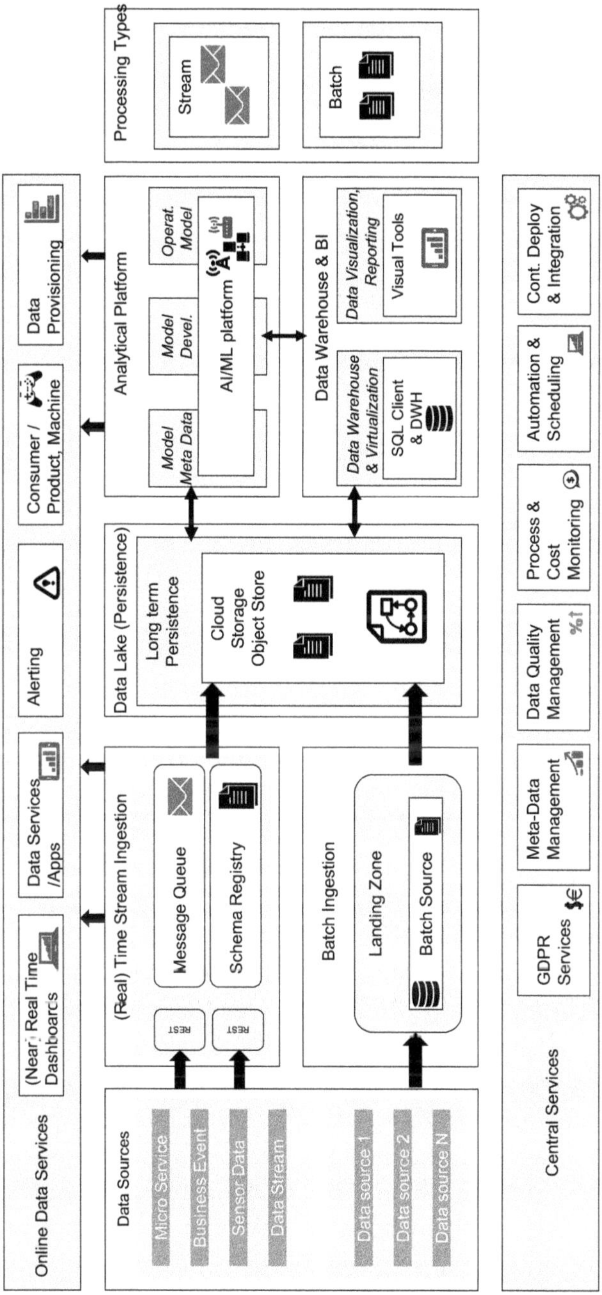

Fig. 9.1 Example data platform framework

API layer. Our API layer platforms support various digital technologies, like RPA bots and process mining tools, but they don't analyse the data, they just act as a middleman to interconnect the tools and technologies and exchange data. The rationale behind this approach is to speed up implementation lead times, which result in reduced operational risks and a smoother transition. We use API layer platforms as an open ecosystem approach, which is commercially termed as an open banking solution for our customers" (Source: Digital solution architect).

9.2.6 Managing Decision Rights

Addressing the relevance of applying digital forms of decision rights, our findings show two perspectives. The first perspective supports the role of digital decision making as part of more common financial business services. To some degree, automation may provide support for digital decision making, specifically in predefined routines. In case rather simple types of decisions have to be made, in which the risks are considered to be low, digital technologies are used in decision making. An example is the use of automated decision making in financial services that corresponds to Know Your Customer (KYC) type of activities. To automate digital decision making with regard to common type of financial services, we find an example in which the provider uses configurable systems. In the context of KYC types of services rule engines are used to configure information systems to automate rather simple type of decisions. Other examples of automated decision making refer to compliance and geographical checks that are required as part of financial transactions.

The second perspective highlights the conscious absence of more complex digital decision making. Interviews revealed that often manual decision making is preferred as governance mechanism. Various digital technologies have a dual option that is, both automated and manual decision-making features. As an example, we did not find that AI is used for automated decision making in a financial services context. Taking financial-related decisions by means of fully automated digitalised decision making, may result in financial risks and compliance issues. The same goes for automated calculations when using AI bots as part of financial services. As customers are still worried about wrong outcomes, the financial services provider decided not to implement digital decision making in the context of complex financial services.

9.3 Analysis

9.3.1 Resource Orchestration Theory

From a resource orchestration theory perspective, we find that senior management decided to apply an internal and external ecosystem approach. On an aggregated level, the internal ecosystem comprises of a delivery arm and sales arm. The delivery arm of the financial services provider exists of multiple delivery centres that are organised at a global level. These product-oriented delivery centres focus on digital technologies and comprise of in-depth knowledge and experience. These centres can be considered as silos as each of them focuses on a specific set of technologies. In addition, the sales arm of the enterprise represents dedicated market teams, such as the financial services sector in which teams interact with their customers directly to ensure that financial services match with agreed contractual agreements. To create alignment between the delivery arm and sales arm, senior management established Centres Of Excellence (COEs) (e.g. data, cloud, digital technologies) that act horizontally across delivery and sales teams. Their main role is to interconnect delivery and sales teams by bundling internal resources. Senior management encourages internal collaboration by sharing knowledge and insights to explore opportunities. As a result, existing financial services may be adjusted, or new type of services initiated. This corresponds to Rai et al. (2012) who argue that knowledge sharing can be seen as a mechanism to overcome uncertainty and as such, enterprises should invest in building knowledge sharing mechanisms to support the exchange of information. These COEs fulfil the role of internal orchestrators as they coordinate the use of internal resources. The COEs are organised as horizontals and the interviews reveal that their employees are highly motivated to work across centres and teams. In doing so, the COEs ensure collaboration between the subject matter experts (SMEs) in the delivery and sales teams, and as such, open up silos instead of breaking them down.

One of the interviewees point out that "*COE topics that are discussed with SMEs focus on customer problem statements, the impact of disruptive technologies on financial services, cost implications, and business benefits. As technologies change rapidly, sometimes we have to educate our customers, such as start small with the use of digital technologies. It's OK to fail in case of innovation projects, and the value of initiating a proof of concept. As a result, customers apply a snowball approach to scale up internally while mitigating business risks*" (Source: Senior Vice President Europe).

In addition, senior management established an external ecosystem approach as their financial services composed of various technical components that are provided by multiple technology partners. Consequently, the financial services provider acts as an orchestrator to coordinate the bundling of internal and external resources. One of the interviewees mentioned that "*A relevant example is our KYC solution that need to be 100% compliant to match regulations. As an example, in case we need multiple tech suppliers, first we define who are the dominant and leading suppliers in their niche. Next, we organise internal labs to build and test the KYC integration platform and corresponding hard and software. Sometimes, we even involve our customers to conduct user acceptance tests. Finally, we initiate a demo to test and validate the solution with our ecosystem partners*" (Source: Director financial services).

The fact that the provider under study uses digital platforms (see KYC example) as a part of their business ecosystem, is consistent with Senyo et al. (2018) who argue that platforms can be considered as a main characteristic of a digital business ecosystem (DBE). Selander et al. (2013) state that a platform "refers to a collection of tools, innovations and services that other DBE partners can use to enhance their performance, create innovations and collaborate" (p. 53). This is consistent with our findings in which digital platforms are used as a foundation for the provider to develop financial services. Interestingly, the provider's ecosystem approach also includes the involvement of their customers as relevant DBE partner (see KYC example). This corresponds to the ecosystem characteristic of openness. Often openness is discussed from a non-digital platform perspective (Eisenman et al., 2006), however, digitality also makes a fundamental difference as 'openness does not merely relate to organisational arrangements like entrance and exit rules but also to openness of technologies such as APIs and software development kits (SDKs) (p. 128)'.

The case study of the financial services provider demonstrates that the external ecosystem of technology suppliers is interwoven with the provider's internal ecosystem and that bundling is used to integrate resources. This corresponds to Edvardsson et al. (2014) concept of institutions that are used to coordinate resource integration. Miller (2014) argues that an institution is "any structure or mechanism of social order and cooperation governing the behaviour of a set of individuals within a given human community" (p. 514). In this case study, we find that the COEs as internal ecosystem orchestrator apply institutions like cultural-cognitive elements (e.g. alignment, knowledge sharing), and normative elements (e.g. platform metrics, measurements). In a similar vein, the provider as a whole acts as an external ecosystem orchestrator towards technology suppliers using institutions like cultural-cognitive elements (e.g. architectural guidelines) and normative elements (e.g. platform specifications) as well.

Our findings on the presence of an internal and external ecosystem approach provide support for the existence of an enterprise ecosystem. Therefore, we argue that the role of institutions can be perceived as critical to specify the rules within the internal and external ecosystem not only to encourage the integration of resources but also to provide enterprise ecosystem stability and meaning.

9.3.2 Boundary Resources

Literature (Eaton et al., 2015; Yoo et al., 2010) demonstrates that the concept of boundary resources is often used in the context of highly distributed arrangements in which independent actors engage in innovations by using opportunities and limitations of digital arrangements. This study shows that the financial services provider established data platforms that are used in distributed arrangements, which bundle internal and external resources. The data platforms consist of information systems that are based on cloud platforms and include additional features, such as data bots and ChatGPT in the AI space. These type of digital innovation arrangements will be both bounded by digital artefacts (Leonardi et al., 2012) and distributed architectures without central control. The latter allows for more complex behaviour by independent actors with emergent side effects. Examples are, challenging existing social categories and control points, by the emergence of new ones (Tilson et al., 2010). More specifically, our findings on data platforms reveal accelerators that include building and deploying frameworks, custom models, and best practices around these technologies. These could thus be conceptualised as boundary resources (cf. Ghazawneh & Henfridsson, 2013) that mediate between the financial services provider (e.g. platform owner) and technical suppliers (e.g. complementors).

One of the interviewees revealed that "*Dealing with proprietary (closed) models is a real challenge as we cannot relate the data to its context. Therefore, there is no meaning to the data and as a result, to its overall use. Furthermore, we noticed that it can take months before we get approval from data owners that may shed some light on the data context*" (Source: Digital solution architect).

Our analysis demonstrates that the introduction of new digital solutions, such as financial driven data platforms, contribute to implementation success of financial business services. Importantly, we find that the complexity to organise financial business services increases as knowledge and skills of subject matter experts is fragmented across the enterprise and external suppliers. We argue that a federated approach may support resource integration tasks in which policies are defined at central level while operational tasks are executed on a decentral level. Boundary resources (e.g. models, architecture blueprints) can be developed at central level to support standardised solutions that can be used at decentral level. One of the interviewees mentioned that "*During the last two years we see data as a product that form a part of common platforms. When using data, we apply a mesh approach as operating model as our main goal is to create scalable solutions. In fact, multiple internal and external data experts contribute to our ecosystem approach. Hence, we use the frame organisation follows the data strategy to underpin that data is the leading factor*" (Source: Delivery manager).

9.4 Conclusion

In this chapter, we studied a financial services provider by focusing on how financial business services are managed and developed by their FSSC. More specifically, we studied the antecedents as described in our research model (see Chap. 4).

The results of the interviews indicate that the provider aim is to develop a business services portfolio in which financial business services are fully digitalised. To achieve this strategic goal financial business processes have been modularised. In doing so, the provider is able to automate all sub-processes steps. From an IS standardisation perspective, we found that the provider's plural sourcing strategy provide opportunities to integrate digital technologies by means of various standardised data platforms. As a result, the provider is able to apply various financial services strategies to their customers, which are affected by their digitalisation appetite and operational risks analysis. Importantly, we found a proactive customer orientation strategy to indicate new customer demands with regard to financial business services. Based on our analysis we found that only routine-based decision rights were digitalised by means of digital technologies. We conclude that the provider's strategy and approach to digitalise their business services portfolio, decreased the implementation effort of business services.

We found that the provider applies an ecosystem approach, in which two orchestrators bundle and integrate both internal and external resources. This approach contributed to decrease business services implementation challenges as information between departments and external suppliers is exchanged by applying collaboration mechanisms. Consequently, financial business services are managed from a holistic view to avoid operational issues. To summarise, we found evidence that the provider, and more specifically the FSSC, paid attention to all antecedents as part of our research model. We conclude that modularised business processes can be seen as an essential antecedent in which they act as a mediator for IS standardisation and customer orientation specifically. The importance of a business services portfolio, modularised business processes and IS standardisation is consistent with the outcomes of our fsQCA analysis. More specifically, modularised business processes were found in three out of seven solutions while once as a core condition. IS standardisation is considered to be an essential condition in four out of seven solutions.

References

Eaton, B. D., Elaluf-Calderwood, S., Sørensen, C., & Yoo, Y. (2015). Distributed tuning of boundary resources: The case of Apple's iOS service system. *MIS Quarterly: Special Issue on Service Innovation in a Digital Age, 39*(1), 217–243.

Edvardsson, B., Kleinaltenkamp, M., Tronvoll, B., McHugh, P., & Windahl, C. (2014). Institutional logics matter when coordinating resource integration. *Marketing Theory, 14*(3), 291–309.

Eisenman, T., Parker, G., & Van Aystyne, M. W. (2006). Strategies for Two-Sided Markets. *Harvard Business Review, 84*(10), 92–101.

Ghazawneh, A., & Henfridsson, O. (2013). Balancing platform control and external contribution in third-party development: The boundary resources model. *Information Systems Journal, 2392)*, 173–192.

Leonardi, P. M., Nardi, B. A., & Kallinikos, J. (Eds.). (2012). *Materiality and organizing*. Oxford University Press.

Miller, S. (2014). Social institutions. In E. Zalta (Ed.), *The Stanford encyclopaedia of philosophy* (pp. 514–518). Stanford University.

Rai, A., Keil, M., Hornyak, R., & Wullenweber, K. (2012). Hybrid relational-contractual governance for business process outsourcing. *Journal of Management Information Systems, 29*(2), 213–256.

Selander, L., Henfridsson, O., & Svahn, F. (2013). Capability search and redeem across digital ecosystems. *Journal of Information Technology, 28*(3), 183–197.

Senyo, P. K., Liu, K., & Effah, J. (2018). A framework for assessing the social impact of interdependencies in digital business ecosystems. In K. Liu, K. Nakata, W. Li, & C. M. C. Baranauskas (Eds.), *Digitalisation, innovation and transformation* (pp. 132–143). Springer.

Tilson, D., Lyytinen, K., & Sørensen, C. (2010). Digital infrastructures: The missing IS research agenda. *Information Systems Research, 21*(5), 748–759.

Yoo, Y., Henfridsson, O., & Lyytinen, K. (2010). Research commentary-The new organizing logic of digital innovation: An agenda for information systems research. *Information Systems Research, 21*(4), 724–735.

10

Cross-Case Analysis

Based on the empirical descriptive results of the four case studies, we relate our findings to the antecedents as described in Chap. 4. Our cross-case analysis comprises of four sections. First, we analyse the antecedents as used in our research model. In addition, we compare the cross-case findings with the outcomes of our fsQCA analysis in Chap. 5. Second, we discuss and show how we use Resource Orchestration Theory (ROT) as a theoretical lens to analyse and explain our findings. Third, we theorise on how enterprises may apply an ecosystem approach to orchestrate the studied antecedents in a coherent manner. Finally, we summarise our findings and provide cross-case study conclusions.

10.1 Analysis of Antecedents

10.1.1 Plural Sourcing Strategy

Our analysis shows that all enterprises under study made a distinction between make and buy decisions, which corresponds with our quantitative findings. As we focus on the impact of digitalisation on financial services, we studied the impact of digital technologies specifically and

A. Plugge, S. Nikou, *Digitalisation of Global Business Services*, Technology, Work and Globalization, https://doi.org/10.1007/978-3-031-51528-6_10

identified three avenues. First, mainstream IT solutions that support financial services are predominantly outsourced to the market, such as IT infrastructure, end-user computing and application maintenance (see the Logistic Service Provider and Employment Agency). These solutions support generic financial services and are applied across enterprise departments. This finding is consistent with literature (Lacity et al., 2017) as enterprises will not be able to achieve competitive advantage when maintaining these solutions in-house.

A second avenue corresponds to a hybrid solution in which platform-oriented application services are outsourced to the market. Examples include functionality like SAP, Salesforce, data analytics, and emerging digital technologies. The management of application functionality, however, is managed by the enterprises in collaboration with service providers (see Construction and Building Company, Financial Service Provider). The main rationale is that various financial services need to be customised to cater for business needs. Hence, this requires specific business insights, knowledge and understanding in order to customise functionality based on ERP and CRM platforms. This avenue corresponds with the findings of Dibbem et al. (2005), which found that the provision of application services requires a large amount of firm-specific human assets. As such, enterprises may distinguish between various options with regard to in-house customisation of functionality and maintenance of outsourced ERP platform services. We find that the decision to provide services in-house or outsourced is affected by the intrinsic motivation of internal and external professionals. For instance, our case studies demonstrate that internal employees were driven to increase the service quality of financial services (see Logistic Service Provider and Employment Agency). Consequently, they support business departments by customising functionality due to their clear perspective on business needs.

The third avenue indicates that digital technologies, which are used as an extension of financial ERP and CRM based applications (e.g. RPA, ML, process mining), are predominantly managed in-house (see all four case studies). Interviewees responded that the rationale to develop and maintain these solutions in-house provide new insights and learnings as experimenting digital technologies contribute to innovate financial services. This finding is consistent with research of Willcocks et al. (2018)

who argued that capabilities required for digital innovations are developed over time, which are in contrast to a transactional or ad-hoc approach.

10.1.2 Orchestration of Business Services Portfolio

Our findings show that the orchestration of business services portfolio as a whole did not change from a financial services perspective. However, the way financial services can be used in practice and accessed by business users changed due to the introduction of digital technologies, such as digitalised business processes, financial services functionality, AI, Robots, and digital portals. The business services portfolio can be considered as an essential antecedent as it acts as a bridging role (boundary spanner) between in-house and outsourced financial services and IT services. When providing business users access through a digitalised business services portfolio, knowledge sharing is perceived to be an important aspect to exchange information of financial services (Jin et al., 2014; Madsen et al., 2015). We find that the role of business services portfolio as boundary spanner is directly related to knowledge transfer in the interplay between in-house and outsourced financial services, which supports communication and trust between an enterprise and its service providers. This approach contributes to a more homogeneous plural sourcing strategy (Wareham et al., 2014).

10.1.3 Modularised Business Processes

Our analysis demonstrates that modularised business processes form an essential antecedent and influencing factor in providing global business services. This finding is consistent with our empirical (quantitative) findings in our study as business processes act as both a mediator and moderator between antecedents and the business services portfolio. All case studies show that business processes are intertwined with financial business services, which means that if business services are adapted due to changing business needs, business processes have to be adjusted as well.

The digitalisation of financial business processes, however, increases the optimalisation of sub-processes. Interestingly, digital modularised business processes (e.g. RPA, ML, AI) contribute to process optimalisation purposes as interdependencies between sub-processes can be coordinated more easily. Based on our analysis, we argue that the digitalisation of business processes contributes to the decomposition of enterprises with a focus on global business services, which operationalise the findings of previous research (Menor & Roth, 2007).

Addressing the importance of business process maturity, our findings can be related to the study of Ulbrich (2012) who identified three categories, namely (1) low process standardisation, (2) balanced process standardisation, and (3) excessive process standardisation. Our analysis shows that the Construction and Building Company is in its early stage of improving financial business process which corresponds to the first category. The Logistic Service Provider on the other hand focuses on the second category by standardising and automating process steps as much as possible. The Employment Agency and Financial Services Provider, however, are in the process of optimising modularised business processes that fits the third category. The latter can be explained by the enterprises digital transformation journey in which optimised processes are a prerequisite to achieve their journey.

As business processes span various organisational entities, digitalisation supports the implementation of GBS functionality as process interdependencies can be automated more easily. This accelerates the GBS implementation acceptance by business users. As such, it is suggested that senior management defines a clear strategy on the decomposition of an enterprise to further reduce organisational and process complexity. Consequently, attention is needed to optimise business process continuously.

10.1.4 Customer Orientation

The interview findings provide evidence that FSSC employees align customer needs with business representatives, although the intensity varies amongst the case studies. At the Logistic Service Provider, for instance,

FSSC and business departments continuously discuss business needs to explore if existing financial services need to be adapted. On the other hand, the Employment Agency also touches upon business requirements, but with less frequency. The Construction and Building Company, however, demands some form of management from the customer perspective in order to align their needs. The Financial Services Provider applies an agile approach in which the COE discusses business needs continuously. As a similarity, all case studies demonstrate that digital technologies are proactively discussed between FSSC and business departments.

We find that knowledge sharing between FSSC, and business departments is an important and yet a vital component in applying customer orientation, which is consistent with literature (Wang & Hou, 2015; Zhang, 2018). More precisely, we find that the FSSCs and COE under study proactively share insights with business departments regarding digital technologies aiming at improving the quality of service by decreasing manual tasks of the employees. By conducting Proofs of Concepts and organising mutual events, business departments create new insights in how digital technologies may improve their daily routines. Hence, knowledge sharing between FSSC, and business departments can be seen as a mechanism to overcome uncertainty. To actualise financial services on a regular basis, it is vital to verify if the required quality of business services (e.g. service levels) still fits with the provided business services functionality (Buell et al., 2016). Therefore, we suggest that organisations invest in building knowledge sharing mechanisms to support the exchange of information. By monitoring customer demands and sensing business changes actively, enterprises are able to improve their own value-generating process.

10.1.5 IS Standardisation

We find evidence that all enterprises focus on reducing routine type of work and simplify business processes by means of IS standardisation. For instance, the Employment Agency standardised their information systems first as a mean to standardise their financial business processes. More specifically, by standardising interfaces between information systems, the

IT department is able to modularise production systems, which reflects the work of Sturgeon (2002).

An essential driver to standardise IS interfaces is the use of data. This is shown in the case of the Employment Agency and the Financial Services Provider as they streamline data flows and visualise data through dashboarding. As a result, they create insight into business operations while increasing their responsiveness and decision making. Importantly, we find that the Logistic Service Provider and Construction and Building Company struggled to establish a data-oriented framework that supports the use of digital technologies such as RPA, ML and AI. Taking legal and regulatory agreements into account, data-oriented frameworks must provide insights demonstrating how data can be exchanged between in-house and outsourced data sources. This reflects the findings of Lee (2020) who also addressed the importance of these frameworks in financial services.

Importantly, enterprises that lack clear data policies may face difficulties with regard to the completeness and correctness of data that may hinder the reliability of AI driven outcomes. Meyer et al. (2015) argued that a data model-driven approach is a necessity condition to automate business processes to support data exchange within and across enterprises. In this regard, the use of data principles like Findable, Accessible, Interoperable and Re-usable (FAIR) are essential in applying digital technologies effectively (Van der Aalst et al., 2017). We find that the Financial Services Provider apply these principles to optimise the use of their data platform that supports their customers' financial services.

Information Systems that are based on the interoperability principle may re-use existing services and assemble them into new business services, which is key to enterprise integration. As such, enterprises are able to decrease the degree of business services complexity, while business services can be more easily adjusted to respond to endogenous developments. We suggest that standardised information systems and clear data policies provide flexibility to support financial business processes and the adaptation of modular business services (Fremantle et al., 2002). As a result, enterprises are better able to apply digital technologies (e.g. ML, AI, process mining) that are supported both in-house and outsourced.

10.1.6 Managing Decision Rights

Our analysis shows that predictive type of decisions has been digitalised as demonstrated in the Logistic Service Provider and Employment Agency of the case studies. Essentially, more routine-based and uniformed process steps can be robotised easily by means of RPA and ML technologies. The example of the Employment Agency study shows that decision rights as part of developed planning tool based on an AI solution can be automated. The case study of the Financial Services Providers shows an example of automated decision making that corresponds to customers Know Your Customer (KYC) type of activities. The case studies did not show examples in which more complex financial decision making is conducted by digital technologies, such as AI. The Financial Services Provider explicitly argues that automated digitalised decision making, such as automated calculations when using AI bots, may result in financial risks and compliance issues in the financial sector. This is consistent with research of Miller (2018) and Duan et al. (2020) in which the authors stated that AI predominantly has been studied from an augmentation perspective, arguing that AI should support humans in decision making. However, when automated decisions rely on low quality, missing or inconsistent data, enterprises are challenged by successfully integrating data. This may result, however, in biased or incorrect decision making. This was found in the Employment Agency study in which AI is not "trusted" when it comes to ethical concerns and profiling. This can be explained by recent studies which show that data-driven decision making relay on the development of predictive models, which are at the core of automated decision-making systems (Brynjolfsson & McElheran, 2016). To overcome data challenges and utilise decision-making opportunities, enterprises are increasingly developing advanced data governance (Ladley, 2020) capabilities as found in all case studies. We suggest that enterprises need to develop policies and frameworks in which data, processes and digital technologies are promoted to control data and as such, enable trusted information sharing within an enterprise.

Summary

Comparing the cross-case analysis with our fsQCA analysis (see Chap. 5), in which we included the size on an enterprise, we found seven solutions. Importantly, all solutions include one of more antecedents in which modularised business processes was found to be a core condition (twice). This is consistent with the findings of the cross-case analysis, which provided evidence that modularised business processes are essential in supporting an enterprise business services portfolio. Although the portfolio as a whole did not change, individual business services did change due to the rise of digital technologies. This finding acknowledges the importance of the orchestration of a business services portfolio and its effect on implementing GBSs. The cross-case analysis demonstrates the importance of the studied antecedents in the context of digitalisation of business services specifically. We found that all antecedents were found to be important, namely: plural sourcing strategy, customer orientation, modularised business processes, managing decision rights, and IS standardisation. We argue that the antecedents under study can be perceived as essential when orchestrating a business services portfolio. Both the qualitative research, the fsQCA analysis, and cross-case analysis support this claim.

10.2 Resource Orchestration Theory

We operationalise Sirmon et al.'s (2011) resource orchestration framework and followed the resource management elements that include structuring, bundling, leveraging processes. We also took asset management elements into account that comprise of search/selection, configuration/deployment processes. Next, the antecedents as analysed in the case studies are mapped to the resource orchestration framework elements. In doing so, we aim to identify how enterprises deal with resource management and asset orchestration tasks in the context of financial global business services.

10.2.1 Resource Management

Structuring Process

The first element of Sirmon et al. (2011) framework corresponds to the structuring of resources that includes the sub-elements acquiring and accumulation resources. These sub-elements predominantly refer to the plural sourcing strategy of an enterprise. At strategic level an enterprise has to make a decision as to what type of resources are needed to be applied and were to attract them. This analysis corresponds to the make and buy decision of an enterprise, for instance, what type of external resources need to be acquired and accumulated. Our analysis demonstrates that enterprise management explicitly develop and implement a plural sourcing strategy with the aim to create and capture value. Managers proactively acquired external resources (e.g. financial and IT services) from the market by structuring them with internal resources while developing new ones. This corresponds to the findings of Carnes et al. (2017) who argued, that in the process of acquiring external resources, firms also eliminate inefficient ones. Our case studies reveal that a balanced mix is created that comprise of value-adding resources both in-house and acquired from the market (i.e. outsourced). Research of Thomke and Kuemmerle (2002) showed that developing resources internally and acquiring external resources are important actions that are independent of an enterprise degree of maturity in orchestrating resources.

Bundling Process

Our observations demonstrate that incremental improvements were made to existing capabilities, such as modelling financial business processes by means of digital technologies (e.g. Logistic Service Provider, Employment Agency, Financial Services Provider). This refers to stabilising activities as a part of bundling resources. We found that current capabilities were enriched by using state-of-the-art digital technologies. An example corresponds to Employment Agency managers that focus on optimising business process by using process mining tools and the Financial Services Provider managers tasks on digitalising their customer's onboarding process. As a result, financial process became more efficient as unnecessary and unvaluable process steps were eliminated. Our interview analysis acknowledges that all enterprises investigated the use and value of latest digital technologies with the aim to understand their value and contribution. This relates to the pioneering sub-element of bundling resources specifically. For instance, Sirmon et al. (2011) argued that pioneering contributes to create new capabilities, which is consistent with our findings. Importantly, the bundling of related activities (e.g. stabilising, enriching and pioneering) all corresponds to an enterprise's business services portfolio in which digital technologies play an essential role. Hence, the stimulation of business and digital innovations strengthens an enterprise business services portfolio. Our findings operationalise the previous findings of Makri et al. (2010) in which the authors underpin the relevance of the mutual influence between a firm's resource portfolio and degree of innovation.

The results of our research go beyond the findings of Sako et al. (2016), who applied a transaction cost lens and found that the design of a service provider portfolio affects an enterprise plural sourcing strategy. We built on this finding by addressing enterprises' orchestration activities towards their business services portfolio, which include the provisioning of both internal and external business services by making use of the ROT framework. Therefore, we argue that a business services portfolio orchestrates the production of in-house and outsourced business services.

Leveraging Process

Based on our analysis, the mobilisation and coordination of resources are crucially influenced by the actions of managers who strategically leverage them to achieve organisational objectives. In particular, we found various examples in which managers mobilised both internal and external resources. For instance, FSSC (Logistic Service Provider case) and COE (Financial Services Provider case) managers proactively aligned their processes with business managers and IT department managers to explore business improvements by means of digital technologies. By mobilising resources, they discussed the way business processes and information systems can be standardised to further improve the effectiveness of financial business services. When creating alignment on the use and applicability of digital technologies, managers were able to foster integration across the enterprise. Addressing the aspect of coordination, we found that managers paid attention how to integrate certain activities and resources in the domain of business processes. By splitting up business process into smaller process steps, corresponding information systems were identified to integrate and automate these steps.

This is consistent with the findings of Grøgaard et al. (2022) who find that firms that integrate certain activities and resources are better able to free up resources that were used for non-value creating activities. We found that agreements were made about who will be responsible to coordinate these activities, which refer to the antecedent managing decision rights. In particular, all case studies illustrated that organisational teams were identified and selected regarding the deployment of digital technologies and information systems. When analysing these findings, we noticed that information systems, business processes and managing decision rights all apply to the leveraging process as described by Sirmon et al. (2011). Our analysis demonstrated the interdependencies between IS standardisation and managing decision rights to business processes, which in turn affect an enterprise business services portfolio.

10.2.2 Asset Management Process

Search/Selection Process

Helfat et al. (2007) argued that managers' goal of the search/selection process is to identify assets, make investments, and design organisational and governance structures for the enterprise. In this study, identifying assets and making investments corresponds to our findings on customer orientation in which enterprise management explores if and to what degree existing financial services need to be adapted and remain fit for purpose. Examples of the Logistic Service Provider and Employment Agency on customer orientation corresponds to the concept of sensing, which is an enterprise ability to detect changes in the direct (internal organisation) and indirect (external service providers) environment. By reaching out to representatives of internal and external departments, insights can be collected to verify if the current plural sourcing strategy still fits to support end users and customers. If required, the enterprises should be able to make a decision to adjust the plural sourcing strategy and create a new resource mix that exists of internal and external resources. Our analysis supports the findings of Teece and Leith (2016) who argued that an early detection of internal and external changes allows an enterprise for more time to prepare and reactive on changes. An example could be seen in the case study of the Financial Services Provider as they explore and align new digital technologies that are provided by multiple technology suppliers. Based on our analysis, we found evidence that managing decision rights and organisational structures are perceived to be essential in developing a plural sourcing strategy and making investments to attract external resources.

We found evidence that the enterprises also grasp opportunities as they arise, which corresponds to seizing. Although seizing is perceived to be complex specifically in large organisations (Haarhuis & Liening, 2020), we found various examples in which the enterprises under study were able to apply an agile business model to restructure their resource mix of internal and external resources. For instance, the intensive collaboration between the FSSC and IT departments of the Logistics Service Provider, Employment Agency and Financial Services Provider shows a sense and seize process to adjust financial services when necessary. When relevant digital technology opportunities were identified the FSSC and IT department explored how financial business processes could be digitalised (e.g. ML and process mining). Importantly, we found that the search/selection process affects the resource management element of the structuring process. This fit demonstrates the dependency between both processes as identified in literature (Sirmon et al., 2011). Enterprises that acknowledge and embrace this fit are more able to realise their potential to attract internal and external resources as part of their plural sourcing strategy, and thus to facilitate the creation of competitive advantages.

Configuration/Deployment Process

The configuration/deployment process as argued by Helfat et al. (2007) requires the coordination of cospecialised assets, providing a vision for those assets, and nurturing innovation. The coordination of cospecialised assets refer to the roles of both the FSSC and IT department as found in our case studies. More specifically, acquiring new digital technologies is predominantly initiated by the FSSCs, while the integration of those technologies with existing information systems was handled by their respective IT department. We found that the FSSCs under study focus on developing a vision in how digital technologies may improve or optimise existing financial business processes. Multiple examples were found that corresponds to RPA, ML, and process mining in particular. Research of Teece (1986) shows that complementary assets are costly to acquire. Consequently, Ceccagnoli and Jiang (2012) argue that "innovative type of firms is more likely to avoid duplicating these assets and ally with incumbents that already possess these assets" (p. 406). Our study shows that the FSSCs in cooperation with their IT departments decide on the make and buy decision (plural sourcing) to determine who should provide those assets. In doing so, they create oversight and avoid the duplication of assets and costs. Importantly, the specialised knowledge that is generated by the FSSCs and IT departments during the exploration and deployment of digital technologies can be considered as cospecialised assets. This type of knowledge is typically developed over time (path dependency) and difficult to acquire in the market.

A relevant example corresponds to the Financial Services Provider case study, who implemented digital technologies as part of financial kiosks in their customers' branch offices. As a result, the customer was better able to support financial customer services while the customer's business services portfolio was extended due to innovations. This example shows that sensing changing environments (e.g. digital technology opportunities), which is part of the search/deployment process, provide input for the configuration and deployment process as digital technologies were seized. In turn, the configuration/deployment process affects the bundling and leveraging process identified by Sirmon et al. (2011) as the enterprises' business portfolio was enriched. In a similar vein, the enterprises experienced the value of new digital technologies that corresponds to the pioneering sub-element of bundling resources specifically.

Summary

With regard to resource management, our study provides insights in to how these antecedents act as a system of complements, which are consistent with our quantitative findings. The findings go beyond the research of Rai et al. (2012) as we demonstrated how IS standardisation and digital technologies, managing decision rights, and modularised business processes affect the concentration and orchestration of a business services portfolio. Addressing asset management, we provided insights in an enterprise transformation approach that is based on sensing and seizing to identify changes that may affect the antecedents in scope. Enterprise management is able to integrate, build and reconfigure internal and external capabilities to cater for business services portfolio changes. Based on the findings of the case studies we created insights in how digitalisation affects the implementation of global business services. Importantly, we found evidence that the enterprises' used an ecosystem approach to orchestrate the antecedents in scope. Therefore, we explore the effects of applying an ecosystem approach to orchestrate an enterprise GBSs in more detail.

10.3 An Enterprise Ecosystem Approach

Today enterprises still struggle how to organise their firm taking the orchestration of a continuous changing resource mix (make and buy) into account. The fact that digital technologies are perceived to be an accelerator of change urges enterprises to pay attention to organisational and collaborative issues. Garten (2002) argued in his bestseller business book "How to organise a company for global operations?" that "internationally experienced business leaders experiment for no one has the right formula", (p. 91). This challenge continues as change within the context of global operating enterprises is here to stay. From a historical perspective, research into the organisation of multinational corporations has been productive, with the development of the integration-responsiveness framework inspiring further exploration into organisational design that was initiated by Prahalad (1975). Although this framework focuses on two distinctive sets of environmental forces (e.g. global and local), the challenging topic is how to integrate and coordinate resources both in-house and outsourced. Many attempts have been made to extend the integration-responsiveness framework to conceptualise the organisational fit of enterprises. Based on the analyses of the case studies, we found that the transactional type of fit still seems to be the more popular organisational form. Benito et al. (2014) argued that the loosely coupled structure of enterprises is based on resource dependency logic where enterprise departments are seen as rather autonomous. Each department has its own network based on strategic decision making. Hence, there is no formal orchestration unit or department that coordinates in-house and outsourced resources. Porter's (1985) value chain model on the other hand, addresses the importance of achieving efficiencies by creating synergies when optimising similar business processes. A central unit or department will perform orchestration activities mainly driven by the logic of cost and value creation. However, the development of a globally siloed organisational structure hinders the implementation of financial services specifically as financial business services requirements and implementations have to be discussed with multiple departments. As such, the traditional organisational forms create various negative effects like extended service lead times, internal disputes about allocating resources, and financial services underperformance.

The enterprises under study are organised in various departments in which they focus on key areas such as, business, FSSC, and IT. This silo-based approach is typical for enterprises as their organisational structure facilitates specialisation, and as a result contributes to value creation. In addition, organisational boundaries are helpful to create focus for each department and avoid internal competition between departments. We argue that traditional approaches, such as the integration-responsiveness framework and value chain model seem to be ripe for change as enterprises need to be more agile to cater for changing circumstances. Implementing financial business services that are supported by digital technologies affect various enterprise departments, thus addressing the aspect of end-to-end business processes. Hence, horizontal collaboration is supposed to be the predominant mechanism. A study conducted by Casciaro et al. (2019) show that colleagues who can reach outside their silo and find complementary knowledge and expertise, lean more and gain skills faster. As such, horizontal collaboration is widely recognised. Consequently, breaking down existing silos virtually is a prerequisite to implement business services effectively and foster innovation. Our analysis shows that enterprises that apply a plural sourcing strategy within a continuous changing environment need some type of coordination unit to orchestrate internal and external resources. Our study reveals two type of coordination units, that we term as the "*business services orchestrator*" and the "*technology orchestrator*".

First, the FSSC, and COE in case of the Financial Services Provider, specifically orchestrates the relationship between both business departments in exploring and improving financial services and the IT department in aligning digital technology solutions. We use the term "*business services orchestrator*" as they focus on financial business services specifically. These orchestration activities comprise of creating digital awareness, exploring how digital technologies may improve financial business processes, and decision making on when to adjust the business service portfolio regularly.

Figure 10.1 shows an example of the relationship between the FSSC and business. In the example of purchasing orders, the FSSC acts as a business services orchestrator while processing process steps. Some process steps require alignment with representatives of business units to complete purchase tasks. The bold arrows show a direct relationship between FSSC and business unit representatives that are based on reciprocity. The dotted lines illustrate an indirect relationship in which the orchestrator exchange information towards business units.

The IT department on the other hand, focus on the integration of technology resources or in other words, various digital solutions and consequently, acts as a "*technology orchestrator*". The technology orchestrator integrates various existing and new technologies, such as applications,

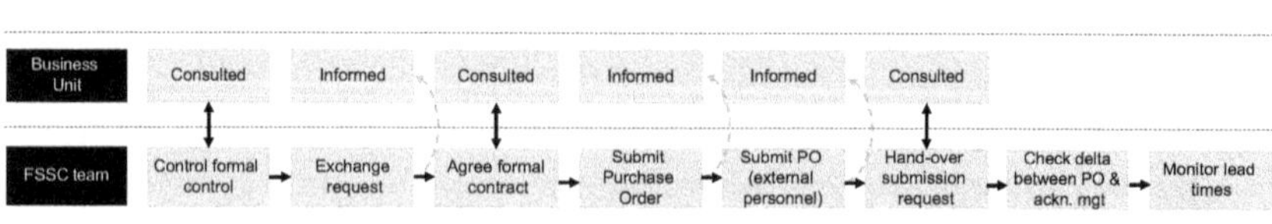

Fig. 10.1 FSSC as business services orchestrator

integration platforms, RPA and ML solutions and process mining solutions, which are provided through in-house and outsourced resources.

Figure 10.2 illustrates the role of the IT department as technology orchestrator when integrating technology related tasks. In this example, the IT department aligns technology related tasks with the FSSC. The bold arrows show a direct relationship between representatives, which are based on reciprocity, to enrich databased business information. The dotted lines illustrate an indirect relationship in which the orchestrator only exchanges information to FSSC representatives.

Both orchestrators are organised separately, however, they intensively coordinate their activities to provide a coherent solution for customers and internal business employees. To support financial business services that spans across departments, the orchestrators did not change the organisational structure and position as this is a risky and time-consuming process. Rather the orchestrators decided to build horizontal mechanisms to exchange information. In doing so, they act as boundary spanners to overcome silo-based thinking.

More specifically, ROT underpins the importance of managers to bundle, structure and leverage resources. In our case studies, FSSC and IT managers initiated horizontal mechanisms, such as joint collaboration meetings and agile PI events across organisational boundaries. We also found that horizontal mechanisms are also supported on an operational level. Subject matter experts, like engineers, business analysts, and RPA developers share their knowledge proactively across departments when exploring new digital technologies. In this regards, Teece (2007) argued that when managerial hierarchies exist, the quality of information that is exchanged between managers commonly decays. Our findings provide evidence that the quality of information; for instance, the applicability of

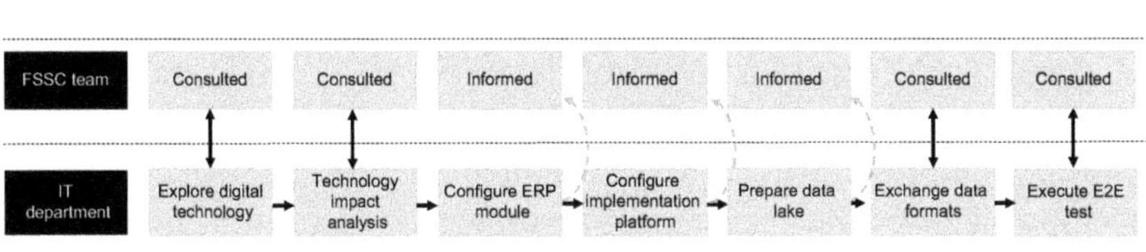

Fig. 10.2 IT department as technology orchestrator

digital technologies, can be improved due to the exchange of knowledge and expertise of involved subject matter experts across departments. As such, information is effectively, and regularly exchanged in agile sprint meetings and impact analyses sessions on financial business processes and digital technologies.

From an organisational perspective, our findings provide support for the coalitional organisational model as described in Chap. 2. The coalitional model corresponds to a market-like partnership where departments are bounded together in a loosely coupled system. Based on the case studies, we found that related tasks and activities in the enterprise system are not directly interdependent and often comprise of specific expertise. The enterprises loosely coupled system model builds on the resource dependency logic where enterprise departments are seen as rather autonomous. Importantly, the ties between departments have become stronger as each of them is aware of dependencies in the enterprise ecosystem. This was found, for instance, in the close alignment between subject matter experts of business, FSSC and IT departments in discussing, exploring, and implementing digital technologies to further improve financial business processes.

Our analysis illustrates four dominant enterprise ecosystem characteristics. First, we found the absence of a formal central actor who orchestrates the enterprise ecosystem as a whole. As a result of an existing power equilibrium the "*business services orchestrator*" and "*technology orchestrator*" filled this gap by orchestrating tasks across departments from a social view. By means of building symbiotic relationships, exploring digital technologies while sharing insights, orchestration took place in practice. Second, the "*business services orchestrator*" and "*technology orchestrator*" showed a collective intension by determining common goals that are supported by all involved organisational departments. This was found to be a necessity to achieve business and technology-driven objectives which is consistent with ecosystem literature (Jacobides et al., 2018; Senyo et al., 2019; Trischler et al., 2020). Third, during an orchestrator's integration resource task, they are likely to learn something new that makes the next iteration slightly different in adapting to a changed context, making the ecosystem self-adjusting and self-organising. This is shown as a part of FSSC's management to develop roadmaps in order to plan data and digital initiatives together with the business and IT departments (e.g. Logistic Service Provider, Employment Agency). Fourth, each department (e.g. Business, FSSC, IT) focuses on a specialisation that ultimately contributes to creating and capturing enterprise value. In doing so, the loosely coupled structure of each department can be seen as a complementor within the enterprise value network.

These four enterprise ecosystem characteristics portray Guggenberger et al. (2020) ecosystem type of a "symbiotic collective ecosystem". The authors described this type of ecosystem as "closed communities focussing on symbiotic relationships to evolve their individual specialisations" (p. 9). When applying an ecological view, the interdependencies between various enterprise departments (e.g. business, FSSC, IT) as shown by their strong social ties, corresponds to the concept of symbiosis. Khanangha et al. (2020) argued that symbiosis is a purely mutualistic approach, in which enterprises provide complementary value by focusing on distinct but nonoverlapping value (symbiosis) between departments. The findings of our research suggest that the benefits of applying a mutualistic approach by the orchestrators (*business services orchestrator* and *technology orchestrator*) contributes to the value an enterprise ecosystem generates. The orchestrators strategy to assure that their relationships between various departments will be one of symbiotic mutualism which safeguards the enterprise ecosystem from closing down silos and thus create internal competition.

10.4 Theoretical Implications

Our case studies findings contribute to the existing literature in several ways. First, we use resource orchestration theory (Sirmon et al., 2007, 2011) as a theoretical lens to study financial services in a plural sourcing context. Our findings of a business services orchestrator and technology orchestrator are congruent with the role of a keystone player or sponsor (Trischler et al., 2020) in a business-oriented ecosystem. Our analysis identified four ecosystem characteristics that underpin the relevance of an enterprise ecosystem. Based on our in-depth findings we suggest that enterprises, which provide services in a plural sourcing context, need to act as an ecosystem to cater for changing circumstances. Consequently, enterprises should apply a systemic approach when organising business services as endogenous and exogenous actors are mutually dependent and as such, affect each other.

Our findings go beyond the ecosystem insights of Fayoumi (2016) who developed a conceptual model of an ecosystem-inspired enterprise in the context of manufacturing enterprises. We empirically demonstrated that enterprises could organise and build an enterprise that is capable to cater for changes and as such, is configurable and adaptive. Consequently, our analysis demonstrates that the various antecedents in scope must be orchestrated as a whole to ensure coherence in case of changing business portfolio needs. This corresponds to the relevance of applying a systemic approach. Therefore, we argue that enterprises need to apply an orchestration lens to manage and coordinate antecedent dependencies in a coherent manner in order to adapt adequately. Recent research (Kristoffersen et al., 2021) indicates similar findings in the context of circular economy in which firms changes from coordinating bilateral relationships between antecedents towards orchestrating antecedents as a whole. Importantly, the antecedents in our study can be perceived as part of an enterprise dynamic capability. Teece et al. (1997) argued that enterprises require dynamic resources to manage and organise both content and processes to achieve sustainability.

This dynamic capability is needed to implement and sustain a business services portfolio in the context of a plural sourcing strategy. We build on the findings of Kristoffersen et al. (2021) and provide evidence that enterprises who coherently orchestrate the antecedents in scope are able to establish a dynamic capability. Our analysis shows how dynamic changes in a distributed sociotechnical system, such as financial services enabled by digital technologies, can be orchestrated effectively.

Second, we found that enterprises that apply an ecosystem strategy based on symbiotic mutualism are better capable to create and capture value creation. When bundling nonoverlapping expertise, an enterprise ecosystem is built on collaboration rather than competition, which is a valuable strategy to overcome silo-based barriers. Silos are not as much a technological phenomenon as they are a cultural phenomenon. Casciaro et al. (2019) studied the phenomenon of cross-silo leadership and found that cultural brokers promote cross-boundary work. The authors made a distinction between the role of a cultural broker as bridge (knowledge exchange) or aversive (build mutual relationships). In contrast to Casciaro et al. (2019) our study suggests that the two orchestrators act both as bridge (i.e. boundary spanner) and aversive as they mutually share and develop knowledge with other departments while strengthen the mutual relationships. In doing so, the orchestrators contribute to an effective synthesis of orchestrating internal as well as external resources.

Research of Serrat (2010) shows that silos are often used as a metaphor to describe organisations "that lack the desire or motivation to coordinate (at worst, even communicate) with other entities in the same organisation, p1–2". Our case studies, however, shows that the business services orchestrator and technology orchestrator act as intrapreneurs bridging the gap across silos to foster business services innovations by exploring digital technologies. Gulati (2007) state that within traditional silo's "collaboration is not rewarded—whether internally among employees of different silos, or externally with customers, suppliers, and partners, p 32". Based on our analysis we argue that collaboration between various departments (silos) must be rewarded as future business services are enabled by digital technologies, which change over time. An essential mechanism is the exchange of knowledge between departments that avoid an "'us versus them' mindset" and ultimately contribute to business services performance.

Third, our analysis sheds new lights on the exchange of information between departments as the case studies demonstrate that orchestration take place on a horizontal level (breadth) as well as vertical level (depth). Hence, the structuring, bundling, and leveraging of subprocesses of resource orchestration differ by managerial level and across organisational departments. Our analysis reveals that the use of digital technologies can be seen as an accelerator to intensify the orchestration of business services portfolio. The complexity of digital technologies and corresponding degree of uncertainty of business and technological effects urges departments to mitigate business and operational risks. This is consistent with research of Kotlarsky et al. (2020) in which the authors found that to manage uncertainties and unanticipated obligations in the provisioning and reliability of business services orchestration is a prerequisite to encourage desirable behaviour in the use of resources.

Our findings are in contrast with previous research of Sirmon et al. (2008) and Holcomb et al. (2009) in which the authors argued that resource orchestration-related research focus on top-level managers that support the exchange of information on a vertical level (depth). The findings of previous research studies can be explained by the organisational strategies that were derived from rational models in which tasks were organised in dedicated subunits (e.g. highly specialised) (Astley & Zajac, 1991). However, our research shows that also subject matter experts exchange information between departments (horizontal level) as part of resource orchestration tasks. We argue that since resource orchestration varies in breadth and depth it can be considered as a multi-level concept spanning various organisational teams.

10.5 Practical Implications

Our research contributes to practitioners and specifically enterprises' management. Our results suggest that leadership must manage the interplay between a plural sourcing strategy, business services portfolio, modularised business processes, IS standardisation, managing decision rights and commercial orientation effectively and simultaneously. We postulate that an enterprise's executive management should pay a close attention to identify and uncover interdependencies across the discussed antecedents. On a practical level, managers must invest in building an orchestration capability to structure, bundle, and leverage internal and external resources to support their business services portfolio. The rationale to establish an orchestration capability is threefold.

First, we may assume that an enterprise business services portfolio will change regularly as a result of plural sourcing strategy changes. As a result, this requires intensive coordination as interdependencies between the antecedents will cause effects. The orchestration capability has to fulfil these coordination tasks to ensure coherence between the antecedents. Second, as change is constant, enterprise management has to develop a transformation approach to structure, bundle, and leverage internal and external resources. Such a transformation approach is based on sensing and seizing to identify changes that may affect antecedents and next, act immediately. In doing so, enterprise management is able to integrate, build and reconfigure internal and external capabilities to cater for rapidly changing environments (Teece et al., 1997).

Third, we suggest organising an internal entity that becomes responsible to orchestrate internal and external resources. This "orchestration hub" needs to identify changes as a result of a dynamic plural sourcing strategy, adapt modularised business processes, allocate enabling digital technologies and so forth. Such an "orchestration hub" requires skilled personnel, adequate tooling, and a transformation mindset as alignment between departments and external parties is essential. In turn, this requires an intensive exchange of knowledge between management and subject matter experts. In other words, an "orchestration hub" is a Centre of Excellence (COE) that has the mandate to interact continuously between departments and external partners and as such, become a dynamic resource. The "orchestration hub" should have the mandate to attract dissimilar service providers and gain various types of external resources, which in turn will contribute to value co-creation by means of information exchange and shared knowledge. The "orchestration hub" must safeguard enterprise ecosystems characteristics, ensures that loosely coupled departments comply to common goals, and apply reciprocal behaviour. As a result, these agreements contribute to the robustness of an enterprise ecosystem. To support an "orchestration hub", enterprise management must define their exact role and boundaries, as otherwise the demarcation between an enterprise ecosystem and their role in an external ecosystem will become obscured. In practice, the role and position of an "orchestration hub" may vary taking various factors into account, like the width and depth of an enterprise business services portfolio, degree of plural sourcing strategy, geographical range, to name a few.

10.6 Conclusions

This section addresses the objective 4: *Demonstrate how digitalisation may overcome business services implementation barriers.*

Based on the analysis of four case studies in the context of financial services, we argue that not only digital technologies will act as an accelerator to overcome organisational boundary challenges (e.g. silo-based structures), but also it requires interdisciplinary skills and knowledge to implement and utilise digital business services effectively. In fact, exploring and implementing digital technologies that enable financial business services caused a disruption that triggered a strategic response. We found that both the FSSC (*business services orchestrator*) and IT department (*technology orchestrator*) apply an enterprise ecosystem strategy to orchestrate activities across organisational boundaries of departments. The orchestrators are supported by four dominant enterprise ecosystem characteristics, which acknowledge the strategic importance of ecosystem thinking. We argue that applying an enterprise ecosystem approach can be considered as a paradigm shift compared to a traditional hierarchal way of organising GBS activities. A traditional silo-based approach neglects horizontal mechanisms to exchange information which result in GBS implementation issues. Our findings demonstrate that by applying an ecosystem approach, enterprises are able to overcome traditional GBS implementation challenges.

The overall results show that the core aim of enterprises is to capture sustainable value from perceived value-creating advantages (e.g. Pitelis & Teece, 2009). The orchestration of a global business services portfolio, which is affected by various antecedents, implicates more than the strategic decision to implement a plural sourcing strategy. In fact, it requires an orchestration capability that focuses on the enterprise ecosystem as a whole rather than on the individual relationships between antecedents and the business service portfolio. Pioneering bundling resources, derive from exploratory learning that represent an avenue through which managers are able to create a new orchestration capability by integrating existing and/or new resources that were previously unrelated (Ahuja & Morris Lampert, 2011). By establishing an "orchestration hub", enterprises are able to structure, bundle, and leverage in-house and outsourced resources that are valuable, rare, imitable, and non-substitutable. Resources that satisfy these criteria become "strategic resources", which help enterprises to outperform their rivals. Therefore, we conclude that enterprises develop and implement an enterprise ecosystem strategy encompassing a multi-perspective approach that contributes to achieve competitive advantage.

References

Ahuja, G., & Morris Lampert, C. (2011). Entrepreneurship in the large corporation: A longitudinal study of how established firms create breakthrough inventions. *Strategic Management Journal, 22*(6–7), 521–543.

Astley, W. G., & Zajac, E. J. (1991). Intraorganizational power and organizational design: Reconciling rational and coalitional models of organization. *Organization Science, 2*(4), 399–411.

Benito, G. R. G., Lunnan, R., & Tomassen, S. (2014). The virtue of in-between pragmatism—A balancing act between responsiveness and integration in a multinational company. *Orchestration of the Global Network Organization Advances in International Management, 27*, 75–97.

Brynjolfsson, E., & McElheran, C. (2016). The rapid adoption of data-driven decision-making. *American Economic Review, 106*(5), 133–139.

Buell, R. W., Campbell, D., & Frei, F. X. (2016). How do customers respond to increased serve quality competition? *Manufacturing & Service Operations Management, 18*(4), 585–607.

Carnes, C. M., Chirico, F., Hitt, M. A., Huh, D. W., & Pisano, V. (2017). Resource orchestration for innovation: Structuring and bundling resources in growth-and maturity-stage firms. *Long range planning, 50*(4), 472–486.

Casciaro, T., Edmondson, A. C., & Jang, S. (2019). Cross-silo leadership. *Harvard Business Review*, May–June.

Ceccagnoli, M., & Jiang, L. (2012). The cost of integrating external technologies: Supply and demand drivers of value creation in the markets for technology. *Strategic Management Journal, 34*(4), 404–425.

Dibbem, J., Chin, W. W., & Heinzl, A. (2005). The Impact of Human Asset Specificity on the Sourcing of Application Services. *ECIS 2005 Proceedings*, p. 114.

Duan, W., Zhang, G., Zhu, Z., et al. (2020). Psychological contract differences for different groups of employees: Big date analysis from China. *Information System and E-Business Management, 18*, 871–889.

Fayoumi, A. (2016). Ecosystem-inspired enterprise modelling framework for collaborative and networked manufacturing systems. *Computers in Industry, 80*, 54–68.

Fremantle, P., Weerawarana, S., & Khalaf, R. (2002). Enterprise services: Examining the emerging files of web services and how it is integrated into existing enterprise infrastructures. *Communications of the ACM, 45*(10), 77–82.

Garten, J. E. (2002). *The politics of fortune: A new agenda for business leaders*. Harvard Business School Press.

Grøgaard, B., Colman, H. L., & Stensaker, I. G. (2022). Legitimizing, leveraging, and launching: Developing dynamic capabilities in the MNE. *Journal of International Business Studies, 53*, 636–656.

Guggenberger, T. M., Möller, F., Haarhuis, T., Gür, I., & Otto, B. (2020). Ecosystem type in information systems. *Twenty-Eight European Conference on Information Systems (ECIS2020)*, Marrakesh, Morocco.

Gulati, R. (2007). Silo busting: How to execute on the promise of customer focus. *Harvard Business Review*, May 1–9.

Haarhuis, T., & Liening, A. (2020). Building dynamic capabilities to cope with environmental uncertainty: The role of strategic foresight. *Technological Forecasting and Social Change, 155*, 120033.

Helfat, C. E., Finkelstein, S., Mitchell, W., Peteraf, M., Singh, H., Teece, D., & Winter, S. G. (2007). *Dynamic capabilities: Understanding strategic change in organizations*. Blackwell.

Holcomb, T. R., Holmes, R. M., & Connelly, B. L. (2009). Making the most of what you have: Managerial ability as a source of resource value creation. *Strategic Management Journal, 30*, 457–485.

Jacobides, M. G., Cennamo, C., & Gawer, A. (2018). Towards a theory of ecosystems. *Strategic Management Journal, 39*(8), 2255–2276.

Jin, X., Kotlarsky, J., & Oshri, I. (2014). Towards understanding knowledge integration in multi-sourcing engagements. In R. Hirschheim, A. Heinzl, & J. Dibbern (Eds.), *Information systems outsourcing: Towards Sustainable Business Value* (pp. 273–287). Springer.

Khanangha, S., Ansari, S. S., Paroutis, S., & Oviedeo, L. (2020). Mutualism and the dynamics of new platform creation: A study of Cisco and fog computing. *Strategic Management Journal, 43*(3), 476–506.

Kotlarsky, J., van den Hooff, B., & Geerts, L. (2020). Under pressure: Understanding the dynamics of coordination in IT functions under business-as-usual and emergency conditions. *Journal of Information Technology, 5*(2), 94–122.

Kristoffersen, E., Mikalef, P., Blomsma, F., & Li, J. (2021). The effects of business analytics capability on circular economy implementation, resource orchestration capability, and firm performance. *International Journal of Production Economics, 39*. https://doi.org/10.1016/j.ijpe.2021.108205

Lacity, M. C., Khan, S. A., & Yan, A. (2017). Review of the empirical business services sourcing literature: An update and future directions. In *Outsourcing and offshoring business services* (pp. 499–651). Palgrave Macmillan.

Ladley, J. (2020). *Data governance: How to design, deploy, and sustain an effective data governance program* (2nd ed.). Academic Press.

Lee, J. (2020). Access to finance for artificial intelligence regulation in the financial services industry. *European Business Organization Law Review, 21*, 731–757.

Madsen, S., Bødker, K., & Tøth, T. (2015). Knowledge transfer planning and execution in offshore outsourcing: An applied approach. *Information Systems Frontiers, 17*, 67–77.

Makri, M., Hitt, M. A., & Lane, P. (2010). Complementary technologies, knowledge relatedness, and invention outcomes in high technology mergers and acquisitions. *Strategic Management Journal, 31*, 602–628.

Menor, L. J., & Roth, A. V. (2007). New service development competence in retail banking: Construct development and measurement validation. *Journal of Operations Management, 25*(4), 825–846.

Meyer, A., Pufahl, L., Batoulis, K., Fahland, D., & Weske, M. (2015). Automating data exchange in process choreographies. *Information Systems, 53*, 296–329.

Miller, S. (2018). AI: Augmentation, more so than automation. *Asian Management Insights, 5*(1), 1–20.

Pitelis, C. N., & Teece, D. J. (2009). The (new) nature and essence of the firm. *European Management Review, 6*(1), 5–15.

Porter, M. E. (1985). *Competitive advantage: Creating and sustaining superior performance*. Free Press.

Prahalad, C. K. (1975). *The strategic process in a multinational corporation*. Unpublished Doctoral dissertation, School of Business Administration, Harvard University.

Rai, A., Keil, M., Hornyak, R., & Wullenweber, K. (2012). Hybrid relational-contractual governance for business process outsourcing. *Journal of Management Information Systems, 29*(2), 213–256.

Sako, M., Chondrakis, G., & Vaaler, P. M. (2016). How do plural-sourcing firms make and buy? The impact of supplier portfolio design. *Organization Science, 27*(5), 1161–1182.

Senyo, P. K., Liu, K., & Effah, J. (2019). Digital business ecosystem: Literature review and a framework for future research. *International Journal of Information Management, 47*, 52–64.

Serrat, O. (2010). *Bridging organizational silos*. Asian Development Bank.

Sirmon, D. G., Gove, S., & Hitt, M. A. (2008). Resource management in dyadic competitive rivalry: The effects of resource bundling and deployment. *Academy of Management Journal, 51*, 919–935.

Sirmon, D. G., Hitt, M. A., & Ireland, R. D. (2007). Managing firm resources in dynamic environments to create value: Looking inside the black box. *Academy of Management Review, 32*(1), 273–292.
Sirmon, D. G., Hitt, M. A., Ireland, R. D., & Gilbert, B. A. (2011). Resource orchestration to create competitive advantage breath, depth, and life cycle effects. *Journal of Management, 37*(5), 1390–1412.
Sturgeon, T. J. (2002). Modular production networks: A new American model of industrial organisation. *Industrial and Corporate Change, 11*(3), 451–496.
Teece, D., & Leith, S. (2016). Uncertainty, innovation, and dynamic capabilities: An introduction. *California Management Review, 58*(4), 5–12.
Teece, D. J. (1986). Profiting from technological innovation: Implications for integration, collaboration, licensing and public policy. *Research Policy, 15*(6), 285–305.
Teece, D. J. (2007). Explicating dynamic capabilities: The nature and microfoundations of (sustainable) enterprise performance. *Strategic Management Journal, 28*(13), 1319–1350.
Teece, D. J., Pisano, G., & Shuen, A. (1997). Dynamic capabilities and strategic management. *Strategic Management Journal, 18*(7), 509–533.
Thomke, S., & Kuemmerle, W. (2002). Assets accumulation, interdependence, and technological change: Evidence from pharmaceutical drug discovery. *Strategic Management Journal, 23*, 619–635.
Trischler, J., Johnson, M., & Kristensson, P. (2020). A service ecosystem perspective on the diffusion of sustainability-oriented user innovations. *Journal of Business Research, 116*, 552–560.
Ulbrich, F. (2012). Preventing the gradual decline of shared service centers. In *Proceedings of the 18th Americas Conference on Information Systems*, Seattle, USA.
Van der Aalst, W. M. P., Bichler, M., & Heinzl, A. (2017). Responsible data science. *Business & Information Systems Engineering, 59*, 311–313.
Wang, W. T., & Hou, Y. P. (2015). Motivations of employees' knowledge sharing behaviours: A self-determination perspective. *Information and Organization, 25*(1), 1–26.
Wareham, J., Fox, P. B., & Cano Giner, J. L. (2014). Technology ecosystem governance. *Organization Science, 25*(4), 1195–1215.
Willcocks, L. P., Oshri, I., & Kotlarsky, J. (2018). Why innovation and why now? In L. Willcocks, I. Oshri, & J. Kotlarsky (Eds.), *Dynamic innovation in outsourcing. Technology, work and globalization*. Palgrave Macmillan.
Zhang, Z. (2018). Organizational culture and knowledge sharing: Design of incentives and business Processes. *Business Process Management Journal, 24*(2), 384–399.

11

Conclusion: Limitations and Future Research

In this book, we introduced four objectives as a direction to explore which antecedents form a part of an enterprise orchestration capability that aims at integrating internal and external resources. We theoretically developed and empirically validated a business services portfolio model and its corresponding antecedents. More specifically, we demonstrated how digitalisation may overcome business services implementation barriers. Overall, we focus on digitalised Global Business Services (GBSs) in the context of a plural sourcing strategy and provided evidence how an enterprise ecosystem approach may decrease GBS implementation challenges. In doing so, we operationalised our definition as described in the introduction "*An enterprise ecosystem is a socio-technical environment in which individuals within organisational units, which are supported by digital interactions, collaborate in co-creating, implementing and orchestrating GBSs in order to create business value*".

In this chapter, we describe the overall theoretical contributions and managerial implications of our research, limitations and suggest avenues for future research.

A. Plugge, S. Nikou, *Digitalisation of Global Business Services*, Technology, Work and Globalization, https://doi.org/10.1007/978-3-031-51528-6_11

11.1 Contribution

To the best of our knowledge, this book is the first attempt of its kind to the analysis of antecedents that influence the orchestration and implementation of an enterprise GBSs portfolio in a plural sourcing context. The result of this research is threefold and contributes to business services and sourcing literature, operation management (OM) and management literature as follows.

First, by applying quantitative research approach in the field of business services, we theoretically developed and empirically evaluated a research model. Based on a unique dataset, we studied GBSs and influencing antecedents within the context of a plural sourcing strategy. The present research investigated the direct and indirect effects of several antecedents on an enterprise's orchestration of business services portfolio. We argue that a fit between these key antecedents is paramount to achieve and sustain a business services portfolio. Consequently, the enterprises' leadership have to manage the coherence between these antecedents and adapt them if necessary. The results contribute to our understanding of the state of current OM practices. Although a number of empirical studies used international samples, only a few of them developed theoretical arguments and hypotheses to study effects across countries or geographical regions (Hitt et al., 2016, p 83). Our study partially fills this gap, as we used an enterprise degree of outsourcing, size, geographical location (e.g. region and country) and enterprise's maturity level as control variables. We examined whether the proposed relationships in the research model are affected by these variables. We identified how these control variables act as moderators and found moderating effects between various path relationships specifically in situations where an enterprise applies a low degree of outsourcing. As a result, we answered the call of Richter and Brühl (2017), who encouraged scholars to identify business services mediators in a context with a larger number of cases (i.e. providing statistical results). We theoretically conceptualised and empirically demonstrated that the antecedent of modularised business processes fully mediates the paths between (a) IS standardisation, (b) managing decision rights, and partially (c) customer orientation to orchestrate a business services portfolio. These findings helped us to understand the importance of modularised business processes to accomplish GBSs portfolio in a plural sourcing context.

Second, applying a qualitative approach and building on the theoretical perspectives of Resource Orchestration Theory (ROT), we examine the dependencies between antecedents and the orchestration of a GBSs portfolio. Literature reveals that many studies that apply an ROT lens are conceptual (Sirmon et al., 2007, 2011). Although OM scholars applied ROT (see e.g. Liu et al., 2016), we argue that the empirical studies may provide additional support for the robustness of ROT. As such, we used the theoretical perspectives of ROT to study the dependencies between antecedents and the orchestration of a business services portfolio. The findings justify why specific antecedents require continuous management attention as they affect orchestrating a GBSs portfolio directly or indirectly. We contribute to OM literature by operationalising Sirmon et al.'s (2011) resource orchestration framework and followed the resource management elements that include structuring, bundling, leveraging processes. We also took asset management elements into account that comprise of search/selection, configuration/deployment processes. Research of Thomke and Kuemmerle (2002) shows that developing resources internally and acquiring external resources are important actions, however, they are independent of an enterprise degree of maturity in orchestrating resources. Our research goes beyond the findings of Thomke and Kuemmerle (2002) as our case studies demonstrates that enterprises need to be mature to orchestrate internal and external resources adequately as the antecedents under study are interdependent. Consequently, maturity can be seen as a prerequisite to create a balanced mix of value-adding resources both in-house and acquired from the market (i.e. outsourced).

Based on our cross-case analysis, we argue that enterprise management have to invest in building a dynamic orchestration capability. Taking the dynamics of a plural sourcing strategy into account enterprises need to focus on a business services portfolio that is sustainable by nature. To deal with this challenge, our research shows that managers have to detect changes in the direct (internal organisation) and indirect (external suppliers) environment, which corresponds to sensing. By reaching out to representatives of internal and external stakeholders, insights can be collected to verify if the current plural sourcing strategy and corresponding business services portfolio still fits to support end users and customers. Subsequently, enterprise management is able to initiate actions to adjust the business services portfolio, if necessary, which addresses an enterprise seizing ability. Importantly, Haarhaus and Liening (2020) found various examples in which enterprises were able to apply an agile business model to restructure their resource mix of internal and external resources. As a result, we build on the authors findings by demonstrating that horizontal and vertical mechanisms are required to exchange information between managers and subject matter experts, both internally and externally. Our results suggest that adapting a business services portfolio requires both sensing and seizing capabilities to cater for changes effectively. As a result, enterprise management needs to use a holistic view to coordinate changes that affect the antecedents under study to ensure coherence.

A third contribution emphasises the dynamics to orchestrate a business services portfolio by means of an ecosystem approach and the enabling role of strategic management. From a management and organisation perspective, we find that a coalitional model creates a better fit to handle enterprise dynamics. Our findings provide novel and powerful insights that enterprises' who apply an ecosystem approach to orchestrate their business services portfolio, taking a plural sourcing strategy and corresponding antecedents into account, are better capable to deal with orchestration complexity. By conducting this study, we extend the research of Holmlund et al. (2016) and examine management and leadership challenges in business services companies during the transition to service orientation (p. 2460). We find that digital technologies accelerated the need to apply an enterprise ecosystem approach, which in turn strengthened the ties between various departments, management, and experts as each of them is aware of mutual dependencies. More specifically, we find enterprise ecosystem roles, such as the orchestrator (e.g. FSSC and IT department), producers (in-house and outsourced delivery units) and consumers (end users and customers) (see Lingens et al., 2022). By applying ecosystem characteristics enterprises were able to adapt to the dynamics to orchestrate a business services portfolio. As far as we know, this is the first study that argues the enterprises can be considered as an ecosystem, taking GBSs in a plural sourcing context into account.

11.2 Managerial Implications

Our findings have direct managerial implications for enterprises that apply GBSs in a plural sourcing context. To overcome barriers in the dynamics of a business services portfolio, we suggest that enterprises need to develop an orchestration approach that is dynamic by nature. It requires an orchestration capability that focuses on the enterprise ecosystem as a whole rather than on the individual relationships between antecedents and the business service portfolio. Pioneering bundling resources, derive from exploratory learning that represent an avenue through which managers are able to create a new orchestration capability by integrating existing and/or new resources that were previously unrelated (Ahuja & Morris Lampert, 2001). We argue that enterprises establish an "orchestration hub" to structure, bundle, and leverage in-house and outsourced resources. Such an "orchestration hub" becomes accountable to coordinate the business services portfolio and in-house and external resources. GBS portfolio changes may impact corresponding business processes, information systems, decision rights and customer orientation which require coordination. The "orchestration hub" coordinates these dynamic changes and develops mechanisms to ensure that managers and subject matter experts of various business and IT departments continue to exchange information. As dependencies between enterprise departments may cause uncertainties with regard to GBS portfolio, traditional hierarchal structures become ineffective to handle the degree of dynamism. Therefore, we suggest that enterprises develop and implement an enterprise ecosystem strategy encompassing a multi-perspective approach that contributes to achieve competitive advantage. By implementing ecosystem characteristics, such as long-term goals, shared fate and reciprocity, enterprises can cater for changing circumstances and adapt the identified critical antecedents to achieve organisational responsiveness. Introducing a more collaborative way of working with suppliers may improve enterprises' performance of their business services. In case of changes in a business services portfolio (i.e. new or adapted functions and services), suppliers may create value by identifying the impact of changes on enterprises' business services. As such, the risk of performance issues can be reduced.

11.3 Limitations and Future Research

While our study provides important implications for enterprises and suppliers involved in providing GBSs in a plural sourcing context, there are also some limitations. Next, we suggest potential research avenues.

First, our study is limited by the general weakness of survey research relying on subjective information as the survey is filled out by one respondent per firm. Our relatively small sample includes only participants with high managerial positions, such as executive management. Although our research included several conditions and control variables, the research model may not be as comprehensive as possible. There may be other antecedents that were not considered in the study, which would have contributed to a deeper understanding of implementing GBSs. We suggest that future studies focus on more diverse respondents and use a large sample survey. A more equal balance of the number of enterprises and responders in various industries as well as more finely grained research related to geography and size may provide more generalisable results. Second, another limitation is that business services antecedents are only studied on a generic level and from a financial services view specifically (see case studies). For instance, we did not specify the in-depth function of financial services, nor did we explore other type of knowledge-intensive business services (e.g. HR, SCM). Based on previous research, it can be assumed that the type of function will influence our findings. Future research may explore the role and effects of specific GBS functions and identify new insights.

Third, because our research primarily represents enterprises, we have not studied other context-related factors that may affect the plural sourcing relationship, such as the role of suppliers. Business services provided by suppliers were not studied, which may create new insights that lead to new antecedents that may affect our research model. Future research may explore the role of suppliers specifically and their perspective on an enterprise business services portfolio would further enrich the findings presented. Fourth, the fact that we used ROT as the main theoretical framework to study an enterprise ecosystem may limit our understanding of moderating and mediating orchestration effects. Due to the dynamics and complexity of resource integration within a plural sourcing strategy, we suggest applying other theories or theoretical frameworks, such as systems theory, to research the effects to which enterprises apply systemic thinking when orchestrating their business services portfolio.

Fifth, the results could be influenced by the specific sampling strategy employed, potentially leading to a skewed representation of the population under investigation and affecting the generalisability of the findings. Different sampling methods may inadvertently exclude certain groups or over-represent others, which could impact the accuracy and applicability of the study's conclusions. Finally, a potential limitation arises from survey items (indicators), and the modification of previously validated measurement items to align with the research context. Thus, these alterations could impact the psychometric properties and comparability of the measurements, potentially affecting the study's internal validity and cross-study comparability.

References

Ahuja, G., & Morris Lampert, C. (2001). Entrepreneurship in the large corporation: A longitudinal study of how established firms create breakthrough inventions. *Strategic Management Journal, 22*(6–7), 521–543.

Haarhaus, T., & Liening, A. (2020). Building dynamic capabilities to cope with environmental uncertainty: The role of strategic foresight. *Technological Forecasting and Social Change, 155.* https://doi.org/10.1016/j.techfore.2020.120033

Hitt, M. A., Xu, K., & Matz Carnes, C. (2016). Resource based theory in operations management research. *Journal of Operations Management, 41*, 77–94.

Holmlund, M., Kowalkowski, C., & Biggemann, S. (2016). Organisational behavior in innovation, marketing, and purchasing in business service contexts: An agenda for academic inquiry. *Journal of Business Research, 69*(7), 2457–2462.

Lingens, B., Huber, F., & Gassmann, O. (2022). Loner or team player: How firms allocate orchestrator tasks amongst ecosystem actors. *European Management Journal, 40*(4), 559–571.

Liu, H., Wei, S., Ke, W., Wei, K. K., & Hua, Z. (2016). The configuration between supply chain integration and information technology competency:

A resource orchestration perspective. *Journal of Operations Management, 44*, 3–29.
Richter, P. C., & Brühl, R. (2017). Shared service centre research: A review of the past, present, and future. *European Management Journal, 35*(3), 26–38.
Sirmon, D. G., Hitt, M. A., & Ireland, R. D. (2007). Managing firm resources in dynamic environments to create value: Looking inside the black box. *Academy of Management Review, 32*(1), 273–292.
Sirmon, D. G., Hitt, M. A., Ireland, R. D., & Gilbert, B. A. (2011). Resource orchestration to create competitive advantage breath, depth, and life cycle effects. *Journal of Management, 37*(5), 1390–1412.
Thomke, S., & Kuemmerle, W. (2002). Asset accumulation, interdependence and technological change: Evidence from pharmaceutical drug discovery. *Strategic Management Journal, 23*(7), 619–635.

Appendix A: Research Methodology

Research Design: Quantitative Research

First, we address the quantitative study in which we used a survey questionnaire that consists of measures (indicators) that relate to our research antecedents. We employ a survey questionnaire. Therefore, it is crucial to determine whether any trends in the events, motivations, and outcomes emerge. This allows us to establish differences in interpretation by respondents so that we can investigate possible explanations. We started by describing GBSs in a plural sourcing context, and secondly, the authors of this book played an active role during the interviews and structured the data to confirm the theory used in the research. Our exploratory study design consists of two stages, (i) face-to-face interviews supported by (ii) an online survey questionnaire. This approach helped to identify and measure the antecedents (e.g. business processes, standardisation, business services portfolio) and collecting complementary data for cross-validation and quantification of specific aspects of the antecedents. One benefit of using survey method is that it allows for the examination of a large number of

A. Plugge, S. Nikou, *Digitalisation of Global Business Services*, Technology, Work and Globalization, https://doi.org/10.1007/978-3-031-51528-6

variables, which can lead to a more comprehensive understanding of a real-world situation from multiple perspectives (Galliers, 1992).

Following the two-stage procedure, we collected data between February 2022 and March 2023. We developed an English questionnaire and pre-tested it with fifteen potential respondents, who represented both scientists and practitioners. Attached to the survey was a short cover letter explaining the purpose of the research. To minimise the risk of non-response bias, the survey was kept brief, and participants were assured that their responses and personal information would be kept anonymous and confidential. We sent out 267 invites and received 121 complete responses (45% response rate). We found three main reasons for not being able to complete the survey: (i) their portfolio did not match the criteria, (ii) not being involved in establishing a plural sourcing strategy, and (iii) lack of time. This rich dataset is rather unique, as it was collected on a global scale, representing firms operating internationally in different industries. We anonymised the data of participants because of confidentiality reasons. The firms represent ten different industries, mostly from Education, Energy & Utilities, Pharma, and Public Sector, and less from Consumer products and Technology & Telecom. Enterprise representatives that participated in the questionnaire held positions like CEO, CIO, CFO, Head of business services, (Senior) Vice President, and Director. While a vast majority of the questions are identical, minor modifications were made to the questionnaire to fit the particular departments, terminology and practices. Considering the need for clarity and given the fact that the terminology can be interpreted differently, a glossary of definitions was included. All items were measured using 5-points Likert scales from validated sources.

Our data set include multiple demographic information including, company name, industry, number of employees, type and introduction date of business services, organisational structure, geographical reach and countries, type and number of information systems, GBS rationales, degree of outsourcing of business services measured by percentage, operating, process owners amongst other aspects. An excerpt is showed in Table B2. The hypotheses, as described in Chap. 3, help to focus attention on the main path relationships between the antecedents and the dependent variable. Our hypotheses also help to organise the case studies by addressing the antecedents.

Survey Instructions

The survey you are about to take will be used to measure your GBS organisation. The survey is organised around four dimensions (see Tables A1, A2, A3 and A4): general information, geographical coverage, functional coverage, and value drivers. Each of which includes a set of key attributes which define the practice and competencies in place in the enterprises in scope. For each of these attributes, participants were asked to define their organisation situation as current as possible. The most important characteristics are highlighted in dark grey. The survey took roughly 60 minutes to complete, and the research team was available to review the results with the participants. All results are kept anonymous and used only for research purposes. The participants were asked to enter the digit 1 to 5 that corresponds with the organisations business services level.

The research team appreciates your time and input in regard to providing data on your organisation's Global Business Services. If some of the features in this survey do not work, please ensure that your MACROS are enabled. Below are instructions on the various types of data. All cells highlighted in dark grey should be filled out. A combination of both manual entry and drop-down boxes are required.

Table A1 General information

Business Services Assessment Survey			
General Information			
Participant Name:	<Insert Name Here>	Company Name:	<Insert Name Here>
Participant email:	<Insert email Here>	Total number of employees in your company	<Pull Down Here>
Participant Title:	<Insert Title Here>	Industry:	<Pull Down Here>
Participant Area of Responsibility:	<Insert Responsibility Here>	*If other Please Specify*	<Specify Here>
Year Started Global Business Services (discreet functionally focused delivery)—See pull down:	<Pull Down Here>	Internal Global Business Services Organisation Headcount—See pull down:	<Pull Down Here>
Year Started Global Business Services (Multi-functional, integrated, end to end process focused)—See pull down:	<Pull Down Here>	Third Party / Service provider Business Organisation Headcount—See pull down:	<Pull Down Here>
Overall Organisation			
What is number of countries in which your organisation has established operations?—See pull down to the right			<Pull Down Here>
What is number of distinct lines of business / business units (BU) that your organisation operates?—See pull down to the right			<Pull Down Here>

Global Business Services Organisation

Please select the operating model that your organisation's BS operates under from options described below.

Decentralised processes within functions performed by Business Units on their own behalf	Centralised processes and outcomes consolidated and owned by centralised functions; BUs are customers	Business Services-processes consolidated to a regional service entity and operated and a business with governance shared with Business Units	GBS Business Services model with global scope and delivery	Multifunctional GBS model extended across multiple functions with end-to-end global process ownership and accountability

Who does head of Global Business Services report to? Please Select from the Boxes below.

CEO	COO	CFO	Functional management	Other executive management

Table A2 Geographical coverage

Business Services Organisation—geographical coverage							
How many unique countries are serviced by your Business Services organisation?—Select appropriate box below.							
1 up to 2	3 up to 5	6 up to 9	10 up to 15	16 or more			
How many unique lines of business / business units are serviced by your GBS organisation?—Select appropriate box below.							
1 up to 2	3 up to 5	6 up to 9	10 up to 15	16 or more			
What are the regions in which your company has captive GBS service centres? Select from below list.							
North America	South America	Europe	Asia/Pacific	Middle East/ Africa			
What are the countries in which your company has captive GBS service centres? Select from below list.							
North America	United States	Canada	Mexico				
South America	Brazil	Chile	Argentina	Colombia	Costa Rica	Panama	Others
Europe	Western Europe	Southern Europe	Nordic region	Poland	Romania	Russia	Others
Asia/Pacific	India	China	Japan	Philippines	Malaysia	Australia	Others
Middle East/ Africa	UAE	Qatar	Other Middle Eastern countries	South Africa	Nigeria	Other African countries	

Table A3 Functional coverage

Functional coverage				
What functional areas fall within GBS today (Please select the boxes below—Check all that apply)				
Finance and Accounting	Information Technology	Human Resources	Supply Chain Management	Other
What total % of GBS delivery is outsourced to a third-party service provider (By function—See pull down)				
Finance and Accounting		<Pull Down Here>		
Information Technology		<Pull Down Here>		
Human Resources		<Pull Down Here>		
Supply Chain Management		<Pull Down Here>		
Other		<Pull Down Here>		

Table A4 Value drivers

Survey Questions
The following questions will be a part of the quantitative survey and will yield more profound information. Six topics will be investigated: Modularised Business Processes, Customer Orientation, IS Standardisation, Decision Rights, Plural Sourcing Strategy, and Orchestration of Business Services Portfolio. The survey was supported by the following statement:
How do you personally evaluate the importance of the following statements on a 5-point rating scale, ranged from 1 being "totally disagree" to 5 being "totally agree"?

Research Design: Qualitative Research

Our qualitative study focuses on naturally occurring, ordinary events in natural settings (Miles & Huberman, 1994). With regard to our key objectives, we prefer the case study method as 'when', 'how' or 'why' questions are being posed when the focus is on a contemporary phenomenon within some real-life context (Yin, 1994, p. 16). The case studies are designed to thoroughly explore how digital technologies affect the implementation and provisioning of GBSs in a plural sourcing context. Importantly, as we would expand and generalise theories (analytical generalisation) and not to enumerate frequencies (statistical generalisation) (Yin, 1994), case studies can be generalised to situations that are sufficiently similar to the observed cases with regard to relevant variables. The results of our empirical research are generalised to the level of the enterprise as a whole.

Case Study Protocol

In order to develop a formal plan for conducting the case studies, a case study protocol needs to be produced to provide guidance and to record the data. The case study protocol consists of the following elements:

- Enterprise related information
- An interview protocol
- A case database

Table A5 Survey questions

Antecedent	Question	Strongly disagree	Disagree	Neither agree nor disagree	Agree	Strongly agree
Modularised Business Processes	MBP_1: Our company applies process management from an end-to-end perspective	O	O	O	O	O
	MBP_2: In our company, process owners are allocated to coordinate end-to-end processes	O	O	O	O	O
	MBP_3: In our company, modularized business processes are supported by Information Systems	O	O	O	O	O
	MBP_4: Our company breaks up end-to-end processes in modularised sub-processes	O	O	O	O	O
	MBP_5: Our company stimulates the standardisation of modularised business processes	O	O	O	O	O
Customer Orientation	CO_1: In our company, managers encourage service level transparency	O	O	O	O	O
	CO_2: In our company, business services are based on competitive pricing	O	O	O	O	O
IS Standardisation	ISS_1: In our company, information systems that support business processes are standardised by design	O	O	O	O	O
	ISS_2: Our company encourages the integration of information systems and business processes	O	O	O	O	O

(continued)

Table A5 (continued)

Antecedent	Question	Strongly disagree	Disagree	Neither agree nor disagree	Agree	Strongly agree
Managing Decision Rights	MDR_1: In our company, business process decision making is allocated to business services teams	O	O	O	O	O
	MDR_2: In our company, managers are supportive to the decisions made by business services	O	O	O	O	O
	MDR_3: Our company encourages business services employees to work in cross functional teams	O	O	O	O	O
	MDR_4: In our company, management facilitates the development of cross business services agreements	O	O	O	O	O
	MDR_5: In our company, management is authorized to apply business services portfolio decision making	O	O	O	O	O

Plural Sourcing Strategy	PSS_1: In our company, the sourcing strategy is based on bundling in-house and outsourced business services	O	O	O	O	O
	PSS_2: In our company, management invest in bundling various business services continuously	O	O	O	O	O
	PSS_3: In our company, we know how to transform our business services over time	O	O	O	O	O
	PSS_4: In our company, executive management is committed to support our sourcing strategy	O	O	O	O	O
Orchestration of Business Services Portfolio	OBSP_1: In our company, management has expertise in building a business services portfolio	O	O	O	O	O
	OBSP_2: In our company, we continuously adapt our business services portfolio based on changing business needs	O	O	O	O	O

With regard to the first element, multiple sources of enterprises' information are identified, which have a direct relationship to the methods (e.g. desk research, interviews) used in our case studies. For each enterprise information is gathered about their history, mission, strategic objectives, and their digitalisation initiatives. The interview protocol, which is the second element, consists of information that relates to the interview preparation and questions. Consequently, the protocol describes the execution of the interviews and the way in which the data is analysed. The third element addresses the role of the case database. The database included interview recordings, desk research documents, and survey outcomes. All documents were codified by a database number, and we developed a table with the different topics corresponding to the case study number applied on the interview form. Each topic is associated with the relevant data collection terms.

The questionnaire will provide more insights about enterprises' GBS organisation, type of services, global research, size, and degree of outsourcing. All the collected data will be stored in the case study database. The database establishes a structure to provide a comprehensive overview of relevant data, qualitative as well as quantitative. Addressing the case study analysis, we group interview information into the format of the case study protocol. The questions of the interviews and surveys are identified by a number. Table A6 shows the different topics and corresponding numbers of the interview form and survey form.

Due to confidentiality requirements of the enterprises, and their participants, we have not disclosed the details (names) of enterprises and their representatives in detail.

The first column refers to the researched aspects, such as plural souring strategy, modularised business processes and IS standardisation. The second column describes the methodology that was used to gather the information denoted as: desk research (D), interviews (I), and survey (S). The third column refers to the number of interview questions that was used (Strategy & Organisation (SO), Digital Technologies (DT), IA related Knowledge and Skills (KS). The fourth column shows the number of the survey questions used.

Table A6 Relationship between research topics and questions

Information	Source	Interview question	Survey question
Plural Sourcing Strategy			
Strategy	D, I, S	SO_1.1; SO_1.2; DT_2.1	PSS_1
Bundling various business services	S		PSS_2
Transform business services	D, I, S	KS_3.1; KS_3.2	PSS_3
Commitment	S		PSS_4
Modularised Business Processes			
Process management	D, I, S	DT_2.3	Mod_1
Process owners	I, S	KS_3.1; KS_3.2	Mod_2
Modularised business processes	D, I, S		Mod_3
Modularised sub-processes	S		Mod_4
Standardisation business processes	D, S		Mod_5
Customer Orientation			
Service level transparency	D, I, S	DT_2.5	CO_1
Competitive pricing	S		CO_2
IS Standardisation			
Standardisation by design	D, S		Stan_1
Integration of information systems	D, I, S	SO_1.3; SO_1.4	Stan_2
Managing Decision Rights			
Decision making	I, S	DT_2.4	MDR_1
Management	D, I, S		MDR_2
Cross functional teams	D, I, S	KS_3.3	MDR_3
Development of cross business services	D, I, S	KS_3.4; KS_3.5	MDR_4
Business services portfolio decision making	D, S		MDR_5
Orchestration of Business Services Portfolio			
Business services portfolio expertise	I, S	DT_2.2	BSP_1
Adaption of business services portfolio	I, S	SO_1.5	BSP_2

Case Study Selection

The unit of observation reflects the relationship between digital technologies and its effects on antecedents (e.g. plural sourcing strategy, business services portfolio, modularised business processes, IS standardisation, managing decision rights customer orientation). We use a set of criteria to select appropriate case studies. First, from a historical view, enterprises that focus on F&A services were some of the first that applied a plural sourcing strategy. We may assume that these enterprises are experienced when it comes to the antecedents in scope. Therefore, we selected four enterprises that have at least 10 years of experience in the F&A domain within the context of a plural sourcing strategy.

Second, in the context of F&A, enterprises increasingly use digital technologies solutions to automate 'the last mile' compared to other focus areas such as HR and SCM. As such, we may assume that they created insights in the use of digital technologies and its effect on the antecedents in scope. Third, consistent with the survey scope, we address the need to select enterprises that are acting in multiple countries, which in turn increase the complexity to orchestrate the business services portfolio. Hence, we selected enterprises that actively use various types of digital technologies solutions such as RPA, ML, IA, process mining solutions amongst others.

Fourth, consistent with the survey scope, we selected enterprises that represent various industries. This creates the opportunity to identify similarities and distinctions as part of a cross-case analysis. Fifth, we select enterprises that apply a plural sourcing strategy, as service providers fulfil an essential role in providing F&A services. As F&A services are based on automation, it is interesting to study how service providers deal with digital technologies. Therefore, we selected a global service provider that is highly experienced in the field of F&A and digital technologies solutions.

In short, we consider including in total four case studies, namely three enterprises (clients) and a global financial service provider. Finally, we will compare the results to the selected various theories and treat them as a data set for comparative analysis (Glaser & Strauss, 1967). As we apply a mixed-method approach, we integrate both qualitative and quantitative data. Miles and Huberman (1994, p. 41) describe this approach as design number one (1). Literature shows that there are three motivations to link qualitative and quantitative data: (1) to enable confirmation of each other via triangulation; (2) to elaborate or develop analysis, providing a richer detail, and (3) to initiate new lines of thinking through attention to surprises or paradoxes (Rossman & Wilson, 1984, 1991).

Therefore, as mentioned earlier, we used three different methods for gathering data: desk research, interviews, and a survey. When analysing antecedents and situational factors, we create a chain of evidence. By using multiple sources of evidence, and seeking confirmation by means of data triangulation, we are able to achieve construct validity. To ensure reliability, we build a research database to create access for other researchers to repeat the case studies with the same results (Yin, 1994). The method of desk research was used to collect background information with regard to the case studies. Background information includes, for instance, the size of the enterprises, geographical research, degree of plural sourcing strategy (outsourcing), business services portfolio, and type of digital technologies solutions. Also, other relevant information such as GBS strategy documents and digital technologies roadmaps were analysed.

Appendix B: Overview Interviews, Excerpts, Interview Questions

Case Study Interviews

Participants were interviewed to better understand the antecedents and degree of digital technologies in scope. To avoid 'elite bias', we interviewed multiple management and subject matter expert representatives. This is relevant because respondents express their personal opinion about how they perceive situations such as automated solutions. Hence, we may assume that their opinions are at least partially subjective.

To select participants, we have used two criteria. First, interviewees were selected from a strategic level as they are involved in plural sourcing arrangements decision making. Senior management is capable of discussing the relation between the antecedents in scope and degree of digital technologies. Therefore, it is valuable to discuss these topics with them. Secondly, senior management is able to create oversight and as such look at their F&A organisation as a whole and identify relationships with business units and IT department. The target groups in our interview relate to senior management of the F&A organisation, subject matter experts of the F&A organisation, representatives of business units (internal customers) and representatives of the IT department.

A. Plugge, S. Nikou, *Digitalisation of Global Business Services*, Technology, Work and Globalization, https://doi.org/10.1007/978-3-031-51528-6

Based on the four case studies, in-depth interviews were conducted with 16 participants who are all directly involved the topics under study. This was to ensure internal consistency within each enterprise and service provider organisation. The interviewed respondents have a minimum of five years of experience with regard to F&A services and digital technology solutions (functionally or technically). Interviewees are located in the Netherlands and India. Interviewee roles, as illustrated in Table B1, are positioned across the firm. In this way we apply a cross-section within the organisations that yield to establish a holistic view. All of the respondents were interviewed in the period May 2022 and June 2023. Interviews varied from 50 minutes to 90 minutes in length and they were conducted via a semi-structured design with many open-ended questions. Applying a semi-structured interview method as a research instrument is useful to select data and information for exploratory-descriptive studies that may be extended later (Denzin, 1978).

Before the interviews started, questions were adjusted to the participant's area of expertise, for instance, digital technologies. All the interviews were recorded and then transcribed, and the text was confirmed by the respondents for approval to ensure accuracy and reliability. The text of the case study as a whole was also reviewed by the enterprises' senior management to avoid uncertainties. Next, the case study outcomes were confirmed by senior management.

Cross-Case Analysis

The cross-case analysis consists of an overview of the various case studies and the identification of business services portfolio and digital technologies patterns. The case studies are compared and assessed based on our research antecedents. As such, a comprehensive picture for the cross-case analysis is provided. Based on the cross-case analysis, we were able to draw conclusions on, e.g. how digital technologies affect the identified antecedents and as such contribute to a decrease of GBS implementation complexity. The results of the four case studies are expected to deliver a valuable contribution both to the scientific community and to practitioners.

Interview Questions

Definition Digitalisation

We define digitalisation as 'use of digital technologies to innovate a business model and provide new revenue streams and value-producing opportunities in an enterprise ecosystem'.

Definition Digital Technologies

We define digital technologies 'as the use of emergent digital technologies, (e.g. AI and its sub-fields), to replace human capabilities, particularly those involving cognition such as learning and problem solving, for the execution of work tasks that were previously carried out by a human.'

Interview Questions

1. Category Strategy & Organisation (SO)

SO_1.1: How does digitalisation affect <client's name> GBS/SSC strategy?
SO_1.2: What strategic goals can be expected or achieved when applying digital technologies?
SO_1.3: How would you define/describe the strategy to implement digital technologies (e.g. defined roadmaps, adjusted architecture)?
SO_1.4: How does <client's name> organises the use of digital technologies (integrated in the GBS/SSC department, separated departments)?
SO_1.5: To what degree does digital technologies overcome or reduce the organisational barriers between business departments/units?

2. Category Digital Technologies (DT)

DT_2.1: How is <client's name> digital technologies strategy developed over time and by whom/department/unit? Is the approach made by one unit or were multiple units involved?
DT_2.2: How does digital technologies affect the GBS/SSC services portfolio? Please do elaborate on the type of digital technologies that is used?
DT_2.3: How does digital technologies affect GBS/SSC business processes? Please do elaborate on the type of digital technologies that is used?
DT_2.4: How does digital technologies affect GBS/SSC governance mechanisms? Please do elaborate on the type of digital technologies that is used?
DT_2.5: How does digital technologies affect GBS/SSC demand management (customer orientation)? Please do elaborate on the type of digital technologies that is used?

3. Category IA related Knowledge and skills (KS)

KS_3.1: When using digital technologies, how does this effect employees' knowledge (or their daily routine processes)?
KS_3.2: How are employees' skills affected when applying digital technologies? Do they need to acquire new skillsets? Did you experience any resistance or hesitation towards implementing IA?
KS_3.3: What types of mechanisms are used to strengthen employees' digital technologies knowledge and skills (e.g. education, leaning on the job)? Specifically, do they need to improve their AI literacy skills through training and workshops?
KS_3.4: What barriers can be identified when adapting employees' knowledge and skills?
KS_3.5: How does the use of digital technologies cause degradation or enhancement of human worker skills over time?

Table B1 Overview of interviewees

Case study	Role	Date	Duration
Logistic Service Provider	Manager FSSC	20/05/2022	60 min
	Manager process & change management	10/06/2022	60 min
	Senior RPA developer	10/06/2022	90 min
	Data specialist	10/06/2022	90 min
	CFO BU customer excellence & digital	15/06/2022	60 min
	manager accounts payable FSSC	15/06/2022	60 min
Employment Agency	Principal staff manager business services	10/06/2022	60 min
	ICT director	10/06/2022	60 min
	Director business unit in-house	20/06/2022	60 min
	Product owner process &RPA	10/07/2022	60 min
Construction and Building Company	Financial Administration	15/07/2022	60 min
	Manager business consultancy	15/07/2022	60 min
Financial Service Provider	Senior Vice President Europe	29/06/2023	60 min
	Director financial services	22/02/2023	50 min
	Delivery manager	10/05/2023	60 min
	Digital solution architect	22/05/2023	60 min

Table B2 Interview extracts

Categories	ID	Key Questions	Interviewee response
Logistic Service provider			
1. Category strategy & organisation	SO_1.1	How does digitalisation affect <client's name> GBS/SSC strategy?	Digitalisation of financial services is key (RPA, ML). As FSSC we are in the lead towards business and top management managing services like chatbots, customer contact. As a result, we are able to proactively offer new services based on digitalisation that contributes to the business directly. We pioneer a lot, and the challenge is to determine the value of digital solutions. What are the benefits? Process mining tools are actually very expensive. What is the value (for instance one-time rights tasks, less frustrations in client processes) of these tools? Most of the times it is always a combination of added value A key question however is: is the organisation ready (adoption). For example: the availability of data and data accuracy is key to create next steps. Is data accessible (data sources), does this align with other department goals and priorities?
	SO_1.2	What strategic goals can be achieved when applying intelligent automation?	New technologies do have a great advantage. They are able to customise some processes, the disadvantage is that we have to separate our processes, modularise them and next automate. The key advantage is that technologies like RPA, process mining and data solutions offer more customisation opportunities (semi standardised). The disadvantage is that we attract more customised solutions (in the end technology will solve anything if it can be designed/developed. As an example, a monthly question to the business is: how many purchase orders (and their value) are in the cue as this is time consuming and costly. These tasks have and can be automated. Conclusion of the FSSC: standardised back office like services is based on ERP type of solutions with some degree of customisation towards the front office and business units by using RPA and ML.

2. Category digital technologies	DT_2.2	How does intelligent automation affect the GBS/SSC services portfolio? Please do elaborate on the type of intelligent automation that is used?	We have to cater for changing circumstances. Business units have the need to upload documents in Salesforce. This could not be done; however, RPA solves this challenge based on a bit of a customised solution. The portfolio as such does not change. However, the collaboration between the FSSC and business units increases (co-develop, search for added value). Technology is bridging the gap between business units and FSSC. For example: automated reading of invoices (OCR: data set based on AI) change from unstructured data to structured data. If we can do this, we do not need an external partner to analyse the data, we just create an in-house sourcing solution. Right now, we have a limited number of external partners: an external vendor provides services like fraud detection and the degree of reliability of clients (do they pay the bill). Based on new digital solutions, the question is: can we do it ourselves? For example: other departments of our firm outsourced business processes to the market.
	DT_2.4	How does intelligent automation affect GBS/SSC governance mechanisms? Please do elaborate on the type of intelligent automation that is used?	Yes and No. Yes, bots conduct tasks that have been predefined including governance decisions that can be uniformed. No, the business units determine the degree of required governance rules and mechanisms due to accountability rules and compliance. We create a governance split: IT is responsible for platforms, and the FSSC is responsible for flexible digital solutions.

(*continued*)

Table B2 (continued)

Categories	ID	Key Questions	Interviewee response
3. Category knowledge and skills	KS_3.1	When using digital technologies, how does this effect employees' knowledge (or their daily routine processes)?	The change of employees to learn new skills was relatively easy. Some were a bit resistant, but we did not experienced job losses. Employees are actually glad that routine-based tasks have disappeared. RPA and Data specialist are enthusiastic, and curious to pioneer (innovate).
	KS_3.2	How are employees' skills affected when applying intelligent automation?	We hired new employees for topics like PowerBI dashboarding and data. They have hardly any experience with PowerBI, but a lot of experience with data (crunching numbers: accuracy, correctness). We hire on the principle of personality of employees (their mindset). Some more technology skills are rather quick to learn. We search for T-shape profiles that include multiple skills and competences. Consequently, we will adapt our function levels and job descriptions and include T-shape tasks. As an example: function Innovation specialist includes the knowledge of RPA tools, process mining, and data. When some technologies change, then we just user other techniques. The main goal is to create 1 main task; besides that, employees will fulfil subtasks.
	KS_3.3	3.3 What types of mechanisms are used to strengthen employee's intelligent automation knowledge and skills (e.g. education, leaning on the job)?	We apply bots at our postal sorting platform and our digital team visits this platform regularly. We also organise courses and visit events (UIPath). We encourage employees to pioneer and innovate. Be aware that pioneering is part of your job and does not only focus on the daily business.

Employment Agency			
1. Category strategy & organisation	SO_1.1	How does digitalisation affect <client's name> GBS/SSC strategy?	From an SSC perspective we provide a P2P example: invoices were handled manually. This is automated right now. We focus on straightforward processes, we do not include manual tasks, and yes, we do check the results (outcomes). The focus is on exceptions handling that contribute to efficiency. Originally 15 FTE we handle P2P tasks but today only 7 FTE will fulfil these tasks. The lead times to provide tasks however are decreased. This was a gradual development as we transformed from manual to automated tasks. Today, we focus on E2E financial process chains. As an example, spend analytics is performed on a global level that is scalable by design. We automated the last mile by adjusting existing platforms such as RPA and OCR.
	S) _1.3	How would you describe the strategy to implement intelligent automation (e.g. defined roadmaps, adjusted architecture)?	We apply various tools to digitalise external client processes like the onboarding of new employees (Government agency for instance). Other examples relate to tools that support credit risks, automated entry of files into BI tooling. The first step is to create a flow design than we automate the process steps. Lot of time savings in automated work, visualisation is done though dashboards. The SSC designed a roadmap for a future design that includes automation. One of the first steps is to determine design principles for a uniform data model and global alignment of the information model. To ensure evidence we test the solutions in practice. We encourage the step towards micro-services and start thinking in modular services which of course require a sound architecture. IT systems include Front office like Salesforce, mid office include time sheets, personnel files and we apply RPA and integration tooling between front and mid office. From a back-office view: it's about accounts payable, salary sheets, bank accounts; core systems (JD Edwards is applied for the harmonisation as we aim to provide these services on a global level.

(*continued*)

Table B2 (continued)

Categories	ID	Key Questions	Interviewee response
2. Category digital technologies	DT_2.2	How does intelligent automation affects the GBS/SSC services portfolio? Please do elaborate on the type of intelligent automation that is used?	Our portfolio has not been automated further. Various business services are already automated in the service portfolio. Changing law and regulations make it difficult as financial services need to be adjusted regularly. This affects the business services portfolio. Sometimes manual tasks need to be fulfilled as some tasks cannot be automated yet (specific expertise). Our conclusion is that financial services can be automated and provided by portals. The portfolio as a whole is not.
	DT_2.3	How does intelligent automation affects GBS/SSC business processes? Please do elaborate on the type of intelligent automation that is used?	As an example, RPA = managing basic tasks (check cost codes on a daily basis), conduct Chamber of Commerce checks, close out order automatically. This provides added value as the quality will increase and make manual work less attractive. The precondition to use automation is to uniform and standardise our business processes.
	DT_2.4	How does intelligent automation affects GBS/SSC governance mechanisms? Please do elaborate on the type of intelligent automation that is used?	From a governance view it is doable to robotise tasks when a simple Y or N is requested. In practice, the impression of the business is that the SSC need to handle exceptions. SSC says: business units are the owner of financial related processes. The question of the day is: who is responsible for a business process (SSC or BU)? Actually, this is an organisational question rather than a technical issue. Importantly, technology raises these types of questions as a result of digitalisation. As such it requires the end-to-end management of financial processes.
3. Category knowledge and skills	KS_3.1	How is employees' knowledge affected when applying intelligent automation?	Mechanisms: regular investments in education and technology for data (SSC employees trained to data specialists. All employees of the RPA (digital team) have been trained, keep on investing (new programme languages). Focus on E2E chains. Future: existing employees have to think and act in E2E chains.
	KS_3.2	How are employees' skills affected when applying intelligent automation?	Sometimes we distrust digitalisation: does it affect my job (will I lose it)? Our goal is to make employees curious about technology.

Construction and building company

1. Category strategy & organisation	SO_1.1	How does digitalisation affect <client's name> GBS/SSC strategy?	The shared service centre is the financial shared service centre, right? So, the impact on the whole company was at the time that. People did not believe that we would need an SSC. All the business units were like entities independent entities. And they found that there was no need for the SSC. So, we started as a pioneer from scratch and trying to do the best we can to concentrate all the financial transaction within the head office. And I must say that after five years now, more than five years, we are running this. Now we are coming down to standardisation and harmonisation of the different transaction and processes. We are using a central software to process incoming invoices from suppliers. The digitalisation has actually impacted the way that the invoices are being delivered and processed.
	SO_1.2	What strategic goals can be achieved when applying intelligent automation?	We are now at the crossroad of saying that we need intelligent automation. We have already made an X-ray on what we can do for, for instance, robotic process automation (RPA). Intelligence automation, for instance. We are now at the crossroad of saying that we need intelligent automation. We've already started just recently. To do an X-ray on what we can do for, for instance, LPA robotic process automation, and when possible, use AI, the management is convinced that we should do this, and they will make a budget regarding this.
	SO_1.3	How would you describe the strategy to implement intelligent automation (e.g. defined roadmaps, adjusted architecture)?	We have seen that there are a lot of areas that can be done. Only our PA is forcing you to think in a different way. So, you know taking logic steps and if the logic steps are not. I think we will start with the first a RPA, and maybe next year with AI. So, the management is convinced that we should do this. And they will make a budget regarding this. And in the long run, we will save more money the comparing to what we will be investing now. So that study is done. I can only say this is adjusting the architecture still in this way because we are trying to what we have already, which is not bad to make it more efficient and shorter and faster and take out the human factor. In fact, that is causing delays.

(*continued*)

Table B2 (continued)

Categories	ID	Key Questions	Interviewee response
2. Category digital technologies	DT_2.1	How is intelligent automation strategy developed over time and by whom, department, unit?	Our director of IT is the one who is in charge of strategies. From the IT department. The IT department director. He knows what is going on. He is this this director, and very well aware through his business. The business consultants are in close contact with all the various departments and business units and they come together and what we have currently. But the strategy is always up to the director to determine that.
	DT_2.2	How does intelligent automation affects the GBS/SSC services portfolio? Please do elaborate on the type of intelligent automation that is used?	Increase of efficiency. Increase of a satisfaction job satisfaction. You are not being frustrated by your colleagues and the delay that we are facing at the moment. Well, also it would help the business to act faster. You also can invoice out to the customer faster and you know where you are and in a more efficient and faster way as well. We are let's say 75% there but the 25% is still has to come. It does have an effect on the customer satisfaction as well as. For the business processes, for instance the number of steps that needs to be taken, currently I am pretty sure that would be decreased by 50%, the process will be shorter. In that respect, it will allow the operations people to add more control points in what they are doing, or it will increase the customer satisfaction in servicing the customer and not waiting for, let's say, information that still needs to be processed. So, all of that will be made shorter and of course efficiency will go higher.
	DT_2.4	How does intelligent automation affects GBS/SSC governance mechanisms? Please do elaborate on the type of intelligent automation that is used?	More efficient, I mean efficiency is the keyword, so that is what I think and expect as well. Areas which the robot may tackle at.

3. Category knowledge and skills	KS_3.1	How is employees' knowledge affected when applying intelligent automation?	The current skill, what they are you applying right now is becoming slowly redundant and they know that. Do they need a training extra training? Yes, although we do not. We have a very small budget in that respect to training. What I did for my people is doing things by example. So, by doing that by example it makes it for them more interesting because they like to see it live as well. We also signed an agreement with the company that provides online training. And this kind of online training, you can do the training on many times you want, but you can go on the site and then start the training and do it.
	KS_3.2	How are employees' skills affected when applying intelligent automation?	I am sorry to the to say so, but those barriers are only applicable for the older. And I tell them that what you have done all those years so far is fine and good, but now we are entering into a new era and you need to slowly change yourself and adopt what is coming. We provide training workshops, and live demonstration.
Financial Services Provider			
1. Category strategy & organisation	SO_1.1:	How does digitalisation affect <client's name> GBS/SSC strategy?	From a customer view, digitalisation provides various solutions/ options such as simulations and calculations. In the end it leads to more empowered client stakeholders. Importantly, the experience which type of digital solutions make sense in the client context. In addition, digitalisation affect clients directly and more instantly due to real time experience and use. Digitalisations provide the option to launce financial services much quicker, the process itself is more automated and straight through that ultimately will result in shorter lead times. Risks are observed in their actual context, such as insurance policy risks: understand the risks much better as controls can be automated, which in turn make reporting easier. From a collaboration view, working between different providers and clients requires an ecosystem model as networks are perceived to be open. This encourages sharing insights. An example from an insurance firm: they collaborate with plumbers/ holds to fix the leak; they collaborate with market suppliers from an ecosystem approach.

(*continued*)

Table B2 (continued)

Categories	ID	Key Questions	Interviewee response
2. Category digital technologies	DT_2.2	How do digital technologies affect the GBS/SSC services portfolio? Please do elaborate on the type of digital technologies that is used??	We see two types of benefits, (a) the customer and (b) our own firm. From a customer view we see cost optimalisations in their IT landscape due to solve inefficiencies as we use extreme automation. That will lead to cost savings as platforms focus on business functionality by means of continuous improvements and continuous monitoring. Benefits in our firm apply to scalable IT solutions like IT platforms (hypervisors, low-code platforms). These support features like logging authentication. Our internal approach is experience driven: engineers are in the lead, for instance in developing technical frameworks and blueprints.
	DT_2.3	How do digital technologies affect GBS/SSC business processes? Please do elaborate on the type of digital technologies that is used?	For instance, our client onboarding process that we developed (check on degree of efficacy). Originally executed in 7 to 8 working days, due to automation of business processes we are able to apply this service in 2 hours. We developed automated workflows based by using automation tooling. Next, we streamlined their onboarding processes. The idea is to reduce redundant tasks. This actually process optimalisation. By constantly measuring our client process outcomes we are able to intervene directly. We created a business dashboard for 20K customers while monitoring business process lead times and suggest improvement when relevant.
	DT_2.4	How does digital technologies affect GBS/SSC governance mechanisms? Please do elaborate on the type of digital technologies that is used?	By using configurable applications and platforms we are able to automate decision making. As an example, decision making within Know Your Customer type of functions can be automated partially, as changes can be implemented fast by developing rule engines for decision rules while we use business rules that are based on parameters). The requirement though is that data must be in place (data lake) in order to use machine leaning and AI to make decisions. In the end it requires a transformation approach as client rely on bots. AI cannot work without a data lake (platform) that means that we have to consolidate the data. On top of that, we use ML and AI engines

3. Category knowledge and skills	KS_3.1	When using digital technologies, how does this effect employees' knowledge (or their daily routine processes)?	Change is always constant you know. Therefore, it is necessary for us to survive. As employees in our teams need to keep up we upskill them regularly to learn new digital trends. This is a job for our internal capability and competency unit. The share new technologies to engineers: a % of the time of our employees is reserved to upskill their skills and capabilities. We also encourage their passion, this even incentive by applying a reward mechanism). So technical recognition for them is key. As a result, our customers acknowledge our way of working as they benefit from faster implementations. There are also options for employees to switch to other type of technologies (we encourage them to keep them interested! It also mitigates retention risks and benefit to clients by our experienced engineers.

Table B3 Extract Survey database

Company Name	Country	Industry	Benchmark Classification	Current maturity	Aspirational maturity	Participant Title
X	USA	Pharma	Pharma	3.0	4.5	Director
X	France	Pharma	Pharma	4.1	5.0	Vice President
X	Finland	Professional Services	Professional Services	2.7	3.1	CIO
X	Finland	Diversified Conglomerate	Diversified Conglomerate	3.0	3.9	Director
X	Brazil—Compartilha	Hospitality	Real Estate & Hospitality	2.5	4.8	Head do CSC
X	Brazil—Compartilha	Manufacturing	Industrial & Manufacturing	2.8		Especialista Financeiro, Gerente de Projetos Financeiros
X	Brazil—Compartilha	Chemicals	Chemicals	2.7	4.8	Head of Shared Services
X	Brazil—Compartilha	Financial Services	Financial Services	1.6	2.1	Diretor
X	Brazil—Compartilha	Education	Education	3.0	4.2	Gerente
X	Brazil—Compartilha	Waste Management	Professional Services	0.9	1.7	Analista de Gestão de Serviços
X	Brazil—Compartilha	Consumer Products	CPG & Beverages	3.7	4.5	Gerente de Contas
X	Brazil—GESC	Energy & Utilities	Energy & Utilities / Oil & Gas	2.9	3.5	Gerente de Relacionamento e Qualidade
X	Brazil—GESC	Manufacturing	Industrial & Manufacturing	3.2	4.2	Gerente Geral
X	Brazil—GESC	Diversified Conglomerate	Industrial & Manufacturing	3.1	3.6	Gerente do Centro de Serviços Compartilhados

X	Brazil—GESC	Pharma	Pharma	2.8	3.0	Coordenador de Controladoria
X	Brazil—GESC	Diversified Conglomerate	Diversified Conglomerate	4.5	4.5	Gerente Planejamento e Gestão
X	Brazil—Somar	Education	Education	3.9	4.0	Diretor Serviços Compartilhados
X	Brazil—Somar	Food & Beverages	CPG & Beverages	3.1	4.2	Gerente Administrativo CSC
X	Brazil—Somar	Energy & Utilities	Energy & Utilities / Oil & Gas	2.6	3.6	Gerente
X	Brazil—Somar	Logistics	Logistics	3.0	3.0	Analista Financeiro
X	Brazil—Somar	Diversified Conglomerate	Diversified Conglomerate	2.6	3.7	Gestor de Serviços
X	Brazil—Somar	Energy & Utilities	Energy & Utilities / Oil & Gas	2.9	3.8	Gerente de Controladoria
X	Brazil—Somar	Cooperative Society	Cooperative Society	3.5	4.3	Gerente de Custos e Eficiência
X	Brazil—Somar	Diversified Conglomerate	Industrial & Manufacturing	3.6	4.5	Supervisor
X	South Africa	Energy & Utilities	Energy & Utilities / Oil & Gas	3.2	5.0	Manager
X	South Africa	Energy & Utilities	Energy & Utilities / Oil & Gas	3.7	4.3	Other
X	South Africa	Telecom	Technology & Telecom	2.3	3.3	Other

(*continued*)

Table B3 (continued)

Company Name	Country	Industry	Participant GBS Functional Responsibility	Total number of employees in the company	Business Services start year	GBS start year	Number of GBS employees	Number of GBS centres	GBS regions
X	USA	Pharma	Multiple Region Responsibility	100001–250,000	1997	NA	501–1000	5	North America, Europe, South America, Asia Pacific
X	France	Pharma	One Function Responsibility	100001–250,000	2009	2011	1001–2000	1	North America
X	Finland	Professional Services	Worldwide GBS	1000–5000	2002	2009	Less than 100	6–10	Europe
X	Finland	Diversified Conglomerate	One function	1000–5000	2014	2014	NA	1	Europe
X	Brazil—Compartilha	Hospitality	Lider	5001–10,000	2009	2014	100 to 500	2	South America, Europe
X	Brazil—Compartilha	Manufacturing	Area de Performance e Processos	1000–5000	2013	2013	Less than 100	1	South America
X	Brazil—Compartilha	Chemicals	NA	5001–10,000	2009	2009	100 to 500	3	North America, South America
X	Brazil—Compartilha	Financial Services	Diretor de Serviços Compartilhados	1000–5000	2009	NA	Less than 100	1	South America
X	Brazil—Compartilha	Education	Gestão de Performance e Integração do CSC	10001–20,000	2009	2009	100 to 500	1	South America

X	Brazil—Compartilha	Waste Management	Report's para o Grupo	10001–20,000	2012	2012	100 to 500	2	South America
X	Brazil—Compartilha	Consumer Products	Gerente	10001–20,000	2000	2000	100 to 500	1	South America
X	Brazil—GESC	Energy & Utilities	Gerente de Departamento	5001–10,000	2009	NA	100 to 500	1	North America
X	Brazil—GESC	Manufacturing	NA	20001–50,000	NA	2014	100 to 500	3	North America, South America
X	Brazil—GESC	Diversified Conglomerate	Principal gestora do Centro de Serviços Compartilhados	10001–20,000	1995 or before	2010	100 to 500	1	South America
X	Brazil—GESC	Pharma	Coordenação	50001–100,000	2004	2004	501–1000	3	North America, Europe, South America
X	Brazil—GESC	Diversified Conglomerate	Modelo de Governança	50001–100,000	2004	2004	501–1000	2	South America
X	Brazil—Somar	Education	Diretor CSC	5001–10,000	2009	NA	100 to 500	1	NA
X	Brazil—Somar	Food & Beverages	Gerente Administrativo CSC	10001–20,000	2008	NA	NA	NA	South America

(continued)

Table B3 (continued)

Company Name	Country	Industry	Participant GBS Functional Responsibility	Total number of employees in the company	Business Services start year	GBS start year	Number of GBS employees	Number of GBS centres	GBS regions
X	Brazil—Somar	Energy & Utilities	Gerente	5001–10,000	2013	NA	Less than 100	1	South America
X	Brazil—Somar	Logistics	Representante	1000–5000	2009	2009	100 to 500	2	South America
X	Brazil—Somar	Diversified Conglomerate	NA	1000–5000	2013	NA	100 to 500	1	South America
X	Brazil—Somar	Energy & Utilities	Gerência	1000–5000	2007	2007	100 to 500	1	South America
X	Brazil—Somar	Cooperative Society	gestor da área de gestão de serviços do CSC	10001–20,000	2001	2001	501–1000	1	South America
X	Brazil—Somar	Diversified Conglomerate	Planejamento, Contabilidade e Call Center Interno	1000–5000	2011	2011	100 to 500	2	South America
X	South Africa	Energy & Utilities	NA	10001–20,000	2012	2012	501–1000	1	Middle East & Africa
X	South Africa	Energy & Utilities	Multiple Functions Responsibility	20001–50,000	2005	2010	1001–2000	3	Middle East & Africa
X	South Africa	Telecom	Worldwide GBS Responsibility	20001–50,000	2013	2013	100 to 500	1	Middle East & Africa

Company Name	Country	Industry	GBS countries	# of ERP systems Deployed	# of ERP Instances	ERP solution provider	# Functions	GBS functions
X	USA	Pharma	US, Costa Rica, India, China, Western Europe	1	1	NA	3	Finance & Accounting, Analytics, Other SG&A
X	France	Pharma	US, Canada	2–3	4–5	SAP	5	Finance & Accounting, IT, HR, Procurement / Supply Chain, Other SG&A
X	Finland	Professional Services	Western Europe	2–3	2–3	Other	3	Finance & Accounting, IT, HR
X	Finland	Diversified Conglomerate	Other Central and Eastern Europe	1	1	Other	2	Finance & Accounting, IT
X	Brazil—Compartilha	Hospitality	Brazil, Other Central and Eastern Europe	2–3	2–3	Oracle	3	Finance & Accounting, HR, Other SG&A

(*continued*)

Table B3 (continued)

Company Name	Country	Industry	GBS countries	# of ERP systems Deployed	# of ERP Instances	ERP solution provider	# Functions	GBS functions
X	Brazil—Compartilha	Manufacturing	Brazil	1	1	Oracle	2	Finance & Accounting, Other SG&A
X	Brazil—Compartilha	Chemicals	US, Brazil, Mexico	1	1	SAP	3	Finance & Accounting, HR, Other SG&A
X	Brazil—Compartilha	Financial Services	Brazil	1	1	SAP	2	Finance & Accounting, Other SG&A
X	Brazil—Compartilha	Education	Brazil	1	2–3	SAP	4	Finance & Accounting, IT, HR, Procurement / Supply Chain
X	Brazil—Compartilha	Waste Management	Brazil	2–3	2–3	Other	2	Finance & Accounting, HR
X	Brazil—Compartilha	Consumer Products	Brazil	4–5	1	SAP	5	Finance & Accounting, IT, HR, Procurement / Supply Chain, Other SG&A

X	Brazil—GESC	Energy & Utilities	Brazil	1	1	SAP	4	Finance & Accounting, IT, HR, Procurement / Supply Chain
X	Brazil—GESC	Manufacturing	US, Mexico, Brazil	4–5	NA	SAP	3	Finance & Accounting, HR, Other SG&A
X	Brazil—GESC	Diversified Conglomerate	Brazil	1	4–5	SAP	2	Finance & Accounting, HR
X	Brazil—GESC	Pharma	US, Hungry, Brazil	1	2–3	SAP	2	Finance & Accounting, HR
X	Brazil—GESC	Diversified Conglomerate	Brazil, Other LATAM	1	1	SAP	2	Finance & Accounting, HR
X	Brazil—Somar	Education	Brazil	1	NA	Other	3	Finance & Accounting, IT, Procurement / Supply Chain
X	Brazil—Somar	Food & Beverages	Brazil	2–3	2–3	SAP	3	Finance & Accounting, HR, Other SG&A
X	Brazil—Somar	Energy & Utilities	Brazil	1	4–5	Other	2	IT, Other SG&A

(*continued*)

Table B3 (continued)

Company Name	Country	Industry	GBS countries	# of ERP systems Deployed	# of ERP Instances	ERP solution provider	# Functions	GBS functions
X	Brazil—Somar	Logistics	Brazil	1	6–10	SAP	4	Finance & Accounting, HR, Procurement / Supply Chain, Other SG&A
X	Brazil—Somar	Diversified Conglomerate	Brazil	1	4–5	Other	3	Finance & Accounting, IT, HR
X	Brazil—Somar	Energy & Utilities	Brazil	1	1	Oracle	4	Finance & Accounting, IT, HR, Procurement / Supply Chain
X	Brazil—Somar	Cooperative Society	Brazil	1	1	SAP	4	Finance & Accounting, HR, Procurement / Supply Chain, Other SG&A
X	Brazil—Somar	Diversified Conglomerate	Brazil	2–3	1	SAP	4	Finance & Accounting, HR, Procurement / Supply Chain, Other SG&A

X	South Africa	Energy & Utilities	South Africa	6–10	1	SAP	5	Finance & Accounting, IT, HR, Procurement / Supply Chain, Other SG&A
X	South Africa	Energy & Utilities	South Africa	1	6–10	SAP	4	Finance & Accounting, HR, Procurement / Supply Chain, Other SG&A
X	South Africa	Telecom	Other Middle East, South Africa, Nigeria, Other Africa	1	1	Oracle	3.00	Finance & Accounting, HR, Procurement / Supply Chain

References

Denzin, N. K. (1978) *The research act: A theoretical introduction to sociological methods.* McGraw-Hill.

Galliers, R. D. (1992) Choosing information systems research approaches. In R. D. Galliers (Eds.), *Information systems research: Issues, methods, and practical guidelines* (pp. 44–162). Blackwell Scientific Publications.

Glaser, B. G., & Strauss, A. L. (1967). *The discovery of grounded theory: Strategies for qualitative research.* Aldine.

Miles, M. B., & Huberman, A. M. (1994). *Qualitative data analysis: An expanded sourcebook* (2nd ed.). Sage Publications.

Rossman, G. B., & Wilson, B. L. (1984). Number and words: Combining quantitative and qualitative methods in a single large-scale evaluation study. *Evaluation Review, 9*, 627–643.

Rossman, G. B., & Wilson, B. L. (1991). Numbers and words revisited: Being 'shamelessly eclectic'. *Evaluation Review, 9*, 627–643.

Yin, R. K. (1994). *Case study research. Design and methods.* Sage Publications.

Appendix C: Curriculum Vitae

Curriculum Vitae Dr. Albert Plugge

Albert Plugge is Professor at Nyenrode Business University in the Netherlands. Albert studied Telecommunications at Delft University of Technology, where he obtained his master's degree in 2001. From 2005 he holds a part-time position at Delft University of Technology where he started his parttime Ph.D. research in the field of Managed of Information Systems, and more on IT outsourcing from a service provider perspective specifically. He completed his Ph.D. research early 2011. In the period 2011 up to 2021 Albert fulfilled various roles at Delft University both in the faculty Technology, Policies and Management and the faculty Industrial Design Engineering. He organised and lectured various courses on the interplay between business, technology and management. He supervised multiple master students and a Ph.D. candidate. Since, 2020, Albert is a research fellow at the Centre Entrepreneurship, Governance, and Stewardship, Nyenrode Business University in the Netherlands. He organises the lecture series Digital Business Ecosystems amongst other lectures as part of master courses. His research interests comprise of

A. Plugge, S. Nikou, *Digitalisation of Global Business Services*, Technology, Work and Globalization, https://doi.org/10.1007/978-3-031-51528-6

digitalisation, digital business ecosystems, ESG, and strategic sourcing and their effect on organisational structures and governance. Recently, he has been appointed to the chair ESG Transformation and Digital Innovation at Nyenrode Business University, which is sponsored by KPMG.

He is involved in various international research projects and presented his work at several conferences. He published papers and book chapters in various scientific and industry journals, for instance, Information & Management, Production, Planning & Control, Information Systems and e-Business Management, Industrial Management and Data Systems, Business Process Management, Journal of Global Information Technology Management, and Journal of Information Technology Teaching Cases. He is a reviewer of various academic journals such as: Journal of Information Technology, European Journal of Information Systems, Information & Management, International Journal of Information Technology & Decision-Making, Journal of Information Technology, Journal of Information Technology Teaching Cases, and Journal of Global Operations and Strategic Sourcing. He is co-chair of the HICSS conference regarding the mini track Socio-Technical Issues in Organisational Information Technologies.

Besides his role at Nyenrode, he is associated with KPMG in the Netherlands supporting organisations in the field of ESG transformations, digital innovations, business ecosystems and sourcing. He has an extensive expertise in these fields and supported more than 85 organisations in the Netherlands and Europe in various industries (e.g. Banking and Insurance, Government, Manufacturing, Retail, Telecommunications).

Curriculum Vitae Dr. Shahrokh Nikou

Shahrokh is currently Assistant Professor at Department of Design, Organisation and Strategy (DOS), at the Faculty Industrial Design Engineering (IDE) at Delft University of Technology. He received a doctorate from Åbo Akademi University in 2012 and became a Docent in Information Systems in 2014. He has MSc. in Computer Networks from the Royal University of Technology (KTH), Stockholm (Sweden), 2008, and MSc. in Computer Sciences from ÅAU 2009. Shahrokh is also affiliated with the Department of Computer and Systems Sciences (DSV), at the Stockholm University, since 2019. His research interests relate to digitalisation, organisational design, innovation, information systems, management, and entrepreneurship. In addition, he is interested in digital platforms, research methods, private and public partnership, digital businesses with a particular focus on the role of digital transformation as enablers for organisational change, both within enterprises and across their entire value network. He has practical and academic experience in business model and business model innovation.

Shahrokh has published more than 125 peer-reviewed articles in academic journals and international conference proceedings, mostly on digitalisation, digital transformation, business models and business model innovation, and research in healthcare, entrepreneurship and higher education using sophisticated and advanced research methods and data analysis techniques. He is an Associate Editor in the Journal of Electronic Markets (Springer) and Digital Business Journal (Elsevier), Academic Editor in PLOSONE, Section Editor in the Journal of Theoretical and Applied Electronic Commerce Research. He is also a member of the editorial board of Telematics and Informatics, Electronic Markets, International Journal of Web Engineering and Technology (IJWET), the Journal of Electronic Commerce in Organizations (JECO) and International Journal of Electronic Business Research (IJEBR).

Index

A. Plugge, S. Nikou, *Digitalisation of Global Business Services*, Technology, Work and Globalization, https://doi.org/10.1007/978-3-031-51528-6

www.ingramcontent.com/pod-product-compliance
Ingram Content Group UK Ltd.
Pitfield, Milton Keynes, MK11 3LW, UK
UKHW020834290926
15470UKWH00004B/1347

* 9 7 8 3 0 3 1 5 1 5 2 7 9 *